WHAT PEOPLE ARE SAYING ABOUT
THE OZ PRINCIPLE^{SM}

"All year long we struggled to show some increase in store sales with no real success. However, after applying *The Oz Principle* Accountability Training, store sales climbed and continued to climb for the next eleven weeks thereafter. Numerous obstacles presented themselves throughout the year, but the team remained '*Above the Line*' and nailed our year-end budget."

—**Kenneth White**
Regional Vice President
Smith's Food and Drug

"We tried for several years to make some basic changes in our Global Manufacturing Group and just couldn't get there. We finally internalized the concept of the accountability process as defined in *The Oz Principle*. It has really turned us around in the direction we wanted and we're now making the progress we've been trying to make for years."

—**Bill Smith**
Executive Director
Global Manufacturing Services,
Eli Lilly

"*The Oz Principle* unlocks your potential and helps you think differently about the way you approach both your personal and your professional life. The language is easily adopted and you can readily identify with the stories and the principles that are taught. If you embrace *The Oz Principle* and you really apply the points that are made, you will change your behavior and become more successful in achieving the results you want."

—**Kelli Fitten**
Director of Human Resources
Brinker International
On the Border Cafes Division

"*The Oz Principle* Accountability Training is a wonderful, incredibly valuable resource. It provided the answers I sought as I strived to meet the challenge of meshing a systems approach (to quality and management) with individual responsibility and accountability."

—**Beth Tolley**
Administrator
Presbyterian Hospital

"*The Oz Principle* Training is making a difference in my life! I didn't even wait to get home, I made a call from the bus station to request an appointment and to move from the 'wait and see' mode to '*Do It*.' Thanks for implementing a great program/principle."

—**Sales Representative**
Pratt Pharmaceuticals,
A Division of Pfizer, Inc.

"It has made a lasting impression on my career, and in my personal life. *The Oz Principle* has made a very positive impact on the way I try to interact with individuals and deal with myself and my interactions, both professionally and personally."

—**Dennis Antinori**
Regional Vice President, Sales
Guidant Corporation

"It will help you approach any new idea or problem and impact your ability to be successful . . . *The Oz Principle* hit the punchline early and then supported it. It introduces a global concept right away, and then the components of each chapter give you a better understanding of that global concept. . . . After our clients' reorganization, we had the worst month we've ever had leading into January (typically a low recruiting month in our industry). We required everyone to submit an *Accountability Plan* and we beat our projected hires by 20%—a direct result of implementing *The Oz Principle* in our organization."

—Mark Wortley
President, Beverly Care Alliance

"*The Oz Principle* has really made accountability very easy to understand and has improved our effectiveness in obvious ways. Our entire organization has not only embraced the concept, but has also made it our culture to operate *Above The Line*. Most importantly, *The Oz Principle* made it very easy for a new representative joining the organization to quickly understand what Pfizer Pratt Pharmaceuticals is all about, both in terms of our culture and how we operate as a group."

—Dick Reggio
Vice President, Sales
Pratt Pharmaceuticals, A Division of Pfizer Inc.

"*The Oz Principle* is very easy reading, practical in its content. The message is so straightforward that it is many times overlooked. . . . We are totally accountable for making things happen. It was extremely well received."

—David Grimes
Vice President, Sales, AT&T

"The concepts in the book are practical and are the things we are living day-to-day. It is well written; in plain talk like a face-to-face discussion. Less theory and more examples and approaches that are immediately usable. We have applied *The Oz Principle* concepts and empowered the people in our whole facility towards the objectives we need to accomplish. The concepts have really served as motivation tools and closed the gap between management and the line workers."

—Vincente Trellis
Vice President, Surgical Operations, Allergan

"Our success rests in our strong culture developed over the years. Our recent addition of new cultural language, i.e., "*Above The Line, Below The Line*" from *The Oz Principle* Accountability Training has enabled our company to be more aligned and riveted us on the targeted results."

—Richard Methany
Director, Human Resources
Friday's Hospitality Worldwide

"*The Oz Principle* eloquently captures the secret to overcoming obstacles and achieving success. It is filled with practical insights essential to the personal and organizational journey of getting results. The book explains an enduring principle that will long outlive the supposed wizardry of the many management fads that melt away with time. I would personally recommend this book to everyone who has tired of wizards and who is anxious to get results."

—Dorothy Browning of Kansas

THE
OZ
PRINCIPLE

GETTING RESULTS
THROUGH INDIVIDUAL
AND ORGANIZATIONAL
ACCOUNTABILITY

ROGER CONNORS • TOM SMITH
CRAIG HICKMAN

PRENTICE HALL PRESS

Library of Congress Cataloging-in-Publication Data

Connors, Roger.
    The Oz principle : Getting Results Through Individual and Organizational
Accountability / Roger Connors, Tom Smith, Craig Hickman.
      p.   cm.
    Includes index.
    ISBN 0-13-032129-X
    1. Management—United States.   2. Responsibility.   3. Success in business—
United States.   I. Smith, Tom (Thomas A.)   II. Hickman, Craig R.   III. Title.
HD70.U5C59   1994   93-38720
658—dc20   CIP

Printed in the United States of America

Partners in Leadership, LLC, has given permission to Prentice Hall to use the following
materials in the book *The Oz Principle*: Steps to Accountability Chart, The Victim Cycle
Chart, The Commitment Process diagram, A List of Clues That Indicate Accountable
Attitudes and Behaviors, *See It* self assessment, *Own It* self assessment, Six Key
Questions to Help You See Your Accountability, *Solve It* self assessment, *Do It* self
assessment, List of Clues to Know When You're in the Victim Cycle, Victim Cycle Self
Examination, The Twenty Tired Excuses, Ways in Which You Can Demonstrate Your
Accountability, List of Keys to Accounting for Progress, Differences Between *Above* and
Below the Line Reporting, The *Above the Line* Leadership Checklist (Do's and Don'ts),
The Organizational Accountability Assessment, Ten More *Above the Line* Questions.
Copyright on these materials is by Partners In Leadership, LLC, 1989-1993.

Selected quotations were taken from the book *The Wonderful Wizard of Oz* by Frank
Baum. The authors of *The Oz Principle* have no affiliation with or connection to the
producers or owners of the movie *The Wizard of Oz*.

"Partners In Leadership," "The Oz Principle," "Creating A Culture of Accountability,"
"Above The Line," "Below The Line," "The Results Pyramid," "Steps To Accountability,"
"See It," "Own It," "Solve It," "Do It," and "Culture Of Accountability" are servicemarks
of Partners In Leadership, LLC.

10 (C)   *10 9 8 7*   *(P)*

ISBN 0-13-032129-X   ISBN 0-7352-0043-2

ATTENTION: CORPORATIONS AND SCHOOLS
Prentice Hall books are available at quantity discounts with bulk purchase for
educational, business, or sales promotional use. For information, please write to:
Prentice Hall Special Sales, 240 Frisch Court, Paramus, New Jersey 07652. Please
supply: title of book, ISBN number, quantity, how the book will be used, date needed.

PRENTICE HALL PRESS
Paramus, NJ 07652

On the World Wide Web at http://www.phdirect.com

PREFACE

▼

In a relatively short space of time, American businesses have moved to new ground, downsizing, flattening, empowering, team-working, liberating, knowledge-basing, networking, quality-imbuing, continuously-improving, process-mapping, transforming, and reengineering their enterprises for the 21st century. For some companies such as General Electric and Motorola the improvements have proved remarkable. For too many others, however, the bewildering array of current success formulas, both theoretical and practical, seems overwhelming or foolish because no one has accurately identified what's really at the core of a GE's or a Motorola's results. We attempt to identify that core in *The Oz Principle*.

Whether you're attempting to reengineer, reinvent, or revitalize your organization, one vital ingredient always determines the success or failure of such efforts: individual and joint accountability for results. In the last three paragraphs of the book, *Control Your Destiny or Someone Else Will: How Jack Welch is Making General Electric The World's Most Competitive Company*, Jack Welch, himself, attempts a final explanation of what's really needed for success:

> "I think any company that's trying to play in the 1990s has got to find a way to engage the mind of every single employee. Whether we make our way successfully down this road is something only time will tell—but I'm sure this is the right road.

"If you're not thinking all the time about making every person more valuable, you don't have a chance. What's the alternative? Wasted minds? Uninvolved people? A labor force that's angry or bored? That doesn't make sense!

"If you've got a better way, show me. I'd love to know what it is."

For now, we believe there is no better way. Only when people in organizations overcome the illusionary trap of victimization and envision the steps to individual accountability can they claim their own destinies and the future of their enterprises.

We wrote *The Oz Principle* to help people become more accountable for their thoughts, feelings, actions, and results, so they can move their organizations to ever greater heights.

We hope you enjoy and gain real value from this new journey through Oz.

Roger Connors
Thomas Smith
Craig Hickman

ACKNOWLEDGMENTS

▼

At the outset, we must first acknowledge what may appear to some as obvious, that we are not the originators of the principle of accountability—a principle that has been around for centuries.

Through our varied experiences in business, and in life, we have gained an understanding of this universal and time-tested principle. There have been many on our continuing road to understanding that have helped shape what we have come to know as perhaps one of the most impactful principles of success. These influences include the examples of our parents, the profound questions clients ask during an engagement, the lessons taught by fellow workers, the principles learned through our faith, and the experiences gained in working to create greater accountability in organizations.

To all of the people who helped shape our understanding we express our heartfelt gratitude and thanks for helping us gain insights that no one of us could ever fully appreciate by ourselves.

Our work with various clients over the years has increased our understanding of how *The Oz Principle* applies in businesses of all types and sizes. We wish to particularly thank Ron Dollens, Mike Eagle, Jay Graf, Steve Johnson, Dick Nordquest, Stan Varner and Joe Cannon for furthering our understanding of what it means to act *Above The Line*.^{SM}

We are indebted to Pat Snell for her suggestion that we use the *Wizard of Oz* as a metaphor to convey the principles of accountability. We also wish to thank our collaborator and agent Michael Snell for his continued tenacity and input throughout this project.

We appreciate the feedback we received that assisted us in improving the manuscript which came from the review of the book by the following individuals: Chris Crall, John Fink, Dr. Michael Geurts, Tom Kasper, Ran Jones, Dave Pliler, and Robert Skaggs. We also appreciate the meticulous review of our work that was given by our fathers Craig Connors, Fred Smith, and Winston Hickman. To these individuals we express our appreciation for their input and for their constant encouragement and continued enthusiasm for this project.

We greatly appreciate Tom Power of Prentice Hall who gave invaluable feedback throughout the development of the manuscript. His insight and experience provided critical suggestions that helped shape the book in a very positive way. *The Oz Principle* is a more powerful book because of his influence.

Most of all we would like to acknowledge the helpful input, candid feedback, and never-ending encouragement of our wives. To Gwen, Becky, and Pam we say thank you, we could not have done this without your support and your participation.

CONTENTS

▼

PART 3
RESULTS THROUGH COLLECTIVE ACCOUNTABILITY: HELPING YOUR ORGANIZATION PERFORM *ABOVE THE LINE*^{SM} 201

ABOUT THE AUTHORS

▼

Roger Connors and Thomas Smith are the principals and founders of *Partners In Leadership, LLC*, a leadership and management consulting firm that has implemented *The Oz Principle*^{SM} in organizations of all sizes, including *Fortune* 500 companies and small "start-ups."

After receiving their MBAs from Brigham Young University, they have spent the last nine years pioneering the implementation of the principles embodied in *The Oz Principle* in a broad array of industries ranging from health care to financial services. They have assisted over 100 clients in ten different countries in implementing *The Oz Principle* at all levels in their organizations. Their varied experience in assisting senior management teams in creating greater accountability in organizations have made them leaders in the struggle of coming to grips with how to create empowerment, employee involvement, continuous improvement, and a culture that fosters accountability. They are authors of the forthcoming book *Journey to the Emerald City: Achieving a Competitive Edge by Creating a Culture of Accountability.*

Craig Hickman is the best-selling author of *The Strategy Game; Mind of a Manager, Soul of a Leader; Creating Excellence; The Future 500;* and *Practical Business Genius.* His work has been featured in *USA Today, Business Week, The New York Times, Industry Week, Nation's Business,* and *Training & Development.* A leading business thinker today, he holds an MBA with honors from the Harvard Business School.

Victor Hugo once said,

There is one thing stronger than all the armies in the world, and that is an idea whose time has come.

I believe *The Oz Principle* is that idea which will transform Corporate America and prepare us for the 21st Century.

Michael L. Eagle, Vice President
Eli Lilly and Co.

THE OZ PRINCIPLE: GETTING RESULTS THROUGH ACCOUNTABILITY

PART 1

The pathway to better results lies in overcoming the deceptive traps of the "victim cycle" by taking the **Steps To Accountability.**[SM] *In Part I we illustrate how the attitude of victimization has captured Americans everywhere in a choking strangle hold. We explain why people in organizations must avoid the debilitating affects of the "victim cycle" in order to get results. Finally, we reveal the* **Steps To Accountability** *as the key to obtaining what you desire, personally and organizationally.*

CHAPTER 1

OFF TO SEE THE WIZARD: BRINGING ACCOUNTABILITY BACK TO THE AMERICAN CHARACTER

"Who are you?" asked the Scarecrow when he had stretched himself and yawned, "and where are you going?"

"My name is Dorothy," said the girl, "and I am going to the Emerald City, to ask the great Oz to send me back to Kansas."

"Where is the Emerald City?" he inquired; "and who is Oz?"

"Why, don't you know?" she returned, in surprise.

"No, indeed; I don't know anything. You see, I am stuffed, so I have no brains at all," he answered sadly.

"Oh," said Dorothy; "I'm awfully sorry for you."

"Do you think," he asked, "if I go to the Emerald City with you that Oz would give me some brains?"

"I cannot tell," she returned; "but you may come with me, if you like. If Oz will not give you any brains you will be no worse off than you are now."

"That is true," said the Scarecrow.

THE WIZARD OF OZ
By L. Frank Baum

3

Like all powerful literature, *The Wizard of Oz* continues to enthrall audiences because its plot strikes a nerve in people. The book recounts a journey toward awareness, and, from the beginning of their journey, the story's main characters gradually learn that they possess the power within themselves to get the results they want. Until the end, they think of themselves as victims of circumstance, skipping down the yellow brick road to the Emerald City where the supposedly all-powerful Wizard will grant them the wisdom, heart, courage, and means to succeed. The journey itself empowers them, and even Dorothy, who could have clicked her red slippers and returned home at any time, must travel the yellow brick road to gain full awareness that only she herself can achieve her desires. People relate to the theme of a journey from ignorance to knowledge, from fear to courage, from insensitivity to caring, from paralysis to powerfulness, from victimization to accountability, because it seems so true. Unfortunately, even the most ardent admirers of the story often fail to learn its simple lesson, never getting off the yellow brick road, blaming others for their circumstances, and waiting for wizards to wave their magic wands and make all the problems disappear. In fact, the temptation to feel and act like victims has become so popular in America that it has created a very real crisis.

THE AMERICAN CHARACTER IN CRISIS

American enterprise may have lost much of its dominance in the world, but it retains the number one position when it comes to what could be considered the "cult" of victimization. *The Economist* magazine calls this cult of victimization "an odd combination of ducking responsibility and telling everyone else what to do." In our society, the cult's adherents argue, people have lost so much of their personal power to affect their circumstances and shape their lives that they must look to others for the means to succeed.

In his enlightening book, *A Nation of Victims: The Decay of the American Character,* author Charles Sykes captures this flaw in the American character: "Crisscrossing by invisible trip wires of emotional, racial, sexual, and psychological grievance, American life is increasingly characterized by the plaintive insistence, I am a victim." He goes on to demonstrate how "victimspeak," "compassion fatigue," "a no-fault, no-pain philosophy," and "an ideology of selfishness" have contributed to an American character crisis that won't go away easily.

A troubling *Time* magazine cover story, "A Nation of Finger Pointers," chalked the phenomenon up to busybodies and crybabies who display, "a nasty intolerance and a desire to blame everyone else for everything." According to the *Time* article, the busybodies "imagine that they would be beautiful and virtuous and live forever, if only you would put out that cigar," while the crybabies "see the American dream not as striving fulfilled but as unachieved entitlement." Both the busybody and the crybaby feel victimized, unable to get the results they want because someone or something else has gotten in their way.

When Clark Clifford appeared before Congress to explain his role in the BCCI scandal, he claimed he was an unwitting pawn. When 296 members of the U.S. Congress were exposed for years of overdrafts at the now-defunct House Bank, they blamed it on their spouses, their colleagues, the system, the lack of information, the House Bank, their religion, and, as *The Wall Street Journal* decried, "on just about everything but the bossa nova." Fully aware of the growing accountability crisis and mounting social and economic problems in America, President Clinton pleaded with both Congress and the American people in his first State of the Union address, February 17, 1993, to stop pointing the finger of blame at one another and begin working together to solve the country's problems; he exclaimed,"We can no longer deny the reality of our condition."

According to author John Taylor in a *New York* magazine article entitled, "Don't Blame Me," the attitude of victimization is becoming more and more widespread. Taylor claims "that a double-barreled social phenomenon now threatens the real exercise of civil liberties." The first barrel is "victimology," the second is the rights industry. Taylor goes on to suggest that "the creation by individuals and special-interest groups of freshly minted freedoms and prerogatives that must be upheld even when they are foolishly asserted" fuels the out-of-control finger-pointing in America today. While this sort of attitude may infect people worldwide, it seems to have become a real epidemic in America.

Ironically, at a time in world history of unprecedented opportunity, several recent national surveys reveal that a growing number of Americans perceive themselves as victims who should be compensated for their misery. Rising insurance rates, insurance company failures, high attorneys' fees and overburdened judicial caseloads, coupled with record numbers of law school graduates and escalating punitive damage awards—all have conspired to create a litigious society that thrives on assigning blame. Americans account for 70 percent of the world's lawyers. Not surprisingly, the average punitive damages awarded by juries in the United States have increased 20-fold in the past 20 years. Donna Roberts of Ventura, California, blaming her veterinarian for injuring her pet iguana and causing her great emotional stress, sued for $1 million in damages, and Tom Morgan, a cashier for a grocery store in Portland, Oregon, blamed a fellow worker for inflicting $100,000 worth of torment and mental stress upon him.

The "blame game" has become the new national pastime, and at the heart of it sits the "rights industry." As Harvard Law School professor, Mary Ann Glendon, points out in her recent book, *Rights Talk,* the legal language in this country dealing with rights has become extremely well developed, while the language dealing with responsibility and accountability lags far behind, a gap that accounts for a chorus of blaming and rights proclaiming, but very few songs of personal responsibility and accountability.

With the "blame game" being played for high stakes, the media rushes to quench our "thirst for exposure" with detailed and titillating tales of society's victims. Any modern victim who can gain visibility in the media stands the chance of turning that visibility into easy money or, at the very least, fame and justification. Each tabloid headline nominates its Victim-of-the-Week. You may recall the Amy Fisher case which illustrates this beautifully: her tragic posture as both victim and victimizer not only captured the attention of prime-time news and tabloids every day for weeks, but all three networks rushed movies to the TV screen. Wretched excess! Such exposure for the victims of schemes, deals, mismanagement, neglect, abuse, incompetence, lies, mistakes, manipulations, and a host of other circumstances reinforces victimization attitudes. The better your case for victimization, the more visibility and exposure you get, and, consequently, the greater the psychological or monetary reward you receive. Popular television exposés such as "60 Minutes" have spawned a proliferation of programs that showcase some of America's most notable and scintillating victims: "Exposé," "48 Hours," "Donahue," "Geraldo," "Oprah Winfrey," "Hard Copy," "A Current Affair." And that's on top of thousands of magazine and newspaper articles from *The New York Times* and *Newsweek* to *The Star* and *The National Inquirer.* According to Larry Sabato, author of *Feeding Frenzy: How Attack Journalism Has Transformed American Politics,* the media, and particularly the press, have become "junkyard dogs," instead of "watch dogs," furthering the cult of victimization by turning ordinary people into victims and victims into celebrities.

The "blame game," as well as the seemingly unquenchable "thirst for exposure," are just two symptoms of a widespread "responsibility avoiding" syndrome, which, not surprisingly, has afflicted business organizations as well. The majority of people in organizations today, when confronted with poor performance or unsatisfactory results, immediately begin to formulate excuses, rationalizations, and arguments for why they cannot be held accountable, or, at least, not fully accountable for the problems. In Congress, fingers point every which way as the excesses of the 1980s continue to burden the 1990s with unprecedented debt and calls for sacrifice. John Gutfreund, former chairman of Salomon Brothers, excuses his failure to report a serious trading violation by claiming "a lack of sufficient attention" to the issue, a little slip-up that brought his fabled career to a tragic end. The computer industry blames Japanese chip manufacturers for unfairly dominating the market, Boeing decries unfair European subsidies for Airbus, and IBM points to the volatility in currency markets. This sort of "responsibility-ducking" renders those who practice it powerless in difficult times, because they spend their time preparing victimization stories instead of determining what they themselves can do to get better results.

The culture of victimization has weakened the American character, stressing ease over difficulty, feeling good over being good, appearance over substance, saving face over solving problems, illusion over reality. It threatens to destroy the American corporate character by emphasizing quick fixes over long-term solutions, immediate gains over enduring progress, total quality programs over total quality attitudes, and process over results. If left unresolved, the accountability crisis can so erode productivity, competitiveness, morale, and well-being that "Made in America" will not refer to quality goods and services but to excuses for shoddy performance.

CAN THE WIZARDS HELP?

Corporate America has long been searching for management wizards who could bring them greater productivity, lower costs, expanded market shares, world-class quality, shorter cycle times, continuous improvement, and the ability to exploit change swiftly. With great excitement and fanfare, these wizards have taken America's best corporations on adventure after adventure down interesting, but imaginary, paths to lands of Oz where they make proclamations that are more "make believe" than "make it happen." When you pull back the curtains you discover the "truth" and realize, as did the characters in Oz, that corporate success springs from the willingness of an organization's people to embrace accountability.

Too often, however, companies employ the latest management program only to abandon it when an even more up-to-the-minute new program comes along. New management "solutions" are routinely heralded as the way to bring an organization great success and force its competitors to their knees. However, even more routinely, such "solutions" get abandoned in a year or two in favor of the next wave of management wizardry, because the old "solutions" just did not seem to fix the problems. Moving from one illusion of what it takes to achieve organizational effectiveness to another, executives never stop long enough to discover the truth. In reality when you strip away all the trappings, gimmicks, tricks, techniques, methods, and philosophies of the latest management "fads," you find them all, albeit awkwardly, striving to accomplish the same thing: to produce greater accountability for results. Programs will continue to come and go, fads will fade in and out, processes will continue evolving, and management wizards will keep on multiplying, but the essence of organizational success will always be found in the accountable actions and attitudes of individuals. Regardless of the shape and texture of your organization's structure, the scope and sophistication of its systems, or the completeness and profoundness of its latest strategy, your organization will not succeed in the long run unless accountable people implement and sustain your organization's structures, systems, and strategies. Until the executives in America's organizations stop fooling around with the symptoms of organizational malaise and abandon their preoccupation with programs and new-fangled philosophies that emerge each season, and start uncovering and putting to work the fundamental cause of success, they will simply continue to move from one distraction to the next.

In our view, corporate America's quest for greater results has culminated in little more than a series of smokescreens and mirrors because it has failed to follow *The Oz Principle*. Not surprisingly, the ever-burgeoning army of experts working to correct America's productivity ailments through preaching such gospels as total quality management, total employee involvement, total customer satisfaction, and total liberation has brought little real or lasting progress. The corporate congregations who listen to all the priests of change remain confused. Given the huge compensation received by America's top chief executive officers, you'd think they'd be turning in stunning leadership performances. Unfortunately, too many CEOs hand off accountability to subordinates without acknowledging their own responsibility for creating results. Too many businesspeople today, at all levels in their organizations, behave like Dorothy, the Tin Man, the Lion, and the Scarecrow, searching for wizards in the form of quick fixes, easy solutions, new programs, the "latest thinking," or high-priced executives who can give them the heart, wisdom, courage, or means to get the results they desire. Eventually, and often too late, such wizard-seeking leads to a realization of the Oz Principle ultimately discovered by Dorothy and her companions: that the power to rise above victimizing circumstances and obtain desired results lies within oneself.

In this book, we want to go beyond current management and leadership fads and push to the very heart of what it takes to have success in business. To do so we'll draw upon the stories and experiences of hundreds of individuals and teams from a wide variety of established and emerging companies whose stories will, we hope, strike a nerve the same way *The Wizard of Oz* has for decades.

For instance, you'll meet an executive who tells how he and his associates consciously ignored the eroding competitiveness of their company's products and marketing programs over the years, pretending that things would get better without putting in a huge amount of effort. He describes in his own words how the company finally came to face reality and began fighting for its life, the first step toward getting the results it once took for granted. Many of the best run, most admired corporations succumb from time to time to attitudes of victimization, failing to understand and apply the basic principles and attitudes that get results. Even the brilliant Jack Welch, chief executive officer of General Electric and font of wisdom for many American executives, failed to see the impending calamity in the refrigerator compressor disaster that cost his company $450 million.

You'll also hear from people at lower levels in their organizations, who, while experiencing very real obstacles to performance, allow themselves to get "stuck" in attitudes of victimization when they themselves possess the power to break out and get results. For example, there are a growing number of people in organizations, like Bob, who claims he can't advance within his company because his boss won't provide the coaching he needs; Maria, a director of financial analysis, who worries that she's been taken off the fast track because she's a woman and needs more time with her children; Judith, a cake decorator, who becomes distressed when her boss tells her to "get the lead out" and "get your butt into high gear," prompting her to sue the company; John, a marketing manager, who blames R&D's late product introduction for his division's loss of market share and his own flagging performance; Brewster, a CEO, who argues that too much shareholder oversight has stifled the risk taking of companies like his; Terri, a department store buyer, who fumes daily because it's just too hard to get anything done in the kind of bureaucracy she confronts everyday.

Then you'll meet people with attitudes of accountability who work hard to hold themselves and others responsible for achieving the results they want. For example, at AES, the builder and operator of electricity-producing co-generation plants, CEO Roger Sant implemented a "theybusters" campaign with all the necessary buttons, posters, and flyers to help workers stop blaming the elusive "they" who always seem to stifle results. "They" represent all the finger-pointing, denying, ignoring, pretending, and waiting habits that grow up in organizations and keep people from taking charge of their own destinies. It worked, and AES's productivity has been climbing ever since. However, even in this era of self-managed teams, people at supercompanies such as 3M, Corning, and Procter & Gamble may on occasion point the finger at "them," blaming their own teams for chewing up time, thwarting career advancement, and making it difficult to get the "real" job done.

The latest, most up-to-date management concepts and techniques won't help if you've neglected the basic principles that empower people and organizations to turn in exceptional performances. With humor, satire, and war stories so close to home they'll shock you with recognition, this book explores the very foundation of America's productivity woes, providing insight into the undernourished American character and presenting a proven program for rebuilding it into a world-class force. In addition to its case studies, you'll find valuable lists (such as the "top 20 excuses people in organizations make today"), self-tests, salient tips, and one-on-one feedback exercises, all designed to keep you off the road of victim thinking and on the path toward full accountability. First, however, you must recognize and appreciate the basic difference between victimization and accountability.

THE DESTRUCTIVE FORCE
OF VICTIMIZATION

The greatest destruction visited upon our society by the current cult of victimization stems from its subtle dogma that people cannot become what they desire to become because of their *circumstance*. In essence, this attitude of victimization prevents a person from growing and developing. Returning to Charles Sykes's work, *A Nation of Victims,* he says, "A society that insists on stressing self-expression over self-control generally gets exactly what it deserves. The sulking teenager who insists, 'It's not fair!' is not referring to a standard of equity and justice that any ethicist would recognize. He is, instead, giving voice to the vaguely conceived but firmly held conviction that the world in general and his family in particular serve no legitimate function except to supply his immediate needs and desires. In a culture that celebrates self-absorption and instant gratification, however, this selfishness quickly becomes a dominant and persistent theme. No wonder, then, that the rage of the eternal victim—both black and white, male and female, 'abled' and 'disabled'—is so often expressed in the plaintive cry of disappointed adolescence. When I refer to America's "youth culture," I do not mean merely one that worships the young. I mean a culture that refuses to grow up."

The S&L bailout, which has so severely damaged our economy, could cost American taxpayers $1 trillion over the next 30 years. Who's responsible for this catastrophe? Who could and should have prevented it? Unfortunately, as so often happens in such cases, *Democrats point the finger at Republicans only to get the finger pointed back at them.* Owners and executives deny responsibility and pretend they didn't do anything wrong, while government officials wait and see if the bailout won't cost as much as the experts predict. Such behavior really doesn't surprise us. In fact, many people in American organizations, wanting to feel good about themselves when results don't materialize, would rather offer excuses for why they didn't get the expected results than find ways to overcome the obstacles keeping them from those results. The truth is, the S&L crisis would never have occurred had politicians, government officials, and S&L owners and executives assumed, from the outset, full accountability for the long-term health of the industry. Unfortunately, the S&L crisis offers but one example of the many problems for which no one seems accountable today. From a beleaguered economy and a bankrupt educational system to an abused environment and a burdensome health care system, American society continues to succeed more at pointing the blaming finger than at assuming responsibility for making things better.

A thin line separates success from failure, the great companies from the ordinary ones. Below that line lies excuse making, blaming others, confusion, and an attitude of helplessness, while above that line lies a sense of reality, ownership, commitment, solutions to problems, and determined action. While losers languish *Below The Line*, preparing stories that explain why past efforts went awry, winners reside *Above The Line*, powered by commitment and hard work.

The diagram on the next page will help you visualize the difference between *Below The Line* victimization and *Above The Line* accountability.

People and organizations find themselves thinking and behaving *Below The Line* whenever they consciously or unconsciously avoid accountability for individual or collective results. Stuck in what we call the "victim cycle," they begin to lose their spirit and will, until, eventually, they feel completely powerless. Only by moving *Above The Line* and climbing the *Steps To Accountability* can they become powerful again. When individuals, teams, or entire organizations remain *Below The Line*, unaware or unconscious of reality, things get worse, not better, without anyone knowing why. Rather than face reality, sufferers of this malady oftentimes begin ignoring or pretending not to know about their accountability, denying their responsibility, blaming others for their predicament, citing confusion as a reason for inaction, asking others to tell them what to do, claiming that they can't do it, or just waiting to see if the situation will miraculously resolve itself.

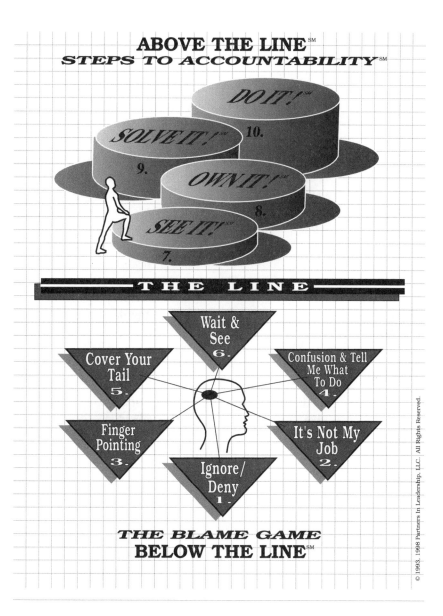

This process, if unabated, can wreak both personal and pro-fessional havoc, as it did for both Exxon and Joseph Hazelwood, former captain of the supertanker Exxon *Valdez*. On March 24, 1989, in what became the worst oil disaster in U.S. history, the Exxon *Valdez* struck a reef, burst a hole in its hull, and poured millions of gallons of crude oil into the pristine waters of Prince William Sound, Alaska. In early reports it became apparent that Exxon was feeling betrayed and victimized by Hazelwood. In fact, Exxon was rather predictably traveling through each stage of the victim cycle, beginning with pretending not to know about Hazelwood's history of drinking problems, to blaming Hazel-wood, to hoping that the initial reports were overstated and exaggerated. Investigators showed that Hazelwood did suffer from a drinking problem and ten hours after the accident his blood alcohol registered 50 percent higher than the limit set by the Coast Guard for seamen operating a moving ship. Strangely enough, Exxon itself supplied low-alcohol beer to tanker crew-men even though doing so violated the company's ban on drink-ing aboard ship, making matters worse. Exxon's sharp cuts in crew size had left the Valdez crew shorthanded and fatigued. Hazelwood's and Exxon's *Below The Line* attitude not only caused great difficulties for themselves but resulted in an enor-mous environmental problem for us all. Even during the exten-sive clean-up of Prince William Sound, when Exxon had the opportunity to pull itself back up *Above The Line*, the company failed to provide employees and volunteers with the necessary breathing masks to prevent the inhalation of toxic petroleum fumes and used cleaning chemicals that some experts say did more damage than good.

In another example, a survey of U.S. workers conducted by Northwestern National Life Insurance Company found that over one-third of the surveyed workers expected to quit their jobs soon because of high stress and "burnout." Almost 50 percent of those surveyed considered their jobs highly stressful, double the per-centage who felt that way in 1985. Northwestern analysts concluded that the major cause of employee stress and burnout was the "lack of control over one's job." Ironically, our own research and experience suggest that the majority of workers who feel they have no control over their jobs choose to feel that way. Rather than accept accountability for making things different and better, they actually behave like victims of circumstance.

Consider, from an expanded viewpoint, the demise of Michael Milken and his investment banking firm, Drexel Burnham. In what, for many, has come to symbolize the greed of the 1980s, Michael Milken reigned as the junk bond king, spreading the philosophy of his kingdom, Drexel Burnham, across corporate America and ushering in an era of debt financing that has proven ruinous to many companies and industries. When corporate America finally sagged under the burdensome debt created by junk bonds, the house of cards came tumbling down, and Drexel Burnham with it. The investment banking firm filed bankruptcy, Michael Milken went to jail, and everyone on Wall Street blamed Milken and his company for their own sad fates. Throughout the country, investors—mutual funds, insurance companies, corporations, and individuals—wriggled off the hook by claiming they had been victimized by evil forces beyond their control. Their once unabashed praise for the wizardry of Michael Milken now turned to universal condemnation. And what about the other respectable investment banking firms that had jumped into the junk bond game—Goldman Sachs, First Boston, Merrill Lynch, Shearson Lehman Hutton? Not their fault, they cried, they were "lured" into it.

Well, that's only half the story. The other half, the rarely told half, reveals a saga of greed that caused mutual funds to own 30 percent of all junk bonds during their heyday. Insurance companies owned another 30 percent, pension funds 15 percent, and savings and loans 7 percent. With junk bonds paying five to six percentage points above conventional bonds, greedy investors just couldn't resist the temptation, even when it didn't take a degree in finance to see the imprudence of excessive debt and the shortsightedness of inflated returns. But, then, why accept any blame for the ultimate disaster, when it's so easy to find someone else on whom to heap it? It's so natural to excuse yourself from blame. It's so human to pretend you really didn't understand the risks or the circumstances. And it's so common to wait and see if things will somehow, someway get better, without any undo effort on your part. In truth, however, many of the so-called Drexel Burnham victims chose their own fates by avoiding accountability every step of the way.

To get *Above The Line* and out of the "victim cycle" you must climb the *Steps To Accountability* by adopting *See It*SM, *Own It*SM, *Solve It*SM, *Do It*SM attitudes. The first step—*See It*—involves recognizing and acknowledging the full reality of a situation. As you'll soon see, this step poses the greatest hurdle because it's so hard for most people to undertake an honest self-appraisal and acknowledge that you can do more to get results. The second step—*Own It*—means accepting responsibility for the experiences and realities you create for yourself and others. With this step, you pave the road to action. The third step—*Solve It*—entails changing reality by finding and implementing solutions to problems that you may not have thought of before, while avoiding the trap of falling back *Below The Line* when obstacles present themselves. And fourth, the *Do It* step entails mustering the commitment and courage to follow-through with the solutions you have identified, even if those solutions involve a lot of risk. Happily, these four steps make enormously good sense—common sense. And ultimately, we believe that common sense provides a major force for moving people *Above The Line*.

▲
―――――――――――――――――――――――――――――――――

THE TRANSFORMING POWER OF ACCOUNTABILITY

However much we may try to believe differently, however hard we may try to shake it off, we all know that we are on the line for results. We know we have responsibilities and that we are required to learn them and to perform at expected levels. While its perfectly normal to have bad days, to be down or to get sick, we all know intuitively that most the work in this world gets done by those who don't feel well. Down deep, we know that others are not at fault when we have made mistakes or "dropped the ball." And we know ever so poignantly that we alone determine the course of our lives and the measure of happiness that we derive from them.

We have spent years studying, thinking about, and struggling to improve the ways individuals and organizations get results. Over the years we've followed all the major developments in management thought, from the technology of quality control to the art of leadership. Although we've learned something from each new trend and have even added to them a few twists of our own, we've concluded that success in business boils down to one simple principle: you can either get stuck or get results. Period. Case closed.

Accountability for results rests at the very core of the total quality, employee empowerment, customer satisfaction, and continuous improvement movements so popular today. Interestingly, the essence of these programs boils down to getting people to become personally *accountable*—rising above their circumstances and doing whatever it takes (within the bounds of ethical behavior) to get the results they want. Creating this individual accountability is the number one managerial and leadership challenge facing organizations today. However, while many people and organizations recognize the pervasive and urgent need for such accountability, few know how to create it or maintain it, as evidenced by the vast number of creative excuses promulgated every day for why affairs have deteriorated to such a sorry state. A debt-burdened economy, drug-plagued and violence-torn inner cities, businesses pounded by European and Japanese competitors, a crumbling health care system, underpaid teachers and overbureaucratized school systems, a record number of personal and corporate bankruptcies? "Hey, it's not my fault!" Unfortunately, even when well-documented, legally defensible or logically compelling excuses let people "off the hook" for poor results, those "responsibility duckers" do nothing but reinforce a habit of side-stepping problems rather than facing up to and solving them. It's no wonder why America currently suffers from an unprecedented confidence crisis.

All of us at one time or another succumb to the urge to take ourselves "off the hook" with one excuse or another: "I didn't have enough time," "If we only had the resources," "The schedule is too tight," "That's not my job," "It's the boss's fault," "I didn't know," "The competition outsmarted us," "The whole economy's in trouble," "Things will get better tomorrow." Whatever the wording, all our justifications for failure focus on "why it can't be done," rather than on "what *else* I can do." To be sure, people really do fall victim every day to manipulating bosses, unscrupulous competitors, conniving colleagues, economic calamities and all manner of liars, cheats and villains. Things do happen to people over which they have little or no control. Sometimes, people do not deserve what happens to them because they did not contribute to it nor are they legitimately accountable for it. But even in the worst of such circumstances, people can't move forward if they just sit around feeling powerless and blaming others for their misery. Regardless of the situation, you cannot even begin to turn things around until you take charge of your circumstances and accept your own responsibility for better results in the future. You must get *Above The Line* that separates success from failure.

When individuals and organizations assume accountability for their own success and results, they naturally rise *Above The Line*, even when the going gets extremely rough. Former CEO Ken Olsen and his company Digital Equipment Corporation illustrate the point. Digital Equipment's popular VAX minicomputers, after reaching their zenith in the late 1980s, soon fell prey to powerful desktop microcomputers, called workstations, that began luring away Digital's prize customers. DEC faced a serious crisis. Ken Olsen's now-famous quote, "You can be sure our plan was perfect—it's just that the assumptions were wrong," shows that rather than playing the victim, he assumed an accountable attitude, one that's still helping reshape the beleaguered company. Instead of blaming others, denying responsibility, acting confused, or waiting for things to get better, Olsen took the bull by the horns, and got the company working productively above the line, incorporating the key features of the workstation into his company's VAX computers in a new product line codenamed Alpha. Many obstacles, from technology and design to marketing and finance, arose as Olsen worked to reshape the entire company and culture. As the culture shifted, his can-do, get-results attitude took hold throughout the company, laying the groundwork for a comeback. In the face of tough and even grueling obstacles, Olsen helped the company stay *Above The Line* and get back on track toward future success. However, in late 1992, after a $3 billion loss for the year, Olsen was asked to resign. Admirably, Olsen never played "the victim." He assumed his accountability for the overall results of the company and rather than leaving the company deeply entrenched in the victim cycle, he left them working diligently *Above The Line.* In our view, the results of Ken Olsen's efforts to keep DEC *Above The Line* will continue to inspire thousands of DEC workers for many years to come, instilling within them a desire to ultimately make the company's fledgling comeback a success. As DEC continues forward, Ken Olsen, at age 66, finds no shortage of opportunities to apply his vision and commitment elsewhere as he serves on the board of directors of two corporations, three institutions of higher education, and a museum.

The transforming power of accountability is real as illustrated by Ford's Taurus plant in Atlanta, Georgia, which has become the most productive automobile plant in America, if not the world. A new Ford Taurus rolls off the assembly line every 17.6 worker-hours, compared to the average European mark of

35 worker-hours, General Motors' standard of 27 worker-hours, and the Japanese 21 worker-hours. How do Ford executives and Taurus plant workers explain this world-class production efficiency? To their minds, it's not the new plant, young workers, state-of-the-art technology, just-in-time inventories, or teamwork that's made the difference. According to plant manager Robert Anderson, what has made the difference is an attitude among plant workers that "they can overcome any obstacle that gets in the way." Exemplifying the value of climbing the *Steps To Accountability* at work, people in the Atlanta plant welcome individual responsibility for results. First, they strive to see any situation clearly and honestly. Knowing that Ford faces stiff competition that the automaker cannot meet or beat with its head in the sand, the Taurus people try hard to maintain a strong sense of reality. Second, having come to "own" the situation and the expected results, knowing they will share in the profits, they muster an amazing commitment to get things right, not because Ford wants it that way, but because they do. Third, these workers continuously "solve" problems and remove obstacles. When a small scratch was appearing occasionally on the hood of one Taurus model, the group responsible promised to find the cause and eliminate it, no if's, and's, or but's. Fourth, and finally, Taurus people "do" whatever it takes to get desired results. When the workers discovered that it was an alcohol wiping machine that was damaging cars during the paint-stripping process, they took the time and effort to find a better way to get the job done, a better way that ultimately achieved higher quality and lower repair costs. In another instance, workers purchased five diesel generators to supplement their power needs during peak load hours, saving themselves $800,000 a year.

This sort of attitude of accountability lies at the core of any effort to improve quality, satisfy customers, empower people, build teams, maximize effectiveness, and get results. Simple? Yes and no. It's a simple message, but it takes a tremendous investment of time and courage to make accountability an integral part of an organization. Whether you confront your own self-diminishing attitudes in your small start-up enterprise or in the management ranks of a *Fortune* 500 firm, you cannot expect to create a better future unless you begin to take the time and find the courage to get *Above The Line.*

THE JOURNEY BEGINS

Part One of this book explores *The Oz Principle*SM, revealing how many American businesspeople and organizations the world over suffer from the same feelings of anxiety and helplessness that beset Dorothy, the Scarecrow, the Lion, and the Tin Man on their trek down the yellow brick road to Oz. In these early chapters we show how people who use their victimization to justify inaction, excuse ineffectiveness, or rationalize poor performance unwittingly stifle their own progress, while in later chapters we demonstrate how people who accept accountability for making things better move beyond their victimization to overcome obstacles, deal with setbacks, and rise to new heights. By the end of the journey you will not only have learned how to become more accountable for results, you will know how to create organizational cultures that develop and reward the sort of accountability needed to rebuild the American character.

An understanding of the seriousness of our current American character crisis will help you travel the real path to results and prepare you to discern the subtle, often obscure, line between victimization and accountability. Once you come to distinguish *Below The Line* attitudes and behavior from *Above The Line* performance, you'll find yourself so much more able to tap the transforming power of accountability for yourself and your organization, the subjects of Parts Two and Three.

The book's broad mix of examples will detail exactly how people and organizations, armed with attitudes of accountability, can overcome the obstacles, excuses, and biases that keep them from getting the results they want. Drawing from the sometimes startling and always eye-opening experiences of individuals and groups in a wide array of organizations, we hope to show how people and organizations can overcome victim attitudes and behavior and step *Above The Line* to attain superior performance. Our aim is to transcend the conventional literature on quality, productivity, customer service, empowerment, and team performance by striking at the core of what causes people to get results in all their endeavors, something so desperately needed in today's organizations. By focusing on the fundamental cause of poor quality, low productivity, customer dissatisfaction, ineffectiveness, wasted talent, dysfunctional teams, or a general lack of accountability, we hope to move you beyond explaining why you didn't or can't do better to what you can do to make your future brighter.

THE YELLOW BRICK ROAD: GETTING STUCK IN THE VICTIM CYCLE

The next morning the sun was behind a cloud, but they started on, as if they were quite sure which way they were going.

"If we walk far enough," said Dorothy, "we shall sometime come to some place, I am sure."

But day by day passed away, and they still saw nothing before them but the scarlet fields. The Scarecrow began to grumble a bit.

"We have surely lost our way," he said, "and unless we find it again in time to reach the Emerald City I shall never get my brains."

"Nor I my heart," declared the Tin Woodsman. "It seems to me I can scarcely wait till I get to Oz, and you must admit this is a very long journey."

"You see," said the Cowardly Lion, with a whimper, "I haven't the courage to keep tramping forever, without getting anywhere at all."

Then Dorothy lost heart. She sat down on the grass and looked at her companions, and they sat down and looked at her, and Toto found that for the first time in his life he was too tired to chase a butterfly that flew past his head; so he put out his tongue and panted and looked at Dorothy as if to ask what they should do next.

THE WIZARD OF OZ
By L. Frank Baum

Victimization has infected so much of our modern society, from small, inconsequential acts to life-destroying abuses, that it affects everyone each and every day. To be sure, the suffering a person inflicts on another poses one of the greatest dilemmas of modern life, yet the shelter of victimization can render the sufferer completely ineffective. Even the most successful people and organizations can fall prey to the virus of victimization, even Supreme Court justices. *The Wall Street Journal* recently reported: "Clarence Thomas tells his friends that he intends to serve on the Supreme Court for 43 years. Why 43, exactly? Because, he figures, that's how old he was when he survived his confirmation-hearing storm over Anita Hill's harassment charges in 1991. The world stuck it to him for 43 years; now it's payback time. As his edgy humor suggests, Justice Thomas's anger didn't begin with Ms. Hill's allegations. It was kindled in a segregation-marred boyhood and smoldered for years as he encountered accusations that, as a black conservative, he was necessarily a hypocrite." One might ask, "Is any man big enough to overcome these circumstances?" Imagine the price the American people would pay should a Justice of the Supreme Court adjudicate law from a position of resentment rather than from a position of justice. Only by offering role models of accountability can judicial leaders hope to stem the tide of professional victims who are clogging the American courts. According to another recent *Wall Street Journal* article, "Since 1977, Barbara Conway (a disguised name), who has a law degree but hasn't been admitted to the bar, has filed more than 30 lawsuits on her own behalf, many of them personal injury claims, and pursued numerous additional complaints privately or through nonjudicial arbitration. She has taken on tenants, neighbors, major corporations, the U.S. government, and has been successful in receiving cash settlements or other relief in roughly half the cases that have reached a conclusion." Like most habitual victims, Ms. Conway thinks she's right, but the attorneys and judges who have dealt with her find her claims greatly exaggerated. Who's responsible for such exaggeration? Certainly, Ms. Conway deserves some of the credit, but so do the attorneys, the judges, the insurance companies, and everyone else who contributes to this litigious society. According to *The Wall Street Journal* article, "By her account—in court files, testimony and medical records—she has been the target of a number of vicious assaults by, among others, a drunk, a postal worker, a private investigator, a hospital employee and the wife of a colleague at a university where Ms. Conway worked. She says she has taken serious falls in two San Francisco department stores, been injured by a door at a Bank of America branch and had her foot run over by a shopping cart at a grocery store." In the injured foot suit, Ms. Conway won $17,500 from Liberty Mutual, the insurer of R. H. Macy & Company. Some of the money covered "rental maintenance activities, such as painting and plumbing work on her house, manicures and grooming services for her dogs." The attorney who represented Ms. Conway and settled the foot-injury case described Ms. Conway's accusation as "just your typical exaggerated claim." One superior court judge, Judge Jack Berman, declared her a "vexatious litigant," hoping, perhaps, to thwart her future lawsuits, but Conway protested and the judge reversed his ruling because, in his words, "It just became too much of a pain. . . . To be perfectly candid with you, I didn't want to be bothered with all the secondary motions that would follow. . . . She was the worst. . . . [But] it is hard to stop anybody in our culture from getting their day in court."

Another front-page *Wall Street Journal* article dubbed a 44-year-old nurse, Sherrol Miller, the "queen of the talk shows." According to the article, "So far, Ms. Miller has to her credit three 'Donahues,' two 'Sally Jessy Raphaels,' one 'Geraldo,' one 'Joan Rivers' and a 'Montel Williams,' not to mention an 'Attitudes' before that show was canceled." What makes Sherrol Miller such a popular TV guest? As she explains, "I was the tenth wife of a gay, con-man bigamist." As the TV talk shows scramble to maintain their ratings, they gladly pay fees to victims like Miller who love to tell their stories to an audience hungry for tabloid tales of abuse. According to Pat Priest who wrote a doctoral dissertation on "Self Disclosure on Television," the victims who tell their stories on TV achieve a new status: "They see it as being chosen." Sherrol Miller herself describes her TV appearances as a kind of therapy, "I've had a happy life ever since," she boasts. And when she meets new friends, "I tell them, Don't mess around with me, or I'll talk about you on a talk show." In Pat Priest's view, telling victim stories on TV makes a lot of economic sense: " 'Oprah' set off the tabloid talk deluge almost seven years ago, and since then a few dozen clones have tried to cash in on the format's low overhead and tremendous upside. It costs the shows about $12 million to produce a 40-week season, the industry average, yet a perennial winner like 'Oprah' brings in revenue of $190 million a year. A dozen syndicated daytime talk shows now vie with one another on the air, three others are in development, while still more are on the storyboards." Now victimization not only claims its day in court, it also demands its afternoon on the tube.

In this chapter we want to deepen your understanding of the dangers inherent in these widespread victimization attitudes, particularly as they relate to business and management situations, because our experience has taught us that it's very difficult to climb the steps to accountability unless you fully understand how and why people get stuck *Below The Line*.

THE LINE BETWEEN VICTIMIZATION AND ACCOUNTABILITY

There is a line between accountability and victimization that separates rising above your circumstances to get the results you want and falling into the victim cycle where you can easily get stuck. Neither individuals nor organizations can stay on the line between these two realms because events will inexorably push them in one direction or the other. While both people and organizations can exhibit accountability in some situations yet manifest victim behavior in others, some issue or circumstance will arise to influence them to think and act from either an *Above The Line* or *Below The Line* perspective.

Even the strongest commitment to accountability will not prevent you from ever falling *Below The Line*. That sort of perfection is not humanly possible. Everyone, even the highest achievers, can get stuck in the victim cycle on occasion, but those who are truly accountable never remain there for long.

People and organizations operating *Below The Line* consciously or unconsciously avoid accountability for results. Languishing in the victim cycle, they begin to lose their "spirit" and "will," until eventually, they feel powerless, just as Dorothy and her friends did. If they choose to continue feeling victimized, they will move through predictable stages in an unending cycle that thwarts individual and organizational productivity: ignoring or pretending not to know about their accountability, claiming it's not their job, ducking their responsibility, blaming others for their predicament, citing confusion as an excuse for inaction, asking others to tell them what to do, claiming that they can't do it, developing their story for why they are not at fault, and finally waiting to see if some hoped-for miracle will be bestowed by an imaginary wizard.

▲
_____

EVEN THE BEST COMPANIES SOMETIMES FALL *BELOW THE LINE*SM

Getting trapped in the victim cycle can afflict even the most admired corporations, as it did a few years ago at General Electric. *Fortune* magazine's 1993 survey of the most admired companies in America ranked General Electric as second in the

Electronics and Electrical Equipment Industry and the ninth overall in terms of financial performance. Almost 100 years ago, on January 1, 1900, *The Wall Street Journal* identified GE as one of America's top 12 companies. Today, only General Electric remains from that original list of 12, and for many businesspeople, the company represents the epitome of continuous corporate transformation. However, GE isn't perfect.

Several years ago General Electric felt pressure to increase the market share and profits of its appliance division. To get the ball rolling, the company hired consultant Ira Magaziner to analyze GE's refrigerator business. As part of his recommendations, Magaziner suggested that GE either buy refrigerator compressors abroad or figure out how to make better ones at home. Opting for the latter course, GE assigned its chief design engineer, John Truscott, the task of assembling a team to design a new rotary compressor. In 1983, after Truscott and another engineer, Tom Blunt, and division head Roger Schipke presented the results to Jack Welch, chairman and chief executive officer of the company, Welch authorized the construction of a $120 million factory to produce the new compressors. The board of directors gave its full approval to the decision. In 1984, 20 senior executives met to review test data on the new compressor before initiating production. Finding no faults, they decided to go forward. In the spring of 1986, full-scale production began in the new Tennessee plant, where a new rotary compressor came off the assembly line every 6 seconds (compared to the 65 minutes it took to produce the old compressor).

In the summer of 1987, the first compressor failure occurred in Philadelphia, followed shortly thereafter by thousands more. Then, in 1988, engineers found the problem: the use of powdered metal instead of hardened steel or cast iron in the compressors. Ironically, GE had tried powdered metal parts in its air conditioners a decade earlier and had found the material unacceptable. At this point, Schipke decided to drop the new compressor in favor of foreign models, causing GE to report a $450 million pre-tax charge in 1989 for resolving the fiasco.

A closer examination of this situation reveals how GE went through every stage of the victim cycle. Executives overlooked earlier problems with rotary compressor technology. Although Japanese companies had already experienced severe difficulties with rotary compressors, no one at GE could recall that fact. Ditto with problems involving powdered metal parts.

All the hints that rotary compressors might not work were denied. Even early reports of excessive heat, worn bearing surfaces, and the breakdown of the sealed lubricating oil fell on deaf ears up and down the line.

Once the failure of the compressor became a stark reality, fingers began pointing in every direction. Senior executives, division management, design engineers, consultants, and manufacturers all took turns blaming others for the problem. Engineers, initially concerned that the new compressor wasn't getting enough field testing, set aside their worries by doing what they were told to do, namely, keeping the project on schedule. When concerns became more widespread, people seemed to think, "We can't tell Jack the bad news" and "We can't let the schedule slip."

Finally, everyone in the appliance division determined that the best course of action was to "wait and see" if things would get better on their own. Many people thought that perhaps things would never really get that bad; after all, this was General Electric, one of the most effective organizations on earth.

Even one of the most effective organizations on earth can find itself *Below The Line* on occasion. Whenever it does, the bill comes due sooner or later. In GE's case, the price tag for their dip *Below The Line* accumulated an estimated $450 million in direct expenditures and eight years of lost opportunity.

HOW TO RECOGNIZE WHEN YOU'RE *BELOW THE LINE*^{SM}

Whenever you get stuck in the victim cycle, you can't get unstuck until you first acknowledge that you're functioning *Below The*

Line and paying a high price for it. Only with that acknowledgment can you begin assuming a *See It* attitude that gives you the perspective you need to get *Above The Line*. Oftentimes, unable to overcome the inertia of the victim cycle on your own, you need feedback from an objective person such as a friend, spouse or, as in the case of GE, a customer in Philadelphia with a failed refrigerator compressor. However, you can greatly improve your ability to recognize when you've become stuck in the victim cycle by looking for one or more of the following telltale clues:

▾ You feel "held captive" by your circumstances.

▾ You feel you have no control over your present circumstances.

▾ You don't listen when others tell you, directly or indirectly, that they think you could have done more to achieve better results.

▾ You find yourself blaming others and pointing fingers.

▾ Your discussions of problems focus more on what you cannot do, rather than what you can do.

▾ You fail to confront the toughest issues you face.

▾ You find yourself being "sought out" by others so they can tell you what someone else did to them this time.

▾ You find yourself unwilling to ask probing questions about your own accountability.

▾ You feel you are being treated unfairly and you don't think you can do anything about it.

▾ You repeatedly find yourself in a defensive posture.

▾ You spend a lot of time talking about things you cannot change (e.g., your boss, shareholders, the economy's performance, government regulations).

▾ You cite your confusion as a reason for not taking action.

- ▼ You avoid the people, the meetings, and the situations that require you to report on your responsibilities.
- ▼ You find yourself saying:

  "It's not my job."

  "There's nothing I can do about it."

  "Someone ought to tell him."

  "All we can do is wait and see."

  "Just tell me what you want me to do."

  "If it were me, I'd do it differently."

- ▼ You frequently waste time and energy "boss or colleague bashing."
- ▼ You find yourself spending valuable time crafting a compelling story detailing why you were not at fault.
- ▼ You repeatedly tell the same old story about how someone took advantage of you.
- ▼ You view the world with a pessimistic attitude.

If you detect any of these signs in yourself, your team, or your organization, act immediately to help yourself or someone else recognize those excuses for what they are: impediments to accountability and results. Once this recognition occurs, you and others can begin to understand the nuances and subtleties of the victim cycle, just as Dorothy and her companions ultimately did.

COMMON STAGES OF THE VICTIM CYCLE

While the victim cycle runs through many stages, we have identified six basic ones common to most people and organizations. As you consider the following descriptions, ask yourself if you see any of your own or your organization's behavior in them.

1. IGNORE/DENY. A typical beginning point for those who become ensnared in the victim cycle is the "Ignore" or "Deny" stage where people pretend not to know that there is a problem, remain unaware that the problem affects them, or choose to altogether deny the problem.

For instance, many of us have witnessed this stage of the victim cycle play itself out when American industries fell prey to smart and worthy competitors who took advantage of the opportunity presented to them by a "nation in denial." First it was the steel industry which denied the need to change and procrastinated their efforts to be more competitive; thus losing their predominance in the marketplace to the more advanced technology of foreign competitors. Then, during the 1970s and even the early 1980s, American auto makers began paying a terrible price for ignoring the trends and pretending not to know that customers wanted higher-quality, more fuel-efficient cars. Choosing to deny the changes in consumer preferences, Detroit continued to believe that "customers will drive whatever we build for them." Japanese auto makers, on the other hand, operated from *Above The Line* and designed cars which were better suited to the world's customers.

How many industries will become victims of their own denial by continuing to pretend not to know what will one day be most obvious? The dangerous thing about this stage in the victim cycle is the devastating price people pay when they get stuck in "Ignore" or "Deny." It almost seems impossible for those in the "denial mode" to see what is really going on around them. Only after the price has begun to be paid, and often when it is too late, does one begin to truly recognize the extent of their own denial and the damage that has been done.

Not long ago the nation was forced to acknowledge a dilemma which the recent *Adult Literacy in America* survey released by the Department of Education brought out into the open. The four-year survey concluded that nearly half of the adults in the United States lack the literacy necessary for dealing effectively with modern life. A *Time* magazine article on the subject reports that "roughly 90 million Americans over age 16—almost half that category's total population—are, as far as most workplaces are concerned, basically unfit for employment. Who is included in that definition? Those who can sign a credit-card receipt but are incapable of writing a letter when they think their bill is wrong; those who can pay the correct change at the supermarket but have difficulty calculating the difference between regular and sale prices; those who can scan a newspaper story but cannot paraphrase its contents." What of the price American business is paying for this lack of literacy? What of the price America will pay in the future for the inability to compete with other nations that have come to recognize their most important national resource—their people? The article continues, "...Perhaps the worst news from the survey was the hubris expressed by those who were tested: when asked if they read well or very well, 71% of those in the bottom grade said yes. If the ETS survey is accurate, the U.S. is not only significantly populated by people unprepared for current and advancing technologies, but most of them do not know that they do not know."

In another example, studies have shown that 70 to 80 percent of graduating MBAs leave their first job within the first 12 months out of school. The study showed that most MBAs leave their first job, not because they lack technical competence, but because they cannot function effectively in the work environment, get along with people, and fit into the company's culture. Both graduating MBAs and business schools continue to deny the organizational reality that it's not just what you do or what you know, but how you do it that determines success in business. When confronted with this reality, most business schools, management professors, and MBAs claim they appreciate the problem, but the facts suggest that perhaps they don't.

In 1993, *The Wall Street Journal* reported that the Chambers Development Company, an acclaimed waste management firm, had overstated its profits by $362 million and had perpetuated many other accounting errors for several years since it went public in 1985. Reporter Gabriella Stern characterized John G. Rangos, Sr., the company's 63-year-old founder and CEO, as a man "obsessed with making his garbage company a star and insistent on managers' meeting his lofty profit goals," leading to an "environment in which manipulating numbers was tolerated." After one executive told Rangos that the company would fall short of projected profits, Rangos told the executive to "Go find the rest of it." However, when auditors Grant Thornton refused to continue signing off on Chambers' numbers, the company's bright track record dimmed. In a report submitted by the accounting firm of Deloitte & Touche, auditors revealed that Chambers Development "covered its losses by grossly understating expenses and in the process violated generally accepted accounting principles." In response, John G. Rangos, Jr., denied "that his family in any way encouraged subordinates to manipulate earnings figures or use inappropriate accounting practices." Chambers Development Company and its CEO obviously ducked its accountability and denied their *involvement in any wrongdoing.*

The challenge of the "Ignore/Deny" stage of the victim cycle is captured in the words of Mark Twain, "it's not what you don't know, it's what you know that just ain't so." Pretending not to know or ignoring a problem will keep you *Below The Line* and impair your ability to get results.

2. IT'S NOT MY JOB. How many times have we heard, and perhaps even spoken, the words, "It's not my job?" This age-old excuse is a well-worn phrase that has been used in countless discussions to excuse inaction, to redirect blame, and to avoid responsibility. In this stage there is an awareness that something needs to be done to get the result but there is also an obvious lack of responsibility or desire to involve oneself. People assuming this victim attitude seek shelter from what they perceive to be additional effort without sufficient reward and personal sacrifice without benefit. They believe that it is not in their best interest for them to take on this "added" responsibility. "It's not my job" is a phrase that gained legitimacy in a past era in which job descriptions set the boundaries across which the worker dared not step, performance expectations focused on individuals' ability to "do their jobs" rather than on their ability to contribute to "getting the result," and organizations assumed it was okay for departments to fight for what they needed instead of working for what was really best for the company.

No matter where you go, at work or at home, if you look, you will see examples of this stage of the victim cycle every day. To illustrate, recall a time when you were on the "other side" of "it's not my job." Have you experienced something like the following scenario? You walk into a store needing to get some help. Encouraged by the company's slogan which reads "we do what it takes to make you happy," you become very disappointed when you only hear, "I'm sorry, but I can't help you, that's not my job." For many people there is nothing more infuriating than becoming a pawn in an endless cycle of "it's not my job," bouncing from one person to the next, finding no one willing to take responsibility. The price of such *Below The Line* behavior becomes onerous when you have to pay it, which is precisely the point. Whenever people use this phrase to duck responsibility, avoiding the opportunity to play a role in getting results, someone pays the price. It may be an indirect price, it may even be difficult to trace, but ultimately someone pays a price. Perhaps the price will be in how others perceive you, perhaps it will be in how the company's performance ultimately affects your pay, perhaps it will be in what someone could have done to help you but didn't, because "it's their job." In the end, "It's not my job" is a universal excuse that says "don't blame me, I had nothing to do with it."

3. FINGER-POINTING. In this well-practiced stage of the victim cycle people deny their own responsibility for poor results and seek to shift the blame to others. "Don't blame me" becomes the catch phrase for transferring fault to the other guy. For instance, the chief operating officer of a leading health care company publicly admitted that a problem with its polyurethane extrusion process was "perplexing everyone in the company." As soon as company employees became aware of the COO's admission, they began using the "extrusion process" excuse for all sorts of product defects, schedule delays, and inefficiencies. Productivity and profitability plummeted as hundreds of employees pointed their fingers in every direction but at themselves.

Blaming can take many forms, and it occurs in even the best of companies. Herman Miller, the furniture manufacturer named by *Fortune* magazine as one of the ten "best managed" and "most innovative" companies and listed by Levering and Moskowitz as one of The Best 100 Companies to Work for in America, recently engaged in a bit of finger-pointing. The company's marketing copy writers, keeping in mind the company's heralded commitment to customer satisfaction as outlined in the best-selling book *Leadership Is an Art* by CEO Max DuPree, prepared the following statement for placement on all Herman Miller shipping cartons:

> This furniture has been carefully inspected before being packed for shipment. It was in perfect condition when packed and received by the transportation company for shipment and delivery to you. If, when you open this crate or carton, you find that the piece of furniture has been damaged, hold shipment intact and call the transportation company immediately, requesting that they send an agent to supply you with an inspection report. This report is necessary, along with the original freight bill, to support a claim. Damage received during transit is the responsibility of the transportation company. If the above instructions are followed, we will be glad to assist in handling claims. Herman Miller, Inc.

That disclaimer lays the groundwork for Herman Miller to point the finger at the transportation company if anything goes wrong, and it reveals a *Below The Line* attitude toward customer satisfaction. To Herman Miller's credit, the company's vice president of corporate quality made the following statement in response to specific customer feedback: "The notice as it now stands communicates a feeling of 'we did our jobs; if it's wrong it must be the other guy's fault.'" Not desiring to play the "victim game" by blaming or appearing to blame others, the company changed the label to read:

> This furniture has been crafted with pride and care and reflects our commitment to supply you with the best products available in the world. If, when you open this crate or carton, you notice that the piece of furniture has been damaged, hold the shipment and the original freight bill intact and call your Herman Miller dealer immediately. The transportation company should send an agent to supply you with an inspection report. This report is necessary, along with the original freight bill, to support a damage claim. We are fully committed to your complete satisfaction and ask only that you follow the above procedure in the event of product damage during shipment.

Unfortunately, many other companies engage in "blame games" every day: marketing blames R&D for designing products or features the market doesn't need instead of the ones marketing knows the customer wants; sales attacks marketing for such inadequate support as ill-conceived brochures or mistargeted commercials; manufacturing accuses sales of signing off on poor forecasts that cause either too many back-orders or too much inventory; R&D points the finger at manufacturing for not resolving manufacturability problems on the factory floor; vice presidents heap scorn on directors for not taking more responsibility, while directors chide vice presidents for either not providing sufficient guidelines or not letting go. Around and around it goes, a merry-go-round of accusations that do nothing to solve an organization's problems.

4. CONFUSION/TELL ME WHAT TO DO. At this more subtle stage of the victim cycle people cite confusion as an excuse to relieve themselves of their accountability. If they don't understand the problem or the situation, surely they can't be expected to do anything about it. For example, a quality assurance manager at a major chemical company received from his superiors comprehensive and confidential feedback about his department's poor performance. After he had thoroughly researched the problem himself, however, he heard so many conflicting reasons for it that he felt completely baffled. Approaching his boss, he confessed his confusion saying, "Given all these mixed signals, how can you hold me responsible for this mess?"

Another manager at a large food processing company received a "mixed review" from her boss during a performance appraisal session: "You do some things well, other things not so well." Given the "mixed review," the boss asked the manager to think about the feedback and respond to it within a week. The manager, befuddled by the appraisal, complained to her husband, her peers, and her subordinates during the week that her boss's evaluation made no sense: "He just doesn't understand me." Rather than seek clarification, the manager opted to remain confused and resentful. When she met with her boss to discuss her reactions, she complained that he had sent her such mixed signals she couldn't possibly initiate any changes in her approach to her job.

> "I don't think that's wise," cautioned her boss. "What about the negative feedback I gave you? That was pretty clear."

> "Well, it wasn't to me."

> "I expected the review session to stimulate some changes that would further your growth and development with the company."

> "You just don't understand me."

> "You're right, I don't."

Within a few months the manager left the company to take another job. Unfortunately, she allowed herself to remain as confused as ever, hoping somehow that a change of scenery would make things better. It didn't, and usually doesn't.

Ironically, hundreds of victims lost millions of dollars in recent telemarketing scams, where promoters promised high, risk-free returns to investors if they put their money into second mortgages on commercial and residential properties. The investors found themselves fleeced yet again when they responded to a second round of scams by new promoters claiming they would recover previous losses for a fee. According to *The Wall Street Journal,* investors in these scams included the following: "doctors, airline pilots, attorneys, teachers, retirees—people who ought to know better, but got taken because they failed to do their homework before investing." Confused by all the hype, the disappointment, and the losses, these *Below The Line* investors failed to assume accountability for their own predicament, finding themselves victimized twice by the same scam.

Out of the finger-pointing and confusion stages naturally grows the response: "Just tell me exactly what you want me to do, and I'll do it." Unfortunately, such a plea, while seeming to indicate a willingness to change behavior, simply transfers accountability to a superior or someone else. Too many bosses perpetuate such an attitude by telling their people "exactly" what to do in difficult situations. Asking someone else to tell you exactly what to do represents nothing more than an advanced form of excuse making because it stems from the victim's desire to prepare his or her excuse before ever taking action. Oliver North defended himself in the Iran-Contra trials by claiming that he simply carried out his commanding officer's orders, which presumably took him off the hook for any personal responsibility in the situation.

In the view of co-dependency expert Abe Wagner, author of *The Transactional Manager,* people display three ego states of the child: the natural child, the compliant child, and the rebellious child. The natural child refers to the part of the personality that someone inherits at birth, and it characterizes an individual's inherent needs, wants, and feelings. When children or adults display their natural child, they do what they want to do and don't do what they don't want to do. Such behavior can be natural and positive. However, the behavior of both the compliant and rebellious child reflect co-dependent relationships with respect to mother's wishes. Each of these co-dependent postures lies *Below The Line* in the "tell me what to do" stage of the victim cycle because they depend on someone else assuming responsibility. Compliant children do what a mother or boss tells them to do transferring to mothers or bosses the consequences of the children's actions. Rebellious children find out what mothers or bosses want them to do, and then defy it, all the while blaming mothers or bosses for all negative consequences. Whether co-dependents comply or rebel, their behavior depends on what a superior tells them to do. They never assume their own accountability. Unfortunately, far too many people in organizations act like compliant or rebellious children.

Disney has adapted the lyrics of an age-old folk song that beautifully characterizes the "tell me what to do" stage of the victim cycle. The song begins with Goofy telling Liza that he has a hole in his bucket. Liza replies, "then mend it, dear Goofy, dear Goofy, then mend it." Goofy, upon hearing this, immediately inquires, "with what shall I mend it dear Liza, dear Liza, with what shall I mend it." Liza, with some amazement at Goofy's predicament replies, "with some straw, dear Goofy, dear Goofy, with some straw." Of course, at this point, Goofy says, the straw is too long. And on the song goes, Liza providing guidance, and Goofy presenting problems until the end, when Goofy needs to retrieve some water, to wet a stone, to sharpen a knife, to cut the straw, to fix the bucket; and so he asks Liza for guidance in retrieving the water, upon which she suggests he use his bucket—to which Goofy replies, "There's a hole in my bucket dear Liza, dear Liza, there's a hole in my bucket, dear Liza, a hole."

Most of us have probably found ourselves in a similar endless circular pattern of "tell me what do to." The game of shifting accountability by refusing to take responsibility for our future actions is played out in business every day.

Command and Control cultures of the past provided a paternalistic approach to employee involvement—"you just do what you are told, do it well, and we will take care of you for the rest of your life." Some people still depict their organizations as places where you begin work in the morning by "checking your brain at the front door." However, most organizations today are fleeing from this "tell me what to do" culture in an effort to create an environment that attracts, develops, and retains the best and the brightest people. As accountability deepens and people move *Above The Line* within the organization, a shift occurs from "tell me what to do," to "here is what I am going to do, what do you think?"—a truly profound and empowering approach to getting results.

5. COVER YOUR TAIL. Another practical stage of the victim cycle is "Cover Your Tail." In this stage people continue to seek the imagined protection that comes from behaving in a *Below The Line* manner. Here, people craft elaborate and precise "stories" as to why they couldn't possibly be blamed for something that might go wrong. These stories can be, and often are, generated after the fact. However, as amazing as it may seem, the vast majority of these stories are prepared before the results are even known, "just in case" an eventual problem or potential failure should occur.

There are a number of methods that people use when they "cover their tail." These range from documenting everything in writing to sending back-up E-mail messages that can be saved and used as later proof that they are not to blame. You may have had the experience of someone coming to you to substantiate the sequence of events and the nature of your conversations in order to build an alibi that may prove useful in the future.

Sometimes the "cover your tail" stage of the victim cycle is played out even more subtlely. We have witnessed individuals who actually run-and-hide in order to disassociate themselves from situations they perceive to be particularly fraught with potential problems. They avoid meetings where they might be put "on the line," or fail to open mail that they know might relate to some anticipated bad news. We remember hearing of one such example where a particular company was at a very critical juncture of its development and growth. It was preparing for an upcoming government inspection that would either "make" or "break" the company by the conclusions and directions given as the result of the agency's findings. It was just days prior to the inspection when the president of the company said that he would be going on vacation and would not be available for any communication or decision making during the inspection. Immediately, people felt the burden of potential problems totally shift to them, leaving the president of the company seemingly "in the clear." The effort expended to "cover your tail" is almost always highly unproductive, producing nothing more than stories of "reasons and justifications" for why people are not responsible, not to blame, and not accountable for things that go wrong. There is no question that there are times when such behavior is warranted and even appears quite necessary to defend oneself against unscrupulous people who are set on taking advantage of others. But warranted or not, "cover your tail" behavior is a costly drain on the time and resources of both the individual and the company.

6. *WAIT AND SEE.* People remain mired in the victim cycle when they choose to wait and see if things will get better. In such a climate, however, problems can only get worse. For example, the senior management team of a $300 million personal care products manufacturer and marketer found themselves struggling over the introduction of a new product line. Because the company had grown so rapidly, it lacked clear precedents for such an introduction. After hours of fruitless debate, company officials decided to "wait and see" if the right approach might emerge naturally from the product management group after everyone's emo-

tions cooled down. After months of indecision a smaller competitor beat them to the punch, making the whole product introduction problem moot. The wait-and-see stage of the victim cycle often becomes the "sink hole" of business management as possible solutions get swallowed up in a swamp of inaction.

In an amusing example of this stage of the victim cycle, *The Wall Street Journal,* reported that bird droppings have been piling up for years in the Amherst, Massachusetts, Town Hall attic, posing an increasing health risk to occupants. The Amherst Select Board voted to allocate $125,000 to clean up the mess, but according to contractors, the job could cost as much as $260,000. Enter a local hero, David Keenan, an Amherst real estate broker, who offered to organize a volunteer group called the "pigeon busters," which would clean up the estimated 55 gallons of bird droppings for free. However, one of the Select Board members pointed out that such an effort would require insurance covering each of the volunteers, a far too expensive proposition. After listening to a lot of discussion, Keenan exclaimed in frustration, "Anyone who would volunteer would gladly sign a waiver. It's not a liability issue. The problem with the Amherst government is they won't roll up their sleeves and shovel the poop." When the community leaders hired lawyers to study the liability issue, the lawyers concluded that "regardless of who does the clean-up, the town could still be sued." In the meantime the bird dung keeps piling, with the people who come to Town Hall on business hoping they don't get psittacosis, a viral disease that can be transmitted from bird to man, and develop into pneumonia. As a final resort, Keenan and his "pigeon busters" suggested that the select board allot enough money to fix the hole in the window frame through which the pigeons have been entering.

In a more serious example, we believe the Los Angeles riots of 1992 stemmed from a similar "wait-and-see" attitude that began to take hold in the 1960s when the Watts riot spurred a few quick fixes but no long-term efforts to find and implement real solutions. As a result, the real problems kept simmering under the illusion of progress only to explode three decades later. In fact, America has ignored quite a few troublesome problems, such as the national debt, social security, health care, and the educational system, that never get solved because the government and most of the country's citizens keep waiting to see if somehow, someway a miracle will occur. It won't until Americans get themselves *Above The Line*.

Stuck in the Victim Cycle: The Plight of Bob Jensen

People tend to remain in the victim cycle because they find certain comforting, if not self-defeating, rewards *Below The Line*. Such rewards include "I don't have to admit I was wrong," "I won't lose face," "I don't have to do anything differently in the future," and "I can justify my lack of performance and growth." For whatever reasons a person remains in the victim cycle, however, they will never get out of it unless they learn to recognize the attitudes and behavior that trap them there. Without such recognition, they will most likely never get the results they want. Let's see how one CEO learned to spot the traps.

Because of our desire to protect the privacy of the executive involved, we have altered Bob Jensen's story somewhat, but we assure you it did take place. We want to share it with you because it sheds important light on the inner struggles of executives in America today as they attempt to get and stay *Above The Line*.

Bob Jensen had racked up a string of successes in his last corporate assignment as director of new product development, and his advancements had impressed the higher-ups in his corporation. Everyone above him agreed that Bob would enjoy a spectacular future probably at the top of the corporation's executive ranks. To further his career development, his superiors proposed a lateral move to manufacturing where he could bring his talents to bear on reenergizing a poorly performing manufacturing factory.

As Bob approached the end of his first year of managing the factory, however, he was feeling frustrated at the lack of improvement in its overall performance. Nothing he had tried seemed to be working, and for the first time in his career he feared that he might fail in an assignment.

With the performance issue continuing to frustrate him, Bob decided to explore the feelings of key people in the factory. During his investigations he invited one of the supervisors to lunch, inviting candid feedback about people's perceptions of Bob's impact on the factory over the past year. Seemingly taken aback by this request, the supervisor asked Bob if he really wanted to hear the truth. When Bob insisted he did, the supervisor opened up, detailing how most people attributed lack of improvement to Bob's own behavior. Bob couldn't believe what he was hearing:

"Jensen's in over his head."

"He's not a manufacturing expert, and we need someone who knows our work."

"Bob hasn't made any difference at all."

"He's trying to run manufacturing the way he ran new product development."

"Bob's not doing anything to increase quality."

"He's not communicating clearly."

"He's ignoring significant personality conflicts on his own team."

"Jensen doesn't seem capable of making tough decisions."

Although shocked by the supervisor's observations of people's negative feelings about his management skills, Bob expressed appreciation for the candor of those observations. While he appreciated hearing the feedback, he also found himself really aggravated by it. After all, when he headed up new product development he constantly heard people in manufacturing complaining that: "All we need is for R&D to quit throwing products over the wall before it has solved the design problems that make quality manufacturing impossible." This memory prompted Bob to chalk up his supervisor's feedback as just so many sour grapes. Why couldn't manufacturing accept the blame for its own flaws?

The following Saturday he went sailing with Pete Sanders, one of his old friends from new product development. Peter had left the company to start his own business just as Bob had transferred to manufacturing. It didn't take long after setting sail for Bob and Pete to begin reminiscing about the good times they'd spent together in new product development. As the casual conversation unfolded, Peter asked Bob how things were going at the factory, and since Bob trusted Peter, he told him that the situation had turned into a nightmare. Before long he was venting all his pent-up frustrations to his friend: "Peter, I've inherited a basket case. And it really upsets me that people at the factory expect me to do something to solve their problems. I didn't create the mess! The manufacturing managers did. When I decided to take this position 12 months ago I had no idea what I was getting myself into. No one on the corporate management staff told me how bad it really was. Frankly, I don't think anyone could get management to back a solution to the factory's quality problems. I'm between a rock and a hard place. Factory managers deny responsibility, and so does corporate management. Morale has sunk to a new low in the factory. At least three lower-level people quit every week, no matter what I do. And I've tried everything! But no one communicates with anyone else, and everyone blames everyone else for their problems. It seems like the director before me let things get completely out of control. The volume of new product introduction is extraordinary, and the products we get from new product development aren't ready when we get them. I can't solve all these problems myself. I'm all alone out there. Corporate management doesn't provide any useful direction. They just assume that I'll do the right thing."

For his part, Peter could not believe this was his old friend talking. Back at new product development Bob had been supremely confident, a take-charge guy who felt he could solve any problem thrown his way. Now he was sounding desperate, with his reasoning looping around in circles. He blamed the corporate management team for putting him in this untenable situation, he blamed his own manufacturing management team for not owning up to their problems, and he blamed himself for getting blindsided by a set of circumstances over which he felt no power or control.

Although Peter sympathized with Bob, saying he knew there must be plenty of good reasons for why he was feeling the way he did, he also observed that continuing to feel victimized would not help him move an inch toward the results he wanted. Peter concluded, "You know, Bob, I attended an interesting accountability workshop a few weeks ago, and, based on what I learned there, I'd say you're stuck in what the workshop leaders call the victim cycle. That's the bad news. The good news is that you can do something about it."

Getting Unstuck: Bob Jensen's Recognition

As Bob and Peter sailed north toward the Oregon Coast, Pete continued his explanation: "In this workshop I learned that everyone falls into the victim cycle from time to time.

It's nothing to feel ashamed about. In fact, if you can only learn to see when you're falling into it, you can start getting out of it. Victims never accomplish anything unless they start taking control over their own futures. The key is accountability, but you can't climb what they called the *Steps to Accountability*SM without first developing a full understanding of the victim cycle. Think about it. Have you been claiming to be unaware of certain circumstances, pretending not to know what's really going on, denying that it's your responsibility, blaming others, attempting to get someone else to take you off the hook and tell you what to do, arguing that you can't do anything, or waiting for things to get better tomorrow?"

These words seemed to strike a nerve in his friend, so Peter continued as gently yet forcefully as possible to get Bob to see himself in a more objective light. "Bob, I really respect you. Remember, it's not that getting stuck in the victim cycle is bad, it's just not effective. It keeps you from getting results. Now I can see hundreds of times when I was in the victim cycle, and that's good, Bob! The more quickly I can recognize that fact, the more quickly I can get out of it and start working more productively toward my goals. The problems you face in the factory are real. I saw it myself. But given those problems, try asking yourself what else you can do to rise above those circumstances and get the results you want. When you described your situation, I didn't hear many words expressing ownership on your part for what's happened over the past year. You talk as if the manufacturing managers aren't really your managers, and as if the factory's problems are something you inherited, that you had no choice in the matter. Did you ever really, completely leave new product development for this new position? Have you really shown up to work at the factory?"

Bob thought about what Peter had said, and the more he thought about it, the madder he got. "You make it sound like

I'm to blame for everybody else's problems. I don't buy that!" When Peter remained silent, Bob took a deep breath, then apologized for his tirade. "I'm sorry. I guess if I were totally honest with myself I would have to acknowledge that I haven't really brought my best efforts to bear on the situation at the factory. The only fun I have lately is when I think about the good old days in product development. Things went so smoothly then. Improvements were so visible. It all comes back when I review the weekly update report on my old R&D projects. I always call my old friends to congratulate them and give them advice."

At this point Peter interrupted Bob by saying, "Do you remember the story about Alexander the Great? When Alexander's army reached the coast of what is now called India, he ordered his men to burn their ships. When the men hesitated at such a shocking order, Alexander responded, 'We're either going home in their ships or we're not going home at all.' In other words, burning the ships would cement his army's commitment to conquest because retreat would cease to be an option. Now, victory could become the sole objective." Peter continued by suggesting that it looked to him as if Bob had kept a boat handy for retreat or escape and thus had never completely committed to winning his battle. When he asked Bob if that were the case, Bob confided, with a certain level of pride, that he had several. He'd already hinted to his superiors that he might like to move back to R&D, and he had even interviewed for a job with a competitor. Now, however, he could see that he had been operating lately with one eye on the exit, and he had to admit that his situation demanded that he keep both eyes on the situation at hand. Finally, he was able to see that he really was stuck in an unproductive cycle playing the victim and that there really were things he could do to improve conditions at the factory, if he chose to focus his full attention on the problem.

Specifically, Bob came to realize that he needed to create a more cohesive team with his managers before any meaningful change could occur. To his regret, he had done little over the past year to foster a close team spirit between himself and the managers who reported to him. Instead, he had simply gone around the managers to the supervisors, meeting with them in early morning meetings to get their input and to give them direction. Bob acknowledged that he had essentially skirted his managers, and, in effect, disempowered them as a management team.

Strangely enough, Bob's recognition of his own accountability for the factory's poor performance no longer made him feel angry or depressed but increasingly exhilarated. Wanting to feed the feeling, Bob told Peter, "You know, I really have been getting in my own way and waiting for someone else to solve these problems. While it's true there are a lot of things that have happened to the factory that I had nothing to do with, I've allowed those things to distract me from focusing on the positive action I can take. And, worst of all, my acting like a victim has given everyone else permission to do the same. Thinking about it now, I can even see that a lot of people at the factory are stuck in this cycle, ignoring problems, denying responsibilities, and blaming others. And, as for me, I think I have let myself become so paralyzed by that fact that even if I start acting differently, even if I start accepting full accountability for the factory's performance, I could still fail. That scares me."

Just as it's okay to fall into the victim cycle from time to time, because it's only human to do so, it's also okay to feel a little scared of the possibility of failure. But the accountable person learns to overcome that fear by recognizing that success can only come from getting *Above The Line* and working hard to get better results. Sometimes you must be willing to burn your other ships and grasp the helm of the one under your command. Doing so can stimulate the conviction and create the ownership necessary to get started on a new program of action and determination to help you rise above your circumstances.

With this realization, *The Oz Principle* was beginning to take hold in Bob Jensen's life just as it did for Dorothy when she realized that the wizard wasn't capable of giving her what she wanted.

THE VITAL LESSON: DETECTING SIGNS OF THE VICTIM CYCLE

Over the years, we've worked through a Bob Jensen kind of truth-telling, soul-searching session with hundreds of executives, professionals, friends and family. Every situation is different, every person is unique, but everyone reaches a critical moment when he or she recognizes having been stuck in the victim cycle. Take a minute to think about what happened to Bob Jensen. For 12 months he honestly believed he could not control his circumstances. Dwelling upon the bleakness of the situation, he chose to think he couldn't do anything about it, that no one could expect him to fix all the factory's long-standing problems overnight. As a result, Bob had languished, unhappily and unproductively, until he recognized he was ducking responsibility by blaming former directors and other managers, asking the corporate management team to tell him what to do, claiming that he couldn't do anything more than what he was already doing, and waiting to see if things would get better on their own. Fortunately, when he finally saw how he'd become stuck in the victim cycle, he could commit himself fully to helping everyone at the factory solve their problems and obtain better results.

Like Bob Jensen, every human being can fall *Below The Line* from time to time, but whenever you do so, you can't get back on track until you first acknowledge that you're incurring a high cost for functioning *Below The Line.* That's when you begin assuming a *See It* attitude that gives you the perspective you need to get *Above The Line* and start climbing the accountability ladder. You'll begin reading about the *See It* rung on the *Steps To Accountability* in the next chapter, but before you do, you should pause here to examine your own position within the victim cycle. We have put together a checklist you should find useful for spotting *Below The Line* attitudes. Take a few minutes to examine your experiences by honestly answering these questions:

**VICTIM CYCLE
SELF-EXAMINATION**
▼

Answer the following questions either "yes" or "no," depending on whether the scenario in a given question has *ever* happened to you. As you read each question, be sure to ask yourself "Has this ever happened to me?" or "Have I ever felt this way?" Try to play your own best friend, answering the question as frankly as possible.

1. Were you ever surprised by negative feedback from someone else when you thought all along you were doing your very best to solve a problem?

   Yes _____ No _____

2. Have you ever spent time blaming others and pointing fingers when things did not go the way you wanted them to go?

   Yes _____ No _____

3. Did you ever suspect something would become a problem for someone else or for your organization but did nothing about it?

   Yes _____No _____

4. Have you ever spent time "covering your tail" just in case things went wrong?

   Yes _____ No _____

5. Have you ever said, "It's not my job" and expected someone else to solve a problem?

   Yes _____ No _____

6. Did you ever feel totally powerless, with no control over your circumstances or situation?

   Yes _____ No _____

7. Have you ever found yourself "waiting to see if" a situation would miraculously resolve itself?

   Yes _____ No _____

8. Have you ever said, "Just tell me what you want me to do and I'll do it?"

   Yes _____ No _____

9. Have you ever felt that you would have done things differently if it were your own company?

   Yes _____ No _____

10. Do you ever tell stories about how someone took advantage of you (a boss, a friend, a contractor, a salesperson, etc.)?

    Yes _____ No _____

Once you have completed the Victim Cycle Self-examination, total up your scores. Give yourself one point for every "Yes" response and no points for every "No" response. After totaling your points, compare your total to the scoring table that follows.

Scoring

If you scored "0" points: You are not being honest with yourself. Go back and try it again, but this time sit in a closet so no one can see your results.

If you scored only "1" point: You know you are capable of falling *Below The Line*, but you probably do so more often than you're willing to admit.

If you scored "2–4" points: You should take some satisfaction from the fact that you're only human.

If you scored "5–7" points: You realize that you can easily fall *Below The Line*.

If you scored "8–10" points: You are very honest, pretty normal, and should be extremely interested in the rest of this book!

Your actual score matters less than the recognition that, as a normal human being, you can be tempted at almost any time to avoid accountability for the false security and imagined safety of the victim cycle, where it's always someone else's fault that you're not getting results. The recognition that you have the capability to fall *Below The Line* sets the stage for you to experience *The Oz Principle*: to rise above your circumstances and achieve the results you desire.

MOVING OUT OF THE VICTIM CYCLE

Throughout this chapter you have seen examples of *Below The Line* attitudes and behavior that will help you more fully appreciate the difference between victimization and accountability. However, just as Dorothy discovered on the yellow brick road to the Emerald City, you will have to work hard to spot victimization attitudes and behavior in your own life and in the operations of your organization. In the next chapter you'll begin seeing accountability in a whole new light as you prepare yourself to climb the four steps to greater accountability.

CHAPTER 3

THERE'S NO PLACE LIKE HOME: FOCUSING ON RESULTS

▼

"But you have not yet told me how to get back to Kansas."

"Your Silver Shoes will carry you over the desert," replied Glinda. "If you had known their power you could have gone back to your Aunt Em the very first day you came to this country."

"But then I should not have had my wonderful brains!" cried the Scarecrow. "I might have passed my whole life in the farmer's cornfield."

"And I should not have had my lovely heart," said the Tin Woodsman. "I might have stood and rusted in the forest till the end of the world."

"And I should have lived a coward forever," declared the Lion, "and no beast in all the forest would have had a good word to say to me."

"This is all true," said Dorothy, "and I am glad I was of use to these good friends. But now that each of them has had what he most desired, and each is happy in having a kingdom to rule beside, I think I should like to go back to Kansas."

THE WIZARD OF OZ
By L. Frank Baum

In the aftermath of the David Koresh-Waco, Texas, disaster during the spring of 1993, Congressman John Conyers, Jr., labeled the events "a profound disgrace to law enforcement in the United States of America." He then turned his attention to U.S. Attorney General Janet Reno, saying, "You did the right thing by offering to resign. And now I'd like you to know that there is at least one member of Congress that isn't going to rationalize the death of two dozen children." Janet Reno's now-famous response came with a quavering voice as she replied, "I haven't tried to rationalize the death of children, Congressman. I feel more strongly about it than you will ever know. But I have neither tried to rationalize the death of four agents, and I will not walk away from a compound where ATF agents had been killed by people who knew they were agents and leave them unsurrounded. Most of all, Congressman, I will not engage in recrimination." Because of Reno's unusual willingness to accept blame and disdain recrimination, she quickly became a symbol of accountable leadership in Washington. A *USA Today* headline read "What's this? Washington leaders accepting blame?" The article went on to praise Reno with another question, "Isn't it refreshing to have someone in Washington take responsibility?" *Time* magazine's article "Standing Tall: The Capital Is All Agog at the New Attorney General's Outspoken Honesty," reported that the moment she uttered her honest and courageous response to Congressman Conyers she "achieved full-fledged folk-hero status." In the article *Time* reporters observe, "It is a measure of Washington's leadership drought that Reno—who has, after all, only stood her ground in defense of a decision that led to a disaster, said what she believes, and taken responsibility for her actions—is the toast of the town." The article concludes: "At the end of the long, terrible day on which Ranch Apocalypse was reduced to ashes along with those in it, Janet Reno went home to the furnished apartment she is currently renting near her office. 'I don't think I've ever been so—I guess lonely is the word,' she said. Then she received two phone calls. The first message, from her sister:

'That-a girl.' The second, from the President: 'That-a girl.' By the end of last week's bravura performance, it was a sentiment that even John Conyers admitted sharing."

For not ducking responsibility, we would also push for Janet Reno in the Accountability Hall of Fame. Clearly, she moved and stayed *Above The Line*. If only more government officials would do likewise.

A "Doonesbury" comic strip raised this question when her boss scolded the fictitious administration official Joan Caucus: "Here's the deal, Joan. We were not happy with how the Waco deal played out. The President should have had a chance to shoulder the blame before Reno grabbed it all for herself!" Assuming blame represents a strong first step in the right direction, but it is not the end of the road.

Unfortunately, however, we feel that on the road to results our society has adopted a much too shallow definition of accountability, one that is myopic in scope and that, ultimately, does not create the empowering influence of true accountability—the point of this chapter.

ACCOUNTABILITY POORLY DEFINED

A survey of the popular press, business literature, and societal norms reveals that most people view accountability as something that happens to them or is inflicted upon them, choosing to perceive it as a heavy burden to carry. In fact, many people think about accountability as a concept or principle to be applied only when something goes wrong or when someone else is trying to determine cause and pinpoint blame. Often, when things are sailing along smoothly and failure has not yet sunk the ship, people rarely ask "Who is accountable for this or that?" It seems that only when the hull springs a leak does anyone start looking around for the responsible party.

Not surprisingly, *Webster's* definition promotes this some-what negative view of accountability: "subject to having to report, explain, or justify; being answerable, responsible." Notice how *Webster's* begins its definition with the words, "subject to," implying little choice to the state of accountability. This confession-oriented and powerless definition suggests that accountability is a state someone creates for someone else.

Since the majority of Americans define accountability this way, no wonder they spend so much time explaining and justifying poor results. Even in Janet Reno's case, for example, we honor her willingness to stand up and take the blame but in doing so we risk ignoring the reality that accountability is more than a confession. Such praise may even leave some asking the question, does taking responsibility for failure make up for a lack of success? The answer to us is clear—it does not. Nevertheless, upon encountering a less than hoped-for result, most people begin preparing their explanations, citing such tired excuses as "we were overbudget, overextended, overloaded, underinformed, underfunded, and underutilized." As a result, millions of people in thousands of organizations expend their valuable time and energy justifying their lack of performance instead of focusing on ways to improve performance. One leader, intently focused on improving performance of his people, suggested that his organization could save a lot of time and energy by handing out a list of tired excuses, so that employees would need only recite a number when explaining failure:

TWENTY TIRED EXCUSES
▼

1. "That's the way we've always done it."

2. "It's not my job."

3. "I didn't know you needed it right away."

4. "It wasn't my fault that it's late."

5. "That's not my department."

6. "No one told me what to do."

7. "I'm waiting for approval."

8. "Someone should have told me not to do that."

9. "Don't blame me, it was the boss's idea."

10. "I didn't know."

11. "I forgot."

12. "If you had told me it was that important, I would have done it."

13. "I'm too busy to do it."

14. "Someone told me to do the wrong thing."

15. "I thought I told you."

16. "Why didn't you ask me?"

17. "No one invited me to the meeting—I didn't get the memo."

18. "My people dropped the ball."

19. "Nobody's followed up on me; it can't be that important."

20. "I told someone else to take care of this."

This list sounds pretty silly, doesn't it? Yet in some way or another, people weave these excuses so deeply into the fabric of their lives that they resort to them without really thinking about what they're really saying. To overcome that impulse, people must abandon the "who-done-it" definition of accountability. Almost without exception, whenever something goes wrong in an organization, people often start playing the "who-done-it" game, a not-so-subtle variation of the "blame game," as they immediately begin searching out the person in the group responsible for the failure. All too often the "who-done-it" game excludes any intention of rectifying the situation. Instead, those who play the game seek only to make sure the spotlight shifts to someone else while they themselves dive for the shelter of excuses, explanations, justifications, and disassociations.

A tragic example of the "who-done-it" game received national attention in early 1993 when it was reported that contaminated meat in hamburgers sold at Jack in the Box restaurants caused the death of two children and severe sickness in hundreds of others. Jack in the Box quickly prepared its explanation, pointing the finger at the supplier of the meat, Von's grocery stores, which, of course, had already prepared its own explanation, blaming the meat inspector, the U.S. Department of Agriculture, which, in turn, explained that insufficient funds made it impossible to employ enough meat inspectors. So who's at fault? The taxpayers, who don't want more taxes for more inspectors, but the taxpayers have prepared their own explanation: "If the federal bureaucracy were only more efficient, it wouldn't cost so much to get the services we need." And the game goes on and on, further unraveling the fabric of America's character.

As the downward spiral continues, fueled by a wrong-headed definition of accountability, more and more people are learning to become adept at playing the "who-done-it" game. Even as projects in organizations are launched, people often begin taking copious notes about the unfolding progress, not to document the success but to justify the lack of results just in case the projects fail. The amount of wasted time and energy, even in the most quality conscious organizational environments, continues to rise as the who-done-it game turns into the "craft-your-story" game, which allows its players to build a handy excuse, regardless of the outcome. Sadly, Americans have learned that they live in a litigious and blood-thirsty society that loves to place blame and fix accountability on someone so someone else can pay dearly for any mistakes. In such a society, winning in the game of life includes "covering your tail."

By defining accountability according to *Webster's,* people only perpetuate a reactive perspective of accountability, one obsessed with the past and blissfully ignorant of the future.

Consumed with dotting the "i's" and crossing the "t's" of their elaborate explanations for why they're not responsible, people today are robbing themselves of the power of accountability— a power that *The Oz Principle* defines as the key to a successful future.

A BETTER DEFINITION OF ACCOUNTABILITY

Pop psychology, whether intentional or not, has often encouraged people in contemporary society to blame all their woes and problems on a single or few experiences in their lives, thus promoting a lack of accountability for current and future behaviors, attitudes, and feelings. It is not unusual for people to explain their nightmares, eating disorders, compulsive cleanliness, anxieties, drive for self-improvement, physical ailments, financial problems, and impatience with others on some singular problem or experience that occurred earlier in their lives. Blaming everything on their past physical, emotional, or psychological wounds, they explain their vulnerability to fad diets, their awkwardness in relating to their children, or their feelings of alienation and loneliness, as if no other modern adult had these problems. The fact is, whether you are a true victim or a pseudovictim, you will never overcome a hurtful past until you develop a present and future-oriented view of your own accountability for getting more out of life. To achieve such a shift in how you view things, you must start with a better, more proactive definition of accountability.

The Oz Principle's definition of accountability can, we believe, help revitalize the American character, strengthen the global competitiveness of America's corporations, improve the quality of products and services produced by companies worldwide, increase the responsiveness of organizations to the needs and wants of customers and constituents, reduce abusive behavior in the world, and expand the happiness, fulfillment, and power of individuals. However, before we offer a new definition of accountability, we'd like to cite 2 major reasons that make a redefinition necessary:

First, somewhere along the line, society and organizations have stimulated people to feel more responsible for explaining their results than for achieving them. As we described earlier in this chapter, many people seem to think that a good explanation can excuse a poor result. The contemporary view of accountability tends to emphasize past actions as opposed to current or future efforts. Just as W. Edwards Deming has been telling businesspeople for decades, so it is that most organizations operate on the assumption that the fear of failure will cause people to succeed. To the contrary, we feel such an assumption only causes people to prepare their explanations of history before the fact.

Rather than focusing on proactive accountability, which stresses what you can do now to get better results, the contemporary definition impels people to "account for" what they have done in the past, instead of defining what they will do now and in the future. This has fostered an "after-the-fact" rather than a "before-it's-too-late" application of accountability. It should come as no surprise that the real value and benefit of accountability stems from a person's or an organization's ability to influence events and outcomes before they happen. The contemporary view of accountability fails to recognize that people can gain more from a proactive posture than from a reactive one.

Second, in a complex and changing world, only a complete definition of accountability, one that captures all the historical as well as the current and future aspects of a person's responsibility and one that stresses the proactive instead of reactive, can reverse America's decaying character and revitalize its institutions.

Take for example a situation which has intrigued us for some time. We have constantly been amazed at the manner in which local government officials determine when stop signs and traffic signals should be installed. We recall a particularly dangerous intersection in Southern California where visibility was terrible and traffic speeds were high. Traffic officials had been exceptionally slow to install traffic signals at this intersection. Rather than tracking complaints about the safety of the intersection, officials tracked the number of accidents. After they reach a certain number of accidents a stop sign gets installed. If a few fatalities occur, then it is indisputable that a traffic signal must go up. Many accidents and some fatalities have occurred at that intersection, which is now home to a four-way stop sign. It's disturbing to consider that those who have been entrusted with public safety look at things from a reactive versus a proactive perspective.

This is a great example of the price that is paid when looking at circumstances from only a historical perspective. After-the-fact, it's too late to adjust behavior and avoid the negative consequences that can follow. This is the primary problem with society's commonly accepted view of accountability.

Consider the following new definition of accountability, one that embodies the essence of *The Oz Principle*:

> **Accountability: An attitude of continually asking "what else can I do to rise above my circumstances and achieve the results I desire?" It is the process of "seeing it, owning it, solving it, and doing it." It requires a level of ownership that includes making, keeping, and proactively answering for personal commitments. It is a perspective that embraces both current and future efforts rather than reactive and historical explanations.**

Armed with this new definition, you can help yourself and others do all that is possible and necessary to overcome difficult circumstances and achieve desired results, which leads directly to the next vital element of accountability.

▲

JOINT ACCOUNTABILITY

A *Wall Street Journal* article, "Urban Trauma Mitigates Guilt, Defenders Say," reports that "Lawyers defending inner-city criminals are honing a new and startling psychiatric defense: that their clients suffer from an 'urban psychosis' that reduces their responsibility for their crimes. The lawyers argue that day-to-day urban life can induce post-traumatic stress disorder, a condition courts already have recognized in Vietnam veterans, rape victims and battered spouses and children. Some defense lawyers are asking courts to take this condition into account when they determine the guilt and punishment of inner-city residents." Even if you believe "urban psychosis" should mitigate a person's guilt, the argument makes it all too easy to mask responsibility people should accept for how they respond to their environments and circumstances. People do play a role in their circumstances and environments, and they share joint accountability for what happens in their neighborhoods and on their streets. Unfortunately, the process of defining joint accountability has gone to exacting extremes as lawyers and litigants spend countless hours and dollars trying to determine who's at fault. Luckily, the article goes on to say, "Many legal and psychological experts are skeptical about whether urban psychosis even exists. . . . 'Pretty soon we're going to have to sweep in everybody because they're born, sufferers from post-traumatic stress disorder,' said Karil S. Klinbeil, a professor of social work and psychology at the University of Washington, who frequently testifies about battered-woman, battered-child and battered-person syndromes. 'It's getting out of control.'" According to another expert, Bruce Fein, a constitutional scholar and attorney, "We have a whole raft of lawyers today arguing that individuals are just helpless over their circumstances and don't have a choice over their destiny. That's nonsense." Unchecked, such nonsense will continue to erode America's competitiveness in the world and drain its people of any sense of individual or joint accountability for better results. That would be tragic.

An important aspect of *The Oz Principle's* definition of accountability involves the fact that accountability works best when people share ownership for circumstances and results. The old definition of accountability leads people to assign "individual responsibility," without acknowledging the shared accountability that so often characterizes organizational behavior and modern life. Not surprisingly, whenever a single individual is identified as the one responsible for poor results, everyone else breathes a sigh of relief now that they're "off the hook." Assigning singular responsibility may comfort the majority, but the fact remains, organizational results come from collective, not individual, activity. Hence, when an organization fails to perform well, it's a collective or shared failure. A complete understanding of accountability in organizations must begin with an acceptance of the notion of "joint accountability."

Imagine a baseball team where each defensive player assumes responsibility for covering an area of the field. No hard-and-fast rules prescribe the exact point where one player's area ends and another's begins. Given such overlapping areas of responsibility, getting good results (i.e., covering the whole field) becomes a team effort wherein individual accountability shifts according to circumstances, and players are always trained to go for the ball, whenever they can reach it, even when more than one player can do so. For example, you have probably observed the occasion when a ball is popped up into shallow left-center field. Immediately, the short-stop, the left fielder, and the center fielder converge at the same time with none of them completely sure of who should catch the ball. Sometimes, the ball gets dropped because the players run into one another or, thinking it could be anyone's ball, they all wait for the other guy to make the catch— uncertain as to who is going to take responsibility for it this time.

In many ways, the organizational game is a "team sport" where everyone has his or her individual responsibility, where everyone contributes to the final score, and where joint accountability governs play.

One company president characterized what joint accountability meant to him: "everyone working together so that we don't drop the ball; but when it does get dropped, everyone dives for the ball to pick it up." "Unfortunately," he said, "too many of our people see the ball falling to the ground between players but react by saying 'that was your ball.'" In most organizations it would be easy to recount a litany of projects in which someone had missed a critical deadline, incurred an unexpected expense, quit in the middle of a job or failed to pay attention to a crucial detail. In such cases, no one jumps in to pick up the dropped ball. Everyone just sits smugly on the sideline, saying, "Well, Bob [or Sue] really messed things up this time." How accountability works individually and in organizations is illustrated with the circles on the next page.

When people look at their accountability to the organization they usually view it strictly in terms of their own individual responsibility. As a result, things tend to fall through the cracks because they fall outside of the boundaries they have drawn around independent aspects of their job. Often, organizations try to fix this problem by redefining roles, hiring more people (thus filling in the cracks by adding more circles), or restructuring the organization. However, when people view their accountability as something larger than their responsibility, people find themselves feeling accountable for things beyond what a literal interpretation of their job description might suggest (i.e., profits, customer complaints, sharing information, project deadlines, effective communications, sales, and the success of the overall company). When people assume this attitude of joint accountability for all aspects of a project, the cracks or boundaries disappear, and people then see it as their responsibility to make sure the ball is not dropped.

Individual Responsibility

Joint Accountability

In their instructive account of Jack Welch's transformation of General Electric, *Control Your Destiny or Someone Else Will,* authors Noel Tichy and Stratford Sherman conclude with a chapter wherein Jack Welch himself speaks his mind about GE's future and its need for more joint accountability or "boundarylessness," as he calls it: "If this company is to achieve its goals, we've all got to become boundaryless. Boundaries are crazy. The union is just another boundary, and you have to reach across the same way you want to reach across the boundaries separating you from your customers and your suppliers and your colleagues."

For too many people, the idea of joint accountability is elusive because they have been programmed to think only in terms of the "one" responsible, rather than the "group" responsible. Yet, you may ask, can people in an organization really assume accountability for the same things, the same results? Doesn't that translate to "no one" being responsible? Not at all. The teamwork concept, now popular throughout corporate America, requires a change from the old notion of singular accountability to one in which teammates work together to catch all the balls and score as many runs as possible. Steven Wheelwright and Kim Clark, authors of the book, *Revolutionizing Product Development*, write about the significant strategic and competitive advantages that result when team members understand this concept of joint accountability. After forming product development "core" teams consisting of dedicated personnel from various functional departments in the organization, they observe:

> Each core team member wears a functional hat which makes him or her the focal point and manager responsible for a function that delivers its unique contribution to the overall project.

> But each core team member also wears a team hat. In addition to representing his or her function, each core team member accepts responsibility for overall team results. In this role, the core team shares responsibility with the heavyweight project manager for the development procedures followed by the team, and for the

overall results that those procedures deliver. The core team is accountable for the success of the project, and can blame no one but itself if it fails to manage the project, execute the tasks, and deliver the performance agreed upon at the outset.

What is unique in the core team members' responsibilities is not so much their accountability for tasks in their own function, but the fact that they are responsible for how those tasks are subdivided, organized, and accomplished.

Yes, it is vital that each individual in an organization be accountable, but, in addition, they must also share joint accountability with others.

In a case that recently came to our attention, a worker was assigned to the packaging department of a manufacturing plant. Not too long after arriving she detected serious problems with products coming from the production line. When she approached the manufacturing line supervisor to complain that "you guys are sending us too many defective products," the line supervisor replied, "On this line there is no 'you guys.' You are as much a part of this line as we are." From that point on she never said the words "you guys" again. Even more important, she started looking for solutions and stopped pointing fingers because she now understood that she would be accountable for not just her function but for the manufacturing plant's final result.

In organizations where the idea of individual responsibility has taken root, an issue will arise such as product recalls, missed sales targets, or cost overruns. Each of these issues will prompt "unaffected" departments to sit on the sidelines and rest quietly, relieved that a particular issue lies outside their realm of accountability and grateful they are not the one on the "critical path." In an environment of joint accountability, however, everyone realizes that most issues extend beyond functional lines and require solutions that often necessitate wide-scale involvement. But how does joint accountability really work, and how do you manage it? How do you avoid getting dragged *Below The Line* when someone with whom you share accountability gets stuck in the victim cycle? The answers to these questions come from learning to hold other people as accountable for the desired outcome as you hold yourself.

▲
HOLDING OTHER PEOPLE ACCOUNTABLE

While *The Oz Principle's* definition of accountability stresses a proactive orientation and an understanding of joint accountability, it does not exclude the more traditional, historical aspect, namely, holding someone else responsible for performance and results. However, holding people accountable does not mean playing the same old "who-done-it" game.

While the new notion of accountability deemphasizes confessions of guilt, it does provide for acknowledgment of the role of the individual. It is often said, "If you are not part of the solution, you are part of the problem." Another more accountable way to look at this is, "If you are not part of the problem, you are not part of the solution." Not only must you play a role in solving the problem, you must be able to acknowledge and "own" your contribution to the circumstances. In other words, you will be more powerful in solving the problem when you understand how your actions or inactions helped create the problem. The group may share responsibility, but each individual must shoulder his or her piece.

Throughout the chapters in Part One of this book, we have tried to show how our society has encouraged individuals to seek protection *Below The Line* from being answerable and responsible for their actions." In fact, many people have become experts at concocting explanations and victim stories. While doing so may provide an illusion of safety, that illusion can so easily be shattered by reality. Consider the following story.

A manufacturer of dishwashers and other home appliances ran two parallel assembly lines separated by a row of inventory handling offices and storage units. Each line functioned autonomously for the most part, and each developed its own unique operating culture. Under the leadership of the line supervisor, the workers on assembly line 1 became adept at quickly identifying a faulty subassembly from any one of the 20 workstations on the line. When someone identified a bad subassembly, the supervisor immediately confronted the operator responsible for the problem and, with everyone watching, embarrassed that person into correcting the problem and improving future performance. Naturally, everyone else on the line, protected by an illusion of safety, would blame the erring operator for slowing them down. Over time, however, people began hiding their mistakes, hoping to remain sheltered from blame, and would not acknowledge an error even when confronted by the supervisor. As a result, production output had been declining and defective subassemblies and scrap had been increasing for several months.

Next door on assembly line 2, the workers had developed a markedly different kind of operating culture. When an operator made a mistake at a workstation, other workers would immediately offer assistance in solving the problem quickly and without a lot of discussion. Functioning as part of a team, each worker felt jointly accountable for the end result of assembling quality products on time. Free from the illusion of safety created by explanations and victim stories, the workers appreciated and helped one another, quickly identifying mistakes but never accusing one individual of hurting the group effort. As a result, production on line 2 remained high, with defective subassemblies and scrap near zero.

The workers on assembly line 1 spent a lot of time *Below The Line*, denying their errors, blaming each other for mistakes, and generally walking and talking like victims. In contrast, the workers on assembly line 2 enjoyed their work, liked working with each other, felt fulfilled, and got great results. Organizational behaviorists could speak eloquently about the many differences between these two work cultures, citing innumerable variables that explain the differences in results, but we see one fundamental difference between the two: one practiced joint accountability, the other did not.

There is a widely used exercise called the Broken Squares Game, wherein teams of five people are asked to assemble five equal-sized squares, one in front of each person, from pieces of a puzzle. Each team member receives random pieces of the puzzle he or she must share with teammates to find the pieces needed to complete each of the five squares, but they can't talk to each other. There is only one way to combine all the pieces into five separate squares. It's not unusual for a team member to complete his or her square and then sit back, arms folded, and wait for the other team members to "catch up." The "safe" player usually becomes frustrated when the other members of the team can't complete their own squares, without realizing that the "safely" completed square must be disassembled because the other team members cannot complete their own squares until they break up the erroneously assembled square to obtain the pieces they need. Those who think they've safely done their job, in fact, pose a danger to the rest of the team. They miss the whole point of the exercise: each team member must accept accountability not only for putting his or her own square together, but also for helping the other team members put their squares together. They typically assume that the first team to complete all five squares wins; however, the rules state that the game doesn't end until the last team puts their last square together. When it's all over, the exercise shows that accountability, in the organizational setting, is not fully defined until everyone understands that individual accountability includes an appreciation for joint accountability. In his best-selling book, "The Seven Habits of Highly Effective People," Stephen R. Covey observes:

> On the maturity continuum, *dependence* is the paradigm of *you*—
> *you* take care of me; *you* come through for me; *you* didn't come
> through; I blame *you* for the results.

Independence is the paradigm of *I*—*I* can do it; *I* am responsible; *I* am self-reliant; *I* can choose.

Interdependence is the paradigm of *we*—*we* can do it; *we* can cooperate; *we* can combine our talents and abilities and create something greater together.

Dependent people need others to get what they want. Independent people can get what they want through their own effort. Interdependent people combine their own efforts with the efforts of others to achieve their greatest success.

The most powerful working environments apply the principles of interdependence and joint accountability, the lessons of the Broken Squares Game, where people don't fear accountability but teach and coach each other in order to win whatever game they're playing. While each individual accepts accountability for his or her own performance and results, each also knows that it takes teamwork and a sense of shared responsibility to achieve overall objectives. For people working in such environments, accountability works for them instead of against them. Yes, you still must account for your own mistakes, but you know such an accounting will drive toward a better future. In such an environment, people spend less time and resources creating excuses and more time and resources uncovering problems, taking risks, and initiating positive action to solve problems. Learning replaces punishment, success replaces failure, and victimization gives way to accountability.

THE BENEFITS OF APPLYING ACCOUNTABILITY *THE OZ PRINCIPLE*^SM WAY

Viewing accountability *The Oz Principle* way doesn't come without its costs. You must abandon the "who-done-it" game and the illusion of safety that arises when you pin blame on another individual. You must also become more involved in coaching yourself and others, and you must learn to hold other people accountable—all within the context of joint accountability.

However, the benefits far outweigh the costs. You save the costs of seemingly endless explanations from people hiding *Below The Line*. You save the costs of missed results that stem from insufficient action. You save the costs of all the dropped balls someone must, sooner or later, pick up. And you save the costs of excessive management resulting from a need to micro-manage everything and everybody in sight.

To illustrate the benefits of applying accountability *The Oz Principle* way, consider Jennifer Hanson, the vice president of sales of a large consumer products company (disguised to protect the privacy of one of our clients), who anxiously awaited an upcoming national sales meeting at which the company would launch several new products. Two months before the meeting, Jennifer received word that the new products would be a full 12 months late. Astonished by the news, she struggled with three enormous challenges: (1) how to keep herself *Above The Line* and refrain from blaming the new product development folks for the current situation, (2) how to help her sales management team stay *Above The Line*, and (3) how to assist her sales managers in keeping their sales reps committed to achieving their sales targets despite the lack of new products.

Having learned to operate *Above The Line* and view accountability in a new light, Jennifer met with her 18 sales managers to take a new look at their circumstances. Resting squarely in the victim cycle, the sales managers could concoct plenty of reasons why they felt let down by the rest of the company, but Jennifer consciously moved the discussion *Above The Line*. Viewed from *Above The Line*, the huge obstacles to achieving sales targets still looked formidable, but not impossible. She asked: "Given the obstacles we face, and there is no doubt that we do face them, what else can we do to rise above these circumstances and achieve the results that we want and those that the company needs?" At first the question astonished them.

"How," they asked, "do you solve a new products problem without new products?" "That's not our real problem," she suggested, "the real problem facing *us* is a sales problem, not a new products problem. If you accept the reality that you will receive no new products this year, then you must operate with that reality. Assigning blame to the new product development folks won't remove your responsibility to deliver on budgeted sales." After much lengthy discussion, the team decided to own their circumstances and to ask: "What else can we do to achieve this year's sales targets, despite no new products?"

In the months after this meeting Jennifer Hanson and her sales management team found many new and creative ways to boost sales and meet the sales targets set at the beginning of the year. By year's end the sales organization turned in an astonishing performance; the best in the history of the company, a healthy 15 percent increase in sales over the previous year.

One year after the accountability session, Jennifer and her sales management team met a few weeks before the next national sales meeting. During the discussions Jennifer asked her team: "What most contributed to our sales success last year?" She recounts: "Everyone felt that we took an *Above The Line* approach to the situation, wasted no time blaming new product development, and really challenged ourselves to find and implement solutions, positively rather than negatively. When the bull charged, we took it by the horns and wrestled it to the ground. We rose above our circumstances and made it happen."

LOOKING FOR PEOPLE WHO ARE REAPING, OR FAILING TO REAP, THE BENEFITS OF ACCOUNTABILITY

As we read the newspaper and watch or listen to the news on any given day, we see *The Oz Principle* applied and ignored each day. In fact, we decided to test this theory by choosing a day and then

searching the paper to see how *The Oz Principle* would be manifested. The day we chose was income tax filing day, April 15,
1993, in *The Washington Post,* the *Los Angeles Times, The (Lon-
don) Times, The Globe, The Wall Street Journal,* and *The New
York Times.*

In the *Los Angeles Times,* we found a story about L-tryptophan and Betsy DiRosa. As you read the following excerpt, you
might take a minute to think about who was accountable and who
could have been more accountable in this story:

"Two years after taking the over-the-counter sleeping aid L-
tryptophan, schoolteacher Betsy DiRosa began suffering skin
blotches, joint and muscle cramps, tingling in her arms and legs,
even damage to her heart and lungs. The symptoms remain with
DiRosa and with thousands of other victims of L-tryptophan,
which was lifted from shelves across the country in 1989 and is
now the focal point of about 1500 lawsuits brought by victims of
the debilitating disease EMS, for which L-tryptophan is blamed.
This week, DiRosa, 42, became the first plaintiff in the nation to
win a lawsuit against Showa Denko K.K., the Japanese manufacturer of the pill, but DiRosa and her attorney reacted with disappointment Wednesday, saying they had hoped for more than the
jury's award of slightly more than $1 million." The article goes
on to say, "She was 'upset' about the jury's verdict, saying she
continued taking L-tryptophan after watching a news report that
said a handful of people in New Mexico had developed mild
symptoms as a result of using the pills." DiRosa exclaimed,
"There was no mention of recalls, and I never saw another report.
L-tryptophan was still on the shelves, with no warning sign anywhere in sight. I don't feel the least bit responsible for causing all
of the horrible things that have happened to me. Was it really my
fault?" DiRosa had been seeking $144 million but received less
than even the $1.5 million offered in a proposed settlement by
Showa Denko K.K. The jury found DiRosa partially at fault
because she continued taking the pill after news accounts warning of its dangers. After the case was ended, Showa Denko's

attorney John Nyhan said, "The result should tell the plaintiffs and the plaintiffs' lawyers that jurors do not believe the company should be punished for its conduct." But then, according to DiRosa's attorney Patrick McCormick, "Fault has been established. We clearly showed that Showa Denko K.K. manufactured a defective product, one that never obtained FDA approval, and which has had a devastating impact."

As with most victim stories, there are clearly two sides to this case: both DiRosa and Showa Denko could have done more to avoid the tragedy. Showa Denko could have performed more testing and gained FDA approval before marketing its product. DiRosa could have stopped taking the pill as soon as she learned there might be a problem with the product. The jury rightly faulted Showa Denko for producing a bad product, but, honestly, the amount DiRosa received seems inadequate compensation for the difficulties she has faced and will continue to face throughout her life because of L-tryptophan. However, the jury based its decision on the principle of "what else might DiRosa have done." Think of the situation in light of the Tylenol-tampering scare of a few years ago. How many people, when they first heard of the tampering problems, stopped buying and using the product? How many people waited for the recall before they stopped using Tylenol? In our opinion, accountable consumers immediately discarded their Tylenol capsules and waited until Johnson & Johnson assured them that it had removed the risk of product tampering before they resumed using the product. DiRosa's story highlights an important aspect of *The Oz Principle*: a person can find herself or himself truly victimized, as Betsy DiRosa did, but at the same time that person can and should remain accountable for certain aspects of the situation.

In *The Washington Post* we found two interesting stories, one about President Clinton's promise to Martha Raye and the other about the decline of the Washington Bullets. During the presidential campaign, then candidate Bill Clinton wrote a letter to Martha Raye saying that, if elected, he would be honored to award her the Presidential Medal of Freedom for her many contributions. Martha is now 76 years old and her health is beginning to fail, but she has not yet received her award. After attempting all the traditional ways to prompt the president to keep his word, Martha's husband, Mark, ran a full-page ad in *Daily Variety* with a copy of the letter from President Clinton to Martha. While this may not produce the result Mark envisions, it does provide an example of someone applying *The Oz Principle* in a circumstance many would consider "beyond their control."

The sports section of most newspapers usually assigns blame for the final outcome of a game or season, and *The Washington Post* did so on April 15, 1993, in an article entitled, "Unseld: Icon or Bygone?" The article reviewed the five-year decline of the Washington Bullets that began in 1988 with the appointment of Wes Unseld as coach. "Who would have thought that after all the changes—after Williams, King, Jeff Malone, Ledell Eackles and Darrell Walker were sent out—that the Bullets would be so much worse? Who bears the burden of this?" The article goes on to suggest several reasons for the Bullets' decline, but after several paragraphs, only one thing becomes clear: the future of the Bullets does not depend on determining who should bear the bulk of the blame. A much more meaningful question occurred to us halfway through the article's finger-pointing: "What else can Unseld and the Bullets do to achieve the results they want?" Such a focus might help everybody get *Above The Line*.

In *The Globe* we found the insightful story of two sixth grade conflict managers, Cheryl Mauthe and Carrie McManus: "When Grade 6 students Cheryl Mauthe and Carrie McManus put on their pink baseball hats and head out to patrol the playground at Betty Gibson school, they go looking for trouble. The two girls are conflict managers, part of a program at the Brandon elementary school where students mediate non-physical disputes among their fellow schoolmates during recess. 'It's a good feeling knowing that you're putting effort into making our playgrounds a safer place,' Cheryl says. 'We're helping people instead of them just getting into fights,' adds Carrie. . . . The conflict managers, who have been patrolling the school's playground since March 8, are not supposed to try to solve problems themselves, take sides or break up fights. Instead, they're taught to ask the children involved how the problem can be solved, how to avoid future fights and attempt to get an agreement from everyone involved." What marvelous *Above The Line* behavior! How would schools today change if kids on all our playgrounds helped children talk rather than fight, encouraged those with conflicts to find their own solutions, and identified conflict as something that does not need to mar school life?

All these examples appeared in the news on April 15, 1993. As you read or watch the news today, look yourself for examples of people reaping or failing to reap the benefits of accountability. It won't take long for you to see the need for *The Oz Principle* in virtually every corner of American life.

▲
_____

PREPARING TO CLIMB THE *STEPS TO ACCOUNTABILITY*SM

Throughout this chapter we have redefined accountability and shown how the new definition can help you more fully appreciate the difference between *Below The Line* and *Above The Line* behavior. To summarize all the points we've made, we share the following story.

In the mid-1980s Cardiac Pacemakers Incorporated (CPI), a Minneapolis-based medical device company, found itself on the brink of disaster with a lack of new products and a loss of its market position as number two in the industry. In 1985, Eli Lilly acquired the assets of the Intec Corporation. The acquisition brought with it a revolutionary new technology, the implantable defibrillator. The acquisition of the defibrillator catapulted CPI into what has become the most exciting Medical Device market of recent times, three years ahead of its competition. Between 1985 and 1990, however, CPI not only squandered that lead, but fell behind its most formidable rival. With marketing leverage and reputation in the industry, it became clear that whatever advantage CPI once owned as the technology leader was going up in smoke.

At this juncture Jay Graf, a former military officer, came on the scene as COO of the organization, joining Dr. Robert Hauser, then CEO, in an effort to regain competitive advantage. Jay Graf recalled describing the company as "an organization going 90 miles per hour on an icy road headed toward a cliff because no one is willing to take responsibility for the situation, and, worse, no one really understands how bad things are." Despite all the clear signs of the company's precarious competitive situation, many people in the organization focused on "coping with growth" as its biggest problem, unwilling to recognize or acknowledge the impending product development challenges that could easily knock them *Below The Line*. Jay could foresee the competition's eventual rise to unquestioned market leadership just two years down the line, and he feared that their continuous introduction of high-quality new products into the market would create a game of "leap frog" that would keep CPI in a defensive posture and render its products "also-rans" as soon as they hit the market.

To meet the challenge of this situation, Jay began instilling a new sense of confidence in the organization by focusing the company on new product development. At a time when many people in the company thought that another acquisition funded by parent company Eli Lilly would solve the problem, Jay was resolute: there were not going to be any more therapeutic or resuscitative acquisitions. CPI will stand or fall through its own efforts. We're going to get off the Lilly cash crutches. Jay and the management team then implemented cross-functional product development teams staffed by people from all parts of the company, which refocused on shortening product development cycles and further defined individual accountabilities.

As Wheelwright and Clark observe:

> One of the most striking advantages of the heavyweight team is the ownership and commitment that arise among core team members, enabling tough issues to be addressed and major challenges to be overcome in a timely and effective fashion. Identifying with the product and creating a sense of esprit de corps motivates team members to extend themselves and do what needs to be done to help the team succeed.

Jay and his team also implemented frequent project review meetings which provided more timely coaching and guiding of product development teams. In addition, they put into effect a new system of succession planning which distinguished between "players," who accepted accountability for results, and "skaters," who routinely fashioned excuses for poor performance. Ultimately, they involved the entire company in a process of organizational transition which focused the company on changing the corporate culture from one characterized by "finger-pointing, confusion, and complacency" to one noted for "accountability and ownership."

As a result, today people at CPI operate *Above The Line* with a steadfast concern for new product development. Each person, in every function, understands that he or she must work together for the company to achieve its vision of "revolutionizing the world's approach to cardiac arrhythmias." CPI's higher level of accountability stimulated strong initiative and commitment throughout the organization. In Jay Graf's words, "Any project worth doing involves risk in the unanticipated. In my mind, part of what differentiates organizations that compete with one another is how each deals with and responds to the unanticipated. We still drop balls, but when the ball is on the ground, people don't stand around with their hands in their pockets wondering who is going to be the first to bend over and pick it up. When the unanticipated does happen, and the ball hits the ground, people are diving for it."

Everyone at CPI strives to affect the product development cycle in a positive way. For example, the Regulatory Group, needing to meet a very tight deadline, accelerated the timetable to complete Pre-Market Approval (PMA), a series of documents, required by the FDA, that can sometimes grow to over four feet high. Such documents would typically take many months to complete and submit. However, the Regulatory Group, knowing that it needed to shorten the cycle time of this particular submission to introduce a new product on time, put in 24 hour days, with one team writing during the day, another team proofreading and correcting all night, and a third team rewriting as necessary early the next day. Long hours for everyone were not unusual.

As an organization that operates *Above The Line*, people at CPI now feel confident that new product development will fuel future growth and return the company to market leadership, even though they still face enormous challenges.

CLIMBING THE *STEPS TO ACCOUNTABILITY*SM

It takes time, effort, commitment, and sometimes even emotional trauma, to get onto the *Steps To Accountability* and stay there, but we have never found an individual or organization, who, after experiencing life *Above The Line*, wanted to return to the victim cycle. You may slip. In fact, you will slip. However, you'll know you're slipping and you'll want to catch yourself before you sink too far.

In chapter two we provided some telltale signs of getting stuck in the victim cycle to help you recognize *Below The Line* attitudes and behavior. We'd like to conclude this chapter with some telltale signs of climbing the steps to accountability that can help you remain *Above The Line*. In the next four chapters we will address the various *Steps To Accountability*.

You can improve your own ability to remain *Above The Line* by watching for the following clues that indicate accountable attitudes and behavior:

▼ You invite candid feedback from everyone about your own performance.

▼ You never want anyone, including yourself, to hide the truth from you.

▼ You readily acknowledge reality, including all its problems and challenges.

▼ You don't waste time or energy on things you cannot control or influence.

▼ You always commit yourself 100 percent to what you are doing, and if your commitment begins to wane, you strive to rekindle it.

▼ You "own" your circumstances and your results, even when they seem less than desirable.

▼ You recognize when you are dropping *Below The Line* and act quickly to avoid the traps of the victim cycle.

▼ You delight in the daily opportunity to make things happen.

▼ You constantly ask yourself the question, "What else can I do to rise above my circumstances and get the results I want?"

When you think and act in these ways you're functioning *Above The Line*. Rising above your circumstances to get the results you seek is the empowering principle operating in Frank Baum's land of Oz.

THE POWER OF INDIVIDUAL ACCOUNTABILITY: MOVING YOURSELF *ABOVE THE LINE*^{SM}

The universally applicable **Steps To Accountability**^{SM}, **See It**^{SM}, **Own It**^{SM}, **Solve It**^{SM}, *and* **Do It**^{SM}, *weave the tapestry of every business success scenario, without exception. In Part II, we examine each of the* **Steps To Accountability**, *one at a time, to help you understand, internalize, and apply each step. You'll learn how to muster the courage to see and acknowledge reality; find the heart to own your circumstances, no matter how difficult that may prove to be; obtain the wisdom to solve any problem or overcome any obstacle that stands in your way; and exercise the means to make things happen, allowing you to get the results you want.*

THE LION: MUSTERING THE COURAGE TO SEE IT^{SM}

▼

*"Do you think Oz could give me courage?" asked
the Cowardly Lion.*

"Just as easily as he could give me brains," said the Scarecrow.

"Or give me a heart," said the Tin Woodsman.

"Or send me back to Kansas," said Dorothy.

*"Then, if you don't mind, I'll go with you," said the Lion, "for
my life is simply unbearable without a bit of courage."*

THE WIZARD OF OZ
By L. Frank Baum

It always takes courage to acknowledge the reality of a difficult situation, and even the most heralded institutions can fail to do so. Consider *Time* magazine's account of IBM's recent decline: "For years, IBM stubbornly attempted to ignore the trend away from big mainframes. Instead of adapting, it tried to protect its base. . . . But with sales slowing and price pressure mounting, IBM has finally faced up to the trend. Last week [December 21, 1992] Akers signaled IBM's intention to shift away from its mainframe business, which is down 10 percent this year." The situation did not occur overnight, and a number of IBM's competitors had already paid the price for not mustering the courage to see it coming. In August 1992 once high-flying Wang Laboratories filed for bankruptcy. Unisys, created by the merger of Burroughs and Sperry, suffered $2.5 billion in losses from 1989 to 1991, and Digital Equipment almost sank under similarly huge losses, which resulted in the ouster of Digital's founder and president Kenneth Olsen in 1992. Clearly, the handwriting was on the wall: the old non-mainframe strategies no longer worked. IBM, however, ignored the signals, even when upstart Apple Computer surpassed IBM as the leading PC maker and rounded up a stellar performance in 1992, partly due to a "tiny frame" computer, the laptop Power-Book. Aggressive price cutting in the industry sparked great demand, which Apple and IBM-compatible Compaq rushed to fill. IBM also failed to anticipate the workstation revolution and sat by as Sun Microsystems and Hewlett-Packard took the lead in that market. As the *Time* article concluded, "Although it developed superb technology years ago, the company sat on it out of fear that it would cannibalize IBM's bread-and-butter mainframe business." Failing to see the reality of its situation, IBM lost both the value of its bread-and-butter business and the chance to position itself properly for the future. No longer the undisputed superstar in its field, Big Blue is fast becoming just another talented player.

When did the downfall begin? In an earlier story, *Fortune* magazine pinpointed the time precisely: "To understand fully just what a disaster IBM has been, and just how blind its own management was to the depth of its problems, step back to a moment in late 1986. IBM was more than a year past a boom period and struggling. Revenue growth was miserable, earnings growth was nonexistent, and IBM's stock, then $125 a share, had lost nearly $24 billion in market value from a peak of $99 billion just seven months earlier. In an interview with *Fortune,* Chairman John F. Akers nonetheless exhibited gritty confidence: "Four or five years from now," he asserted, "people will look back and see that the company's performance has been superlative." Almost five years later, reality proved Akers dead wrong. IBM stock continued to fall, losing another 18 billion in market value. Revenues grew at less than half the industry average of the period, and IBM's worldwide market share fell from 30 percent to 21 percent, a whopping $3 billion in sales for each percentage point. When asked by *Fortune* what went wrong and why his prediction of superlative performance had been so unrealistic, Akers replied, "I don't think anything went wrong." *Fortune* reporters responded, "Then why, one might reasonably ask, did he tell his managers in May [1991] that IBM was 'in crisis,' a characterization made in private and quickly leaked to the press? And, if IBM stock has lost $42 billion in value since 1986, just how far would it have fallen if something really had gone wrong?" Akers later claimed he only meant to emphasize that Big Blue's industry is so volatile that no company can anticipate all the unexpected changes that sweep through it. To his credit, however, he admitted that IBM could not blame any outside force for its stupendous loss of market share.

At the time this book went to press, IBM's woes were even worse than imagined in 1991–1992, and the company's new chief executive officer, Louis Gerstner, must have felt much like the Wizard of Oz, from whom everyone expected an impossible miracle. That miracle won't materialize, of course, until everyone at IBM musters the courage to *See It* and move the company back *Above The Line.*

It isn't easy to see such a reality, and you can't do it overnight, but you will get there fairly quickly if you proceed one sure step at a time. As you begin taking the first step *Above The Line*, bear in mind the words of Jack Welch, chief executive officer of General Electric, who defines management as "looking reality straight in the eye and then acting upon it with as much speed as you can."

TAKING THE FIRST STEP *ABOVE THE LINE*^{SM}

Even the most accountable people get stuck in the victim cycle from time to time. And sometimes, people who are otherwise very accountable can get stuck on a particular challenge. Regardless of whether you're stuck *Below The Line* all the time or only on a particularly pesky problem, you must still take the first step out of the victim cycle by recognizing that you are stuck in a circle of denial. That recognition requires the courage to acknowledge the reality of your situation, no matter how unpleasant or unfair that reality may seem. Without such acknowledgment, you can never expect to respond to it effectively. According to Andrew S. Grove, chairman of Intel, as reported in a *Fortune* magazine article, "There is at least one point in the history of any company when you have to change dramatically to rise to the next performance level. Miss the moment, and you start to decline." The key is courage.

It's astonishing to see such giants as IBM, General Motors, Sears and U.S. Steel, who at one time were seen as the unchallenged leaders in their respective world markets, suddenly fall because they were not able to *See It* and respond fast enough to the revolutionary changes that occurred in their marketplaces. Merck, who for several years running, has been named the most admired company in the country in *Fortune* Magazine's annual survey of corporate reputations, appears to be on the same track of decline. Merck's growth in income, which had climbed 24 to 34% per year in the late 1980's, was currently projected by many of the experts to slow to 10% in 1993 and then slide even further into single digits in the years to follow. Some of Merck's most profitable and successful products have begun losing market share to price-cutting competitors and Merck's stock price has dropped 38% from near-record highs the previous year.

But rather than shrinking from the stark reality they faced, Merck mustered the courage to *See It*, to acknowledge the path they were on and in one bold move may have taken the fundamental action necessary to escape the similar fate of many of their peers among the *Fortune* 500. In a recent Fortune article entitled, "Why Merck Married The Enemy," Brian O'Reilly recounts how "Merck had become a victim of its own success. Like a handful of other top drugmakers, its strategy had been to develop so-called annuity drugs—medicines for common chronic diseases that patients had to take every day for years. With pressure mounting on governments and private medical plan sponsors to rein in spending, the yearly bill for Merck's annuity drugs quickly made them the focus of the most aggressive cost cutting in the U.S. and abroad."

Medco, a company that contracts with big medical plan sponsors to lower the cost of prescription drugs used by their 33 million patients was one of the major forces behind Merck's loss in market share and decline in growth. O'Reilly quotes Merck's chief scientist as saying, "The degree to which Medco was able to shift market share away from Mevacor was unthinkable. Adds the head of strategic marketing in the U.S. for Merck: One day it was like all quiet on the western front, and the next day it was war. We concluded that we had to change our fundamental business philosophy."

At a time when others are stuck in the victim-cycle mode of "wait and see," Merck moved with boldness, courage, ownership and vision. The data was clear and Merck was clearly listening.

Merck's first step was to acquire Medco for $6 billion; a move that was and still is seen as risky by many of the "experts" who were advising others to "wait and see" what Clinton's health care policy reforms would include. Merck believes that Medco will be able to help them expand volume dramatically which will help offset the profit pinch created by falling prices. Furthermore, while the drug costs included in some managed health care plans are 50% currently, Merck believes that this percentage will grow to 90% within the next ten years. As O'Reilly states, "Medco gives Merck a chance to play that game, while offering a number of other important revenue-raising opportunities as well." In addition, Medco will allow Merck to cut their extraordinary marketing costs. One final advantage of the acquisition is that Merck may be able to use Medco's computerized patient record system as a real-life laboratory in which they hope to prove that some of Merck's drugs really are worth the premium price the company charges for them.

No one can really know how the Medco purchase will in the end be viewed. But there is no question that Merck is meeting its challenges head on with its eyes wide open to reality. Interestingly, O'Reilly summarizes, "Only two days before the Medco agreement was announced, a top Wall Street analyst was lamenting that there was nothing Merck management could do to escape from devastating price pressure." Obviously, while skeptics are sometimes right in their conclusions, they need no courage to offer their observations and they often tend to be unequivocally *Below The Line* in their conclusions—there is nothing they can do!

▲
WHY PEOPLE FAIL TO *SEE IT*^{SM}

People most frequently fail to see reality because they choose to ignore or resist changes in the external environment. For example, *The Wall Street Journal* recently ran an article entitled, "To Trim Their Costs, Some Companies Cut Space for Employees," in which it reported, "Last year, Connie Plourde and the other sales representatives at American Telephone & Telegraph Co.'s Sacramento, Calif., office lost their desks. They were given laptop computers, cellular telephones and portable printers and told to create 'virtual offices' at home or at their customers' offices. It wasn't an easy change for the extroverted, 19-year AT&T veteran, who delighted in the camaraderie of the workplace. 'Until the real-estate people came in and started moving our cubicles out, we just continued to come in,' she recalls. 'It was a comfort zone, I guess.'" Ignoring or refusing to deal with such a change can quickly thrust you *Below The Line*, when you sit waiting for the "good old days" to return. According to the *Journal* article, "'The office isn't a place to come, sit down and stare at a computer screen or talk on the phone all day,' says Dun & Bradstreet's Michael Bell, one of a new sort of corporate real-estate manager pushing such changes. 'If you want to do that, you can do it at home.' It is far from clear, however, whether corporate decision makers—who climbed the ladder at a time when clout was measured by office size and location—are ready to embrace what Mr. Bell has dubbed the 'un-real-estating' of corporate America." Resistance to such a trend could, however, undermine the competitiveness of a company that has found itself in a dogfight for market share. Larry Ebert, director of real estate at Ernst & Young, says there will be a lot of "cultural resistance" to such office changes. If those changes are inevitable, then those who resist them will inevitably fail.

To illustrate another common reason why people fail to see reality and their own responsibility for that reality, consider the current family "dysfunction game." While most people agree that the home environment affects a person's habits, it has become fashionable, even epidemic, for adult children to blame all their woes on dysfunctional childhood homes. Compulsive shopping disorders, sex addictions, poor eating habits, alcoholism, spouse and child abuse, work ruts, personality disorders, uncontrollable urges to please others? "It's not my fault, it's my family's fault." Talk show hosts from Oprah to Donahue to Geraldo daily exploit America's penchant for playing the "dysfunction game" by parading celebrities such as Roseanne Arnold, Gunnar Nelson, Patti Davis, Kitty Dukakis, and many others across the nation's television screens, perpetuating the notion that none of us need shoulder full responsibility for our problems. The raging popularity of such shows emphasizes just how much the nation's television audiences enjoy hearing other people recount their victim stories. In turn, many TV watchers use such victim stories to justify their own *Below The Line* behavior, making the blame game a new national pastime. After all, according to popular lecturer and author, John Bradshaw, 96 percent of the population comes from "dysfunctional" families.

While we agree that family problems can plague people far beyond their childhoods, we take issue with Bradshaw's claim, not just because we question the accuracy of the percentage, but because reliance on that percentage lets 96 percent of the population off the hook for their current behavior. If you comfort yourself with the knowledge that 96 percent of your fellow Americans can blame their dysfunctional families for their problems, you're probably stuck in the victim cycle. Oh, you may justly feel early experiences have contributed to your problems, but chalking everything up to those problems prevents you from taking charge of your life and doing something about your problems. In this sense, the current dysfunctional fad strikes us as just one more indicator of people's inability and unwillingness to acknowledge their own accountability. Fortunately, many experts and writers, fed up with the extremes to which the dysfunctional game has been taken, are encouraging people to see the reality of their own responsibility. A new book by Wendy Kaminer entitled *I'm Dysfunctional, You're Dysfunctional,* a parody of the best-selling *I'm Okay, You're Okay,* criticizes the popular recovery movement and all the self-help gurus because they too greatly diminish individual accountability.

In a *USA Weekend* article, "Dysfunction Junction," author Tim Larimer chides, "With all due respect to the recovery movement and other self-help trends, some experts say the time has come to grow up, quit whining and give Mom (and Dad) a break." Larimer also quotes Frank Pittman, well-known therapist to communications mogul Ted Turner and many others, who admits that his profession has encouraged the whining of millions of Americans: "A society full of victims is a bunch of people who have a free pass not to take responsibility for their actions."

Given this "It's-not-my-fault" climate, it's not surprising that people find it difficult to see reality and accept their own accountability, but it's also gratifying to see Kaminer, Larimer, Pittman, and the following excerpt from a mortgage company ad that appeared in 1992 poke fun at those who fail to *See It* at a time when it is painfully obvious:

THE TOP TEN EXCUSES FOR NOT REFINANCING
WHILE INTEREST RATES ARE LOWER
▼

1. "I like double-digit interest."

2. "I like higher payments."

3. "The bank needs the money more than I do."

4. "I didn't know I could."

5. "I didn't know who to call."

6. "I'd probably only save a measly few hundred bucks each month."

7. "My current mortgage company never told me about any lower rates."

8. "I couldn't trust myself with any extra cash."

9. "I couldn't think of anything to do with any extra cash."

10. "The dog ate my loan documents."

That ad amused us, and the whole dysfunctional movement would strike us as funny, if it weren't so dangerous to our country's well-being. Sadly, in the long months before election day on November 3, 1992, most Americans grew disheartened with what they perceived to be the endless excuse making of the Bush campaign, which eventually guaranteed the president's election defeat. In the eyes of many Americans, Bush never did face up to the realities of a declining economy. Not surprisingly, President Bush was not the only elected government official who paid a "career limiting" price because of *Below The Line* behavior. Consider, for instance, these excuses for overdrafts at the now-defunct House Bank as reported in *The Wall Street Journal* during 1992:

▼ Representative Mary Rose Oakar, a Democrat of Ohio who sat on the House Administration Committee that oversaw the House Bank and racked up 217 overdrafts, said, "When I came to Congress, they didn't tell us there was another way to get your check."

▼ Representative Robert Mrazek, a Democrat from New York with 972 overdrafts, said, "I have never bounced a check."

▼ Representative Tim Penny, a Democrat from Minnesota, blamed his overdrafts on his office manager.

▼ Representative Edolphus Towns, another Democrat from New York, attributed many of his 403 overdrafts to embezzlement by a former employee.

▼ Representative Newt Gingrich, a Republican from Georgia and House Republican Whip, dismissed his overdrafts as "no big deal."

Such failure to see reality has grown rampant in American society. Again, on the lighter side, look at these actual descriptions people wrote on accident report forms that were published by the Arizona Safety Association:

▼ "Coming home, I drove into the wrong house and collided with a tree I don't have."

▼ "A pedestrian hit me and went under my car."

▼ "The guy was all over the road. I had to swerve a number of times before I hit him."

▼ "I had been shopping for plants all day and was on my way home. As I reached the intersection, a hedge sprang up, obscuring my vision. I did not see the other car."

▼ "As I approached the intersection, a sign suddenly appeared in a place where no stop sign had ever appeared before."

▼ "An invisible car came out of nowhere, struck my vehicle, and vanished."

▼ "The pedestrian had no idea which direction to run, so I ran over him."

▼ "The indirect cause of this accident was a little guy in a small car with a big mouth."

▼ "The telephone pole was approaching. I was attempting to swerve out of the way when it struck my front end."

Each of these drivers, not to mention all the folks in Washington, couldn't come to grips with the reality of their situations. How much better for them, the victims of their negligence, and the country at large, if they could only

1. Recognize when they are in the victim cycle;

2. Realize that remaining in the victim cycle not only ignores the real problem but leads to increasingly poor results; and

3. Acknowledge and accept reality as the first step toward accepting accountability.

Acknowledging *Below The Line* behavior and facing up to "the reality" of your situation takes courage. Failure to muster that courage results in an unwillingness to pay the price for greater accountability and results. In most troublesome situations, people do know, in the back of their minds, that acknowledging reality means they'll have to do something about their situations, first viewing their situations differently, then acting differently to improve their situations. Viewing a situation differently often means getting comfortable with the fact that you did something wrong, admitting that you yourself could have done more and didn't, or deciding that since you can't do anything to remedy the situation you may as well move on. Doing something differently about your situation often requires doing things you dislike doing, such as taking a risk you've been avoiding or confronting an issue or person you've been ignoring. At Hartmarx Corporation, the Chicago-based maker of men's suits, the board of directors failed to confront the inability of the company's chief executive officer, Harvey Weinberg, to halt a string of losses that eventually totaled $320 million. Only then did the board force Weinberg to resign. According to *The Wall Street Journal,* the board didn't act sooner because it "didn't want to be seen as pulling the plug too early." Unfortunately, the "wait-and-see" attitude significantly contributed to the value of the company's stock falling from $600 million to $200 million.

Embracing such realities can prove difficult because doing so involves shedding the protective cocoon of a victim story. It seems so much safer to remain in the victim cycle, but the cocoon really offers only an illusion of safety because eventually the time will come to pay the piper for your inaction. When you give yourself permission to do nothing about your situation, when you don't act, don't learn, don't acknowledge your responsibility, don't admit having done wrong, don't face the facts, don't give up the sympathy that a victim story attracts, and don't look for what else you could do to achieve results, your behavior gets you nowhere. To get somewhere better, to improve your situation, and to solve your problems, you must abandon the illusion of safety *Below The Line* and take the risks associated with rising *Above The Line*.

When you encounter a difficult situation, ask yourself whether you want to remain mired in the difficulty or attempt some sort of breakthrough to extract yourself from the situation. Even the most habitual victim would rather be leading a better life, but achieving a "break through" usually requires a "break with" *past actions* and attitudes. That means that any person feeling victimized must replace his or her victim story with a willingness to see things as they really are and not as they appear to be from the tenuous safety of the victim cycle. To create a better future, you must often break with the past. Failing this, you will, sooner or later, suffer serious consequences for your inaction.

THE CONSEQUENCES OF NOT *SEEING IT*

When Christopher J. Steffen resigned as chief financial officer at Eastman Kodak after less than three months on the job, his exit exposed the growing vulnerability of boards of directors who must assess the reality of their companies' needs in a timely fashion. According to *The Wall Street Journal,* "Management experts say boards of directors everywhere are under greater pressure nowadays to fill top jobs quickly. Directors sometimes fail to gauge whether a new executive—especially below the chief executive officer's level—will mesh with existing senior management." According to the article, in Eastman Kodak's case, Steffen's resignation "knocked $1.7 billion off market value of the company's stock." Not seeing reality, especially at the board level, can deliver serious, and sometimes lightning-swift, consequences.

We recently worked with a client who, because of the sensitive nature of the story and our desire to protect the privacy of the individuals involved, must remain disguised. The story's true, however, and it exposes the inexorable consequences of not seeing reality.

Tim Langley, president and CEO of CET, a $400 million insurance company, had recently hired Jed Simon as his new vice president of underwriting to resolve a sales volume shortfall in the near term, and to build a world-class underwriting organization in the long term. Langley believed he had hired the perfect man, and after the first year together, Langley awarded Simon a rave review for his work and even implied that his protege would someday succeed him as CEO of the company.

Soon after joining CET, Simon had introduced an organizational effectiveness program that created greater openness and productivity throughout the company's underwriting operations and quickly ended the sales shortfall. In addition, Simon drafted a new policy manual, hired new staff, and beefed up the organization's capabilities to meet anticipated future demand. Since his actions enabled the company to surpass all its annual goals, Langley took to calling Simon "the best underwriting vice president in the business."

Then, as the year ended, and the new year began, Langley shifted CET's emphasis from increased sales to quality service; Simon's reputation plummeted almost overnight. In stark contrast to last year's review, his next one nailed him to the wall. From Langley's perspective, Simon had been ignoring vital feedback from the sales force about CET's dismal quality of service. According to the sales force, poor service quality made it impossible for them to sustain and increase sales.

When we dug into the situation, we discovered that Simon responded to this feedback from deep within the victim cycle. Here's how he described his feelings to us: "How can I get a review like this? I have never received such a horrible review. What do these salespeople know anyway? They can't even make accurate sales forecasts for one quarter. The sandbaggers! They want a sure thing in terms of their sales quotas, and they never stretch for higher goals. They haven't even looked at the monthly graphs that clearly show customer complaints down and sales up. Furthermore, we have rolled out so many new products prematurely that we have ended up doing the job of the development people along with our own. You know, I really think Langley's got an ego problem and feels threatened by me. Last year he told me and many others that he thought I was the best underwriting vice president in the industry. He even told me I would succeed him someday. Now he's telling me I'm doing a rotten job. I don't think he knows what he wants. He changes his priorities every time I turn around. He's the one who's got a problem, not me."

While there may have been some truth to Simon's perceptions, he was clearly wallowing *Below The Line* by refusing to acknowledge the reality of his circumstances. Through a series of rationalizations, he convinced himself that the alleged service quality problem shouldn't fall in his lap. Worse, he considers his current course of action productive, appropriate, and destined to yield superior results, when, in fact, it won't.

In Jed Simon's case, before he could *See It* he needed to (1) acknowledge his own *Below The Line* behavior, (2) recognize the reality (and not necessarily the accuracy) of his boss's perception that he has failed in the area of service quality, and (3) realize that as long as he stays *Below The Line* he will remain ineffective. Simon's inability and/or unwillingness to acknowledge the realities created a widening chasm between himself and his boss, and no matter how unjust it may seem to him, when it comes to a showdown, he'll lose, Langley will win. Anyone who fails to see reality and remains *Below The Line* always loses.

With that in mind, let's now look at how you can assess and develop your own ability to acknowledge reality and thereby avoid the unpleasant and inevitable consequences of failing to *See It.*

SEE IT^{SM} SELF-ASSESSMENT

Picture in your mind's eye something we see all too often: the sales vice president of a midsized computer manufacturer telling his colleague, the marketing vice president, that the company's sales are weak because its products don't meet customer needs, but the marketing vice president dismissing the argument. In such a situation, the sales vice president perceives that the marketing vice president never listens to their input while the marketing vice president thinks that the sales vice president is never happy with the support that he is getting. Both feel victimized by the other, and both remain stuck *Below The Line*, unwilling to acknowledge reality. Unless these two executives can "see" reality, they will squander their time and energy blaming each other, fostering confusion, promoting organizational discord, and creating an environment in which their people "wait and see" if their leaders will work things out. So how do these vice presidents begin recognizing their *Below The Line* attitudes and behavior?

The first step requires careful and honest self-assessment. To facilitate your own self-assessment, we have developed the following exam, which will give you a general idea of your ability to recognize a *Below The Line* posture. Take a few minutes to evaluate your ability to *See It* in the context of your work, home, team, club, community, church, or association, answering each question as honestly as you can.

SEE IT℠ SELF-ASSESSMENT

▼

	Never	Seldom	Sometimes	Often	Always
1. You quickly recognize when you are in the victim cycle.	7	5	3	1	0
2. You accept coaching from others who point out ways in which you helped contribute to the problem you currently face.	7	5	3	1	0
3. You willingly acknowledge that you make mistakes that impair your ability to get results.	7	5	3	1	0
4. You openly listen when people offer you perspectives of the problem that are different from yours.	7	5	3	1	0
5. You look first at what you are personally doing, or not doing, that is getting in your way of progress; as opposed to solely looking at how others are preventing your progress.	7	5	3	1	0

	Never	Seldom	Sometimes	Often	Always
6. You strive to broaden your scope of under-standing about the problem you face by seeking greater under-standing from a wide array of resources.	7	5	3	1	0
7. You readily acknowl-edge existing problems and clearly understand the consequences of not resolving them.	7	5	3	1	0
8. You test your view of reality with other peo-ple when faced with a perplexing problem.	7	5	3	1	0
9. You consciously and actively work to get *Above The Line* by objectively acknowl-edging reality.	7	5	3	1	0
10. When explaining your lack of progress, you are quick to acknowl-edge how you con-tributed to a lack of results	7	5	3	1	0

After you have completed the *See It* Self-assessment, total up your score. The following table provides some guidelines for evaluating your ability to recognize when you're stuck *Below The Line*.

Total Score	*Evaluation Guidelines*
50+	Indicates a serious inability or unwillingness to *See It*. You need outside help. Call 911, immediately!
30 to 50	Suggests that you often find it difficult to *See It*. Learn to seek feedback (see next section). Ask someone sitting near you to slap you in the face, right now!
10 to 30	Reveals a fair ability to *See It*. Keep working on it. If you have a victim story write it on a piece of parchment, bury it in the back yard, and move on!
0 to 10	Verifies a strong ability to *See It*. Turn to a person near you and ask them to give you a pat on the back!

Once you have assessed yourself, don't get discouraged if you discover that you need help "seeing it." The greatest help in acknowledging the reality of the circumstances you face can come in the form of feedback from others familiar with your situation.

▲
HOW FEEDBACK IMPROVES YOUR ABILITY TO *SEE IT*^{SM}

You can gain great insight from frequent, regular, and ongoing feedback from other people. Although painful and embarrassing at times, the honest input from others helps create the accurate picture of reality that lies at the core of accountability. Since no one individual can mandate a perfectly accurate description of reality, you must draw from many other people's perceptions to imbue your reality with the deepest possible understanding of its many hues and shades. In our experience, accountable people constantly seek feedback from a wide range of associates, be they friends, family, business partners, consultants, or other advisors. Remember, other peoples' perceptions of reality, whether you agree with them or not, always add important nuances to your own perception of reality. The more perceptions you obtain, the more easily you can recognize when you're stuck *Below The Line*, move *Above The Line*, and then encourage others to do likewise.

The diagram on the following page illustrates the effect that feedback has on creating accountable people.

To better grasp the importance of seeking and giving feedback, picture in your mind a common situation we encountered with one of our clients: Betty Bingham, a corporate staff human resources vice president of a large corporation, has been temporarily reassigned to "clean up" a division's human resources policies and practices. The people in the division naturally view her as an intruder, and she assumes, after a few weeks, that all the "bad press" she's getting automatically comes with such "bad guy" assignments. Several months later when she thinks it's time to return to her corporate staff assignment, she learns that headquarters doesn't want her back. Worse, she receives no salary increase. Devastated by this turn of events, Betty feels victimized and confused because she had received no direct feedback about her performance from headquarters or from the division president to whom she has been temporarily reporting. Instead of feeling sorry for herself, however, she begins seeking direct feedback from the people she's been working with over the last nine months. As she seeks and receives this input she discovers that her "clean-up" methods have caused deep resentments and frustrations. For example, one vice president confided in her that he thought she did not respect others' points of view, that she did not acknowledge the previous accomplishments of the organization or her staff, and that she tended to take credit due others.

This sort of feedback helped Betty gain an awareness of how she had caused much of the "bad press" herself, which made

Feedback Creates Accountability

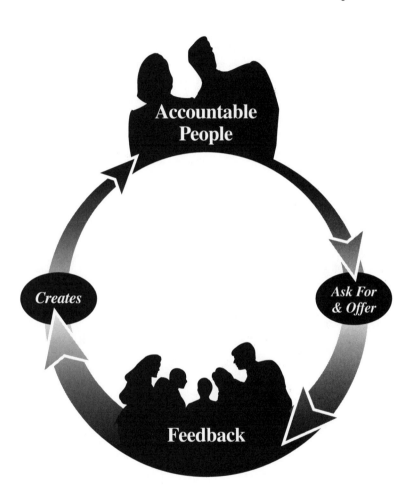

it difficult for her to get the results she wanted. Now, armed with direct feedback, she set about turning around the negative perceptions in an effort to win back the confidence of people in both the division and at headquarters. To her delight, more and more people began to confide in her and she soon built a reputation as a credible and useful executive. Before she got the feedback, she felt victimized, powerless, and unable to change things; truly unaware, and unbelieving, as to how others viewed her. Had she remained stuck in that resentment, she would undoubtedly have sought employment elsewhere. After the feedback, however, she could *See It* more clearly and consequently felt more empowered to do something about her predicament. In short, she had moved herself *Above The Line*.

If you find yourself continually surprised by your performance appraisals, we suggest you do what Betty did and seek more feedback about your performance, not just from your superiors, but from others whom you respect and trust. It's easy to go home and rant against your superiors, over what you perceive as unjust treatment; it's hard to ask your family to help you understand why you've gotten the review you did. Specifically, we recommend that you seek feedback from others. There are right and wrong ways to seek feedback. If you don't do it right, you may only hear what people think you want to hear. To gain the most honest feedback, you should follow these tips:

1. Ask for feedback in the right environment—a comfortable, quiet place free from interruptions and distractions.

2. Tell the person from whom you're seeking feedback that you want honest input about a particular situation or concern. Emphasize your sincerity, and explain your motivation.

3. Remember, the feedback you're requesting represents an important point of view, so don't get defensive, even if you strongly disagree with something the person says.

4. Listen carefully and ask for elaboration (but be sure not to off-handedly invalidate feedback which is not supported by examples).

5. Make sure you express your appreciation for your advisor's time and help.

Once you have more fully examined your own *Above* and *Below The Line* behavior, consider the substantial benefits that automatically flow to someone who has mustered the courage to face reality.

THE BENEFITS OF *SEEING IT*

As we indicated at the beginning of this chapter, even if you consider yourself a highly accountable person, you can still get stuck in the victim cycle when facing a particular challenge, as we ourselves did not long ago with an important client. To protect our client's privacy, we'll refer to the organization as DALCAP.

We always strive for superior customer service with our clients, but something in our consulting engagement with DALCAP over a six-month period caused certain key executives there to perceive us as *Below The Line* in terms of customer service. Had we, somehow, failed to practice what we preach? While we saw them as our most demanding client, we had also felt that we had risen to the occasion time and time again. At the same time while we knew that our client had concerns, it seems, we pretended not to know that our client resented what they saw as inaccessibility. Each time a DALCAP executive referred to some example of our inaccessibility, we were stunned. How could they feel that we were inaccessible after all the extraordinary things we had accomplished at their request? We rationalized what we considered to be DALCAP's false expectations, by convincing ourselves that no matter what we did, we could never make this client happy. Eventually, however, after a lot of discussion, we realized that in order to maintain a successful relationship with this client we had to acknowledge that we were not meeting DALCAP's expectations. We knew that we must get *Above The Line* and demonstrate the *See It* attitude we emphasize so much in our consulting work. As a first step, we wrote the following memo to DALCAP's executive staff:

To: DALCAP Executive Staff Members

From: Partners in Leadership

Date: July 17, 1992

Subject: Customer Orientation

We reviewed our recent proposal to DALCAP with Barbara Kowal this morning and were pleased to hear that there is a good chance that we would be going forward with the project. We appreciate your confidence in our ability to continue to assist DALCAP.

Barbara very graciously shared with us some constructive feedback about our work that came up during one of your recent executive staff meetings. Some people honestly feel Partners in Leadership has not been as accessible as it should. This deeply concerns us because it seems to indicate that some at DALCAP question our commitment to customer service.

We want you to know that we will do everything we can to prove our commitment. Your feedback will help us to grow, and that will help us help you. We promise this: *Partners in Leadership will be accessible.*

We understand that perceptions do not change overnight, but we have already begun to work on establishing this new perception. Specifically:

1. Throughout our engagement, we will call Barbara Kowal weekly to review progress and to determine whether we should meet with any of you or any of the trained facilitators.

2. While our travel and our work in facilitating off-site sessions may prevent us from getting back to you right away, we will personally respond to your voice mail messages no later than the evening of the day on which you call.

3. If you need to reach us for an immediate response please call our office number 909-694-5596. Emphasize that you have an "urgent message" and need to reach us right away. We will make sure our people remain alert for all such calls and that they relay them to us immediately. We will get back to you as soon as possible.

If at any time you doubt our accessibility, tell us so at once. We need your continued feedback to foster our own accountability for results.

We look forward to our ongoing relationship and the growth of both our organizations.

Sincerely,

Partners in Leadership

While this response may not appear extraordinary, it did communicate to our client that we heard their feedback, acknowledged their concern, and desired to respond to their needs. Less than one month after receiving the memo, the president of DALCAP signed a new long-term agreement with us, larger than our two previous agreements with the company.

It would have been much easier for us to continue denying or rationalizing DALCAP's perception of our inaccessibility, but doing so would have robbed us of the substantial benefits we gain from such a valuable client. By acknowledging the "reality" we ran the risk of appearing "wrong," but until we decided to do something about our client's perception, we would not be able to get *Above The Line*, and effect any positive shift in our client's perceptions.

PREPARING FOR THE NEXT STEP
ABOVE THE LINE^{SM}

Oz's Lion symbolizes the first dimension of accountability, mustering the courage to see reality. However, Dorothy would need to understand all four dimensions of accountability before she would fully understand that only she could rise above her circumstances and return to Kansas. Not surprisingly, along her yellow brick road journey she learned to love and cherish her companions for each of their unique qualities. In the end she was able to combine what she had learned from and with her companions to escape feelings of powerlessness and rise *Above The Line* to get the results she wanted. In the next chapter, you will see how the Tin Woodsman symbolizes the heart to *Own It* and in the process learn how to muster your own courage to own the reality you learned to recognize in this chapter. Keep in mind that to get the results you want on your own journey, you'll need what all the Oz companions gained on theirs'.

CHAPTER 5

THE TIN WOODSMAN: FINDING THE HEART TO *OWN IT*^{SM}

▼

"I might have stood there always if you had not come along,"
he said; "so you have certainly saved my life. How did you
happen to be here?"

"We are on our way to the Emerald City, to see the great Oz,"
she answered, "and we stopped at your cottage to pass
the night."

"Why do you wish to see Oz?" he asked.

"I want him to send me back to Kansas; and the Scarecrow
wants him to put a few brains into his head," she replied.

The Tin Woodman appeared to think deeply for a moment.
Then he said:

"Do you suppose Oz could give me a heart?"

"Why, I guess so," Dorothy answered.

THE WIZARD OF OZ
By L. Frank Baum

Too many Americans have lost the heart to own their circumstances, and that loss of heart has begun eroding the very foundation of American competitiveness. A recent *Time* magazine article, *"The Temping of America: As Stable Jobs Disappear, Americans Are Being Forced to Adjust to a Fragile and Frightening New Order,"* details one particularly alarming aspect of that erosion: "This is the new metaphysics of work. Companies are portable, workers are throwaway. The rise of the knowledge economy means a change, in less than 20 years, from an overbuilt system of large, slow-moving economic units to an array of small, widely dispersed economic centers, some as small as the individual boss. In the new economy, geography dissolves, the highways are electronic. Even Wall Street no longer has a reason to be on Wall Street. Companies become concepts and, in their dematerialization, become strangely conscienceless. And jobs are almost as susceptible as electrons to vanishing into thin air. The American economy has turned into a bewilderment of good news, horrible news, depending on your point of view. After two years of record profits, the Bank of America recently announced that thousands of employees will become part-timers, with few benefits. Beneath some of the statistics of economic recovery lies stress and pain."

A companion article in the same *Time* issue, entitled *"Disposable Workers,"* identifies America's growing reliance on temporary staffers as a trend that's shattering the tradition of employee loyalty and commitment: "The corporation that is now the largest private employer in America does not have any smokestacks or conveyor belts or trucks. There is no clanging of metal on metal, no rivets or plastic or steel. In one sense, it does not make anything. But then again, it is in the business of making almost everything. Manpower, Inc., with 560,000 workers, is the world's largest temporary employment agency. Every morning, its people scatter into the offices and factories of America, seeking a day's work for a day's pay."

As behemoth companies like General Motors and IBM strive to "rightsize" themselves by shrinking their payrolls, Manpower, based in Milwaukee, Wisconsin, fills the vacuum supplying the bodies and brains those companies still need to accomplish their goals. The United States has entered a new era, the *free-lance economy,* where the ranks of part-timers, temps, and independent contractors are expanding while the traditional full-time work force is shrinking. According to the *Time* article, "Already, one in every three U.S. workers has joined these shadow brigades carrying out America's business. Their ranks are growing so quickly that they are expected to outnumber permanent full-time workers by the end of this decade." While this trend may benefit the bottom line, it can take its toll not only in terms of alienated relationships among co-workers but also in terms of pride in product quality and customer satisfaction. Will "temps" care as much as full-time workers about the long-term consequences of their jobs? Will they be as willing to go beyond their job description in order to get the result? Or, will they use their job description as justification for why they failed to get results? Will they feel victimized by an organization that wants to "rent" their services, but requires them to "own" their jobs?

The *Time* article continues with Robert Schaen, former controller of Ameritech and now publisher of children's books, observing that "The days of the mammoth corporations are coming to an end. People are going to have to create their own lives, their own careers and their own successes. Some people may go kicking and screaming into the new world, but there is only one message there: You're now in business for yourself." In the free-lance economy "owning" your circumstances, whether for a week temping in an unfamiliar organization or for a few years in a career-enhancing position or for a lifetime in your own business, will become more and more critical for every American.

In this year's "Most Admired Corporations" issue of *Fortune* magazine, reporters highlighted employee involvement, which includes ownership and accountability, as a common thread among the most admired corporations: "Most admired companies treat their employees exceptionally well, which is a factor in, and a result of, their success. Robert Haas, CEO of Levi Strauss Associates, thinks employee engagement and satisfaction are fundamental to running a strong business. Says he: 'You have to create an environment where everyone feels like a representative of the company. Unless you have people who know what you stand for and want to make every transaction the best, you're going to stub your toe.'" As an example of the sense of ownership felt by Levi Strauss employees, *Fortune* describes what happened at a plant in Albuquerque, New Mexico, where factory workers identified a serious problem and began working with a local businessperson to recycle some of the millions of pounds of denim scraps Levi took to the landfill every year. The workers approached Levi headquarters with the idea and won approval for the plan. Today, all Levi Strauss interoffice stationery is blue and is made of recycled denim. And as a result, the plant has cut paper costs 18 percent and a little pressure has been taken off the local landfill. Now that's ownership!

In too many cases, however, an "ownership gap" seems to be widening between executive pay and company performance, a problem that a growing number of shareholder activists have pounced on. According to *The Wall Street Journal,* "To hear some people tell it, corporate chieftains are on the run. Boardroom revolts at giant companies such as GM and IBM (where chief executive officers and top executives received huge salaries and bonuses even while their companies were floundering) give the impression that rising shareholder activism has top executives scared and weakened as they try desperately to hang on to their jobs. The reality, however, is quite different at most U.S. companies. First Mississippi Corp., for example, has made a decade's worth of strategic mistakes. Its earnings have been flat. And its stock price is roughly where it was in 1982, even though the bull market has more than tripled the value of the average company's stock. Yet throughout all that, J. Kelley Williams has remained chief executive officer and even got the added job of chairman. He doesn't seem worried about his job or under any urgent pressure from directors, and he says that's how things should be. Slavish obedience to activist shareholders 'locks you into a short-term time frame,' he says. 'That's bad for technology development, and it's bad for the country and the economy.'" While there may be some truth in what Williams says, there's also some falsehood: no chief executive officer, board member, or senior executive should ever argue for long-term, patient capital to cover up strategic mistakes and avoid accountability. In the end, such lack of ownership for results will only erode America's competitiveness.

No matter what your current circumstances, once you come to *See It*, you must take the next step to *Own It*. Only by accepting full ownership of all past and present behavior that has contributed to current circumstances can you hope to improve your future situation.

TAKING THE SECOND STEP *ABOVE THE LINE*ᔆᴹ

We'll never forget a national sales conference in Hawaii organized by one of our clients where we saw firsthand the power of ownership. Since the schedule called for us to make our presentation on the third day of the week-long conference, we had time to observe the interaction and behavior of the sales reps. Curiously, as we toured the island during scheduled recreational breaks, we saw people happily driving cars over the rough lava beds. The vehicles were taking a real beating. "'Ten to one' those are the sales reps," we joked; "there's no way those people own those cars." Later, during our session, we began the the discussion about "owning it" by suggesting that self-guided tours through Hawaiian lava beds by rental car might exemplify a "no ownership" attitude. The embarrassed laughter in response to this comment was a dead give-away, and it helped us drive home a crucial point: "Ownership of your circumstances isn't circumstantial."

All too often people view unhappy circumstances as positions in which they find themselves stuck; yet when they find themselves in happy circumstances, they tend to take credit for a job well done. Ownership should not depend on the quality of your circumstance. If you selectively assume accountability for some of your circumstances and conveniently reject it for others, you cannot stay on the steps to accountability. Selective perception not only prevents people from owning their contribution to the creation of their circumstances, but it keeps them mired in the victim cycle, as the following disguised but true story aptly illustrates.

Brian Porter and Andy Dowling were driving to work together one morning, when the radio announcer reported the mugging of a 25-year-old man who now lay in a coma at the local hospital.

"Do you ever think that could happen to you?" asked Andy.

Brian thought for a moment, then said, "It did happen to me."

"You're kidding!"

"Well, not the way you might think, but I was definitely mugged."

"Tell me about it."

As Brian told it, during his final year in the MBA program at Northwestern University, he had been interviewing with prospective employers and had almost decided to accept what appeared to be an imminent offer from Citicorp in its international division. Given the fact that it was early May, and many of Brian's classmates had already accepted offers, Brian was feeling a little anxious.

To his surprise, Brian received a telephone call from the owners of a $15 million-a-year southern California-based pool supply distributor where he had worked the previous summer. Sam and Dave, the two founding partners of Sunshine Pool Products, had grown up in southern California and were close friends with Brian's older brother, now a physician in Anaheim. Now, on the telephone, the two men urged Brian to fly to Orange County to "talk over a great opportunity." Although Brian told them he intended to accept an offer from Citicorp, should it materialize, they insisted Brian come along anyway, bring his wife, Christie, with him, all expenses paid, just on the chance that Brian might change his mind. Flattered by this show of interest, Brian decided it wouldn't hurt to listen.

A few days later, Brian and Christie were met at the LAX Terminal by the two partners, who drove the group to a beautiful house in Palos Verdes. If the Mercedes Benz 500 SL hadn't been enough to impress Brian and Christie, the house certainly was: a rambling Spanish-style ranch home nestled among lush gardens and overlooking the Pacific Ocean. To top it off, the two partners' wives welcomed their guests to a festive table set with antique china and stunning silver.

After a wonderful dinner Brian joined Sam and Dave for a walk along the moon-lit ocean cliff, during which he listened to a powerful sales pitch for why he should join Sunshine Pool Products as vice president of marketing and sales. The starting salary and the luxurious benefits, including immediate stock options and any car of his choice, made his head swim. But most alluring was the fact that fresh out of grad school Brian would oversee 30 people. Sam concluded the pitch by putting his arm around Brian's shoulder and saying, "Brian, we have a vision of the three of us building a great company together that will make us all wealthy. You have the skills we need to pull it off. It's the opportunity of a lifetime."

The next day Brian and Christie flew back to Chicago wondering how they could turn down such an offer. Brian especially relished the looks on his classmates' faces when they heard about the salary. Suddenly, Citicorp seemed like a pale prospect by comparison. Later, that same day, Brian called Sam to accept the job.

On July 1, Brian went to work as the Sunshine Pool Products vice president of marketing and sales, and after his first three months he felt things were rolling along beautifully. His summer with the firm had prepared him so well for the new environment, he eased smoothly into his new responsibilities. With his people beating their sales targets, he knew he had made the right career choice. He and Christie were even planning to make an offer on a new home, so they could move out of his brother's house, where they had been staying since moving to southern California.

Then, lightning struck on October 8. When he came to work that day, Brian heard a rumor that the company had been sold. Shocked, Brian confronted Sam and Dave, but they simply said, "That's business, kid. You never know what's gonna happen next!" They went on to assure Brian that his job was secure, hinting that they just might be able to offer him another "opportunity of a lifetime" in the near future.

Brian felt betrayed. What had happened to the vision of the three of them building a great organization? His anger soon gave way to resignation, however, and he decided to hang on and make the situation work.

Over the next few months, Brian watched forlornly as sales took a nosedive. Unaccountably, some of Brian's best salespeople were just not performing. After several weeks of sagging orders, he confronted the two people who seemed to have fallen off the most. As the three sat in Brian's office, Don, the more open of the two salesmen, admitted, "Brian, we have to be honest, the new president of the combined companies doesn't have much confidence in you. He approached us both a couple of months ago and told us we could receive a higher commission rate if we turned our sales directly over to him, rather than through you. What could we do?" Halfheartedly thanking Don for his honesty, Brian immediately called Morgan, the new president, who worked in an office a few miles away, and demanded an appointment. "Sure," said Morgan. "Tomorrow, 10 A.M."

When Brian walked in to the president's office the next day, he didn't mince words. "Morgan, is it true that you're offering more commission to some of my salespeople if they turn over their sales directly to you?"

Morgan's face did not betray any surprise. He chuckled. "Yeah, it's true. Look, Brian, I like you, but you're just out of graduate school, and I really can't afford an inexperienced guy running the marketing and sales side of this business. I've got to keep hold of the reins myself to take this company where I want it to go. But, hey, there's a place for you here. I'm glad you dropped by, I've been wanting to talk about your future."

Brian shot back, "I already know about my future. I quit. Just pay me the $8,500 in commissions you owe me."

Morgan's expression finally cracked with a frown. "Hold on, Brian. Most of that money represents commissions on personal sales, and as far as I'm concerned, those sales are house accounts. No vice president of marketing and sales should get commissions for such sales. We only owe you $5,500."

Without uttering another word Brian spun on his heel and left the office. Reaching his car, he yanked open the door, climbed in, and left a smoking strip of rubber as he shot out of the lot. During his one-hour commute home, he replayed in his mind the illusion of good fortune he once held. Thinking himself the victim of a terrible ruse, Brian found a lot of gut-wrenching questions racing through his mind: What am I going to tell Christie? What will my friends from Northwestern think? Worse, what will my brother think? Brian arrived at his brother's house in a black mood. Anger, confusion, embarrassment boiled up as he felt more and more victimized by Sam and Dave and Morgan. Fuming, he pounded the steering wheel, muttering, "I'll never trust anyone, again."

Three years later, the episode still infuriated him. "So," he sighed, as he finished recounting the story to Andy Dowling, "you can see that a guy can get mugged, and I mean really beaten up by people who are supposed to be looking out for his welfare. I don't know how that guy in the hospital feels about his attacker, but I bet it would be even worse if it had been a friend doing the job on him."

Finally, Andy spoke up. "Don't take this wrong, Brian, but the way you told your story, it sounds like you had nothing to do with the outcome."

Brian frowned. "I didn't!"

"But, Brian, wasn't there something you could have done to prevent what happened to you?"

"Yeah, I could have gone to work at Citicorp in the first place. Hey, what is this? I thought you'd be on my side."

"I am. That's why I think we should talk through what happened to you."

Andy then tried to help Brian consider what he might have done differently. The two continued their discussion for a week as they commuted to and from work. Uncomfortable at first, Brian actually began looking forward to the talks because they afforded an opportunity to examine feelings he had not shared with anyone but his wife.

Gradually, Brian came to see that he had only been looking at the facts from the victim's point of view, while, in fact, another viewpoint actually existed. Such a realization represents a crucial step for anyone who wants to move beyond feeling victimized. While a situation may seem starkly black and white from a victim's angle, within the context of accountability it takes on more shades of gray.

For instance, from the standpoint of accountability, Brian could see how he had let himself get sucked in by the promise of a quick road to wealth and prestige. The luxurious cars and houses owned by the two partners lay just around the corner, or so Brian imagined. He had been seduced by the image of himself as a vice president right out of graduate school, with an income higher than almost everyone in his graduating class. From the victim's point of view, Brian had been sandbagged, but from an accountability point of view, perhaps Brian himself had been too greedy, shortsighted, immature, and vain. Together Brian and Andy reviewed the following questions to help Brian adopt a more accountable attitude:

- ▼ What things did you pretend not to know?
- ▼ What are the things that you could have done differently?
- ▼ What clues or evidence did you ignore?
- ▼ Who or what should you have confronted earlier?
- ▼ What could you have learned from your previous similar experiences that might have helped you avoid or minimize the negative outcome?
- ▼ Can you see how your behavior and actions prevented you from getting the results you wanted?

With Andy's help, Brian tried, sometimes painfully, to answer those questions. Not surprisingly, he began confronting a lot about himself that he had selectively screened out of his consciousness.

One of the things Brian pretended not to know or remember was a conversation that had taken place the summer before with

his boss, Sunshine Pool Product's then vice president of marketing and sales, Bill Wold. When Brian had asked Bill why he was
working for Sunshine and what he expected to happen down the
road, Bill had spoken confidentially of the pact he had made with
Sam and Dave to make great things happen in the future. When
Brian heard Sam suggest a similar pact almost a year later, he had
ignored or suppressed that earlier conversation. This time the two
partners really meant it because, after all, they were talking to
Brian Porter, whiz kid extraordinaire.

Brian had missed other hints as well. During his second
month as marketing and sales VP, he got a speeding ticket driving
his new Corvette, and when he showed the highway patrolman
the car's registration, he discovered that it had been leased on a
temporary, monthly basis. That clue might have tipped off Brian
that his bosses had made something less than a long-term commitment to his career.

When Brian received his first paycheck it turned out to be
somewhat less than the agreed-upon salary. Dave assured Brian
that the difference would quickly come in the form of commissions on personal sales, so Brian chose to overlook the discrepancy. After all, he should lead the way in sales, setting an example for his team.

Why hadn't Brian demanded a written confirmation of his
salary and benefits? Friends should trust friends, he had decided.
When doing so Brian set aside the memory of a partnership he
had formed while in college with a buddy that had soured when
the buddy absconded with $3,000 in profits, saying, "Sue me. We
don't have anything in writing." Unfortunately, Brian elected not
to apply that lesson to Sam and Dave.

Brian came to realize that as soon as he had learned that
Sam and Dave had sold Sunshine Pool Products he should have
sat down, right then, with Morgan to clarify everyone's expectations and commitments. However, because Brian didn't know
Morgan well enough to feel comfortable with him, he decided to

let the situation slide, hoping that things would iron themselves out naturally over time.

Did Brian therefore have accountability for what eventually happened to him? In many ways he did. Even though others did take advantage of him and misled him, he learned through objective self-examination that he himself must shoulder some responsibility. After Brian opened up with Andy and pondered Andy's feedback, he finally came to appreciate both points of view: that of the victim and that of the accountable individual. Finally, Brian was ready to own his circumstances and create a better future. In our experience, however, too few people take this step toward greater accountability.

▲ WHY SO MANY PEOPLE FAIL TO *OWN IT*[SM]

People most often fail to own their circumstances because they cannot bring themselves to accept the accountable side of their story. That's why in our consulting practice we frequently invoke the cliché that "there're two sides to every story." The victim side stresses only one side of the story, the one that suggests you played no role in creating the circumstances. In a difficult situation, it's easy to feel "had" or "let down" and to let yourself "off the hook." But when you "lock-in" on that single perspective, you "lock-out" the other side of the story, which are all the facts that suggest you contributed to creating the circumstances you now face. Victim stories tend to screen out all evidence of accountability.

To establish ownership, then, you must find the heart to tell both sides of the story, linking what you have done or failed to do with your current circumstances. Such a shift in perspective requires that you *replace* your victim story with an accountable one. However, seeing and owning the accountability side of a story does not mean suppressing or ignoring the victim facts;

rather it means acknowledging and possessing the reality that you participate in and do not passively observe your circumstances.

The accountable person who owns his or her circumstances can see both the victim and the accountable side of any story, and that usually means admitting that you've made some mistakes. Those people who consistently achieve results, people like former Chrysler Chairman Lee Iacocca, quickly acknowledge their mistakes and own the resulting circumstances so they can avoid getting bogged down in the victim cycle and set to work improving things. Here's what Iacocca told *Fortune* magazine about one of his mistakes: "I've made a lot of them. Let's say moving the Omni/Horizon cars to one plant and then to another before discontinuing them, at a cost of $100 million, was a mistake. Why argue? We made a $100 million mistake." That sort of willingness to own the whole reality and admit mistakes allowed Lee Iacocca to save Chrysler from bankruptcy and make it a viable automobile manufacturer.

On a personal level, consider the story of Home Mortgage Service Scams reported in *The Wall Street Journal:* "If you get a letter advising you that servicing your mortgage has been taken over by a new company, check it out before you send a check. It may be a scam. That's what homeowners in Texas learned recently after receiving a letter announcing that an outfit calling itself Mortgage Bankers of America had 'acquired ownership of your previous mortgage company.' The letter asked that future payments and other correspondence be sent to a post office box in Houston. Although the letter says Mortgage Bankers is the fifth largest mortgage banking company in the United States, law enforcement authorities say it doesn't exist." While Robert Pratte, a St. Paul, Minnesota, attorney who represents mortgage lenders, says the company's solicitation shouldn't fool people, it does, everyday. People living *Above The Line* would investigate the situation, those living *Below The Line* just assume the scam is above board. The former "own" their circumstances, the latter become willing victims.

At the University of Southern California Business School, Richard B. Chase, professor of business administration, teaches a class on the management of service operations where he offers students a money-back guarantee of $250 if they aren't satisfied with his performance by the end of the course. That offer represents a big risk in an academic environment not known for its emphasis on accountability. Chase wants to impress upon his students, as they study about the superior service practices of companies such as Federal Express and Domino's Pizza, that customers expect the service they pay for. While some of Chase's colleagues worry about the implications of his experiment, we admire it as an example of assuming accountability. Professor Chase owns his circumstances, and even though he could end up paying as much as $13,000, if all his students demanded their money back, he's willing to take the risk. However, just to make sure he doesn't take an inordinate amount of the responsibility for what his students learn, he requires that they request rebates before they obtain their final grades. If Chase makes mistakes in his class or fails to satisfy his customers, he's willing to pay for it.

Some health care businesses are also trying to make sure they please their patients. In a *Wall Street Journal* story entitled, "Pleasing Hospital Patients Can Pay Off," the reporters found a few hospitals owning their circumstances and making it pay off: "As the health-care industry moves into an era of accountability and cost-cutting, the desire to relate patient feedback directly to the bottom line is likely to grow, say hospitals and management service companies." Take St. Barnabas Medical Center in Livingston, New Jersey, for example: "All patients are asked to evaluate quality of food, cleanliness and staff courtesy, using a questionnaire that provides a measuring stick for a novel contract that links profit to patient satisfaction. . . . Hospitals that farm out certain hospital services—including St. Barnabas, Faulkner Hospital in Boston and Park Ridge Hospital in Rochester, N.Y.—are in the forefront of what may be a key operating strategy for the 1990s:

Share the risk. Contracts that contain incentives have been around for years, and so have patient surveys. But 'partnering' has linked the two formally, and raised the ante higher for vendors, who are sometimes expected to invest in state-of-the-art equipment for use in the hospital they have contracted with. A performance-linked contract 'is a vendor's gamble,' concedes Ronald Del Mauro, president and chief executive officer of St. Barnabas. But he adds: 'If we're successful, they're successful.'" For St. Barnabas, owning their circumstances and getting their affiliates and suppliers to do likewise result not only in happier patients but in healthier profits.

Unfortunately, millions of people keep themselves from achieving the results and happiness they so desperately pursue because of their unwillingness to see both sides of the story and "own" their circumstances. According to an Associated Press series of articles entitled, "Are We Happier?" by Leslie Dreyfous, "The number of books on the topic [happiness] has quadrupled in recent years and the therapy industry has more than tripled in size. Excruciatingly frank talk shows dominate afternoon TV, and entire catalogues are devoted to marketing meditational tapes and inspirational videos. People pay hundreds of dollars and travel thousands of miles to retreats like Esalen (the granddaddy of human potential centers in Big Sur, California). Still, baby boomers are four times likelier to say they're not satisfied with their lives than are people of their parents' generation, according to an Associated Press poll. Experts estimate the incidence of psychological depression is ten times what it was pre–World War II." In our increasingly complex and changing world, it seems more and more people think they exert less and less control over their happiness.

Just like Dorothy and her friends in the *Wizard of Oz,* a lot of people take the trek to the Emerald City, where they assume that a personal audience with the wizard will solve all their problems. All too often, such people blame their lack of happiness on perplexing circumstances that seem totally beyond their control.

Rather than own their circumstances by seeing the whole story, they choose to view themselves as incapable of modifying their situations through their own actions, resigning themselves to being "acted upon" by influences and forces rather than the other way around.

It seems ironic that, in this age of information, millions of people feel such a lack of control over their lives. Obviously, the communications revolution has done little to overcome, and may have contributed to, a feeling of detachment and disconnectedness with circumstances and other people. As a result, America has truly come perilously close to becoming "a nation of victims," in which its citizens feel paralyzed rather than empowered by what they observe and learn every day. In such a climate, it's not terribly surprising that so many people resist ownership of the consequences of their own behavior.

A nation of observers is not a nation of participants. If you sit on the sidelines watching "the game of your life" play out before your eyes, you relinquish your ability to affect the outcome just as much as a spectator watching a football or baseball game from the bleachers. To remedy this darkening malaise, people must abandon the bleacher seats and take to the playing field. You can take an important step in that direction by embracing the whole story and accepting ownership for your circumstances, no matter what the condition or history of those circumstances. Failure to do so invites dire consequences.

THE CONSEQUENCES OF NOT OWNING

In June 1990, two months after NASA launched the $2.5 billion Hubble space telescope intended to scan distant stars and galaxies ten times more clearly than previously possible, the space agency discovered a fundamental flaw in the mirrors that blurred the instrument's imagery. Responding to this $2.5 billion mistake, Robert Brown, a former Hubble scientist, argued that NASA could have uncovered the problem years before the launch if it had only built an inexpensive observatory to test it. Edward Weiler, another Hubble scientist, told *The Wall Street Journal* that NASA rejected the best test for evaluating telescopes, "autocollimation," on the grounds that it would cost too much. However, some felt that the additional $10 million could have prevented the mistake. In the same article, Roger Angel, an astronomer designing and building a large observatory on Mt. Graham in Arizona, attributed the fundamental problem to NASA management, which did not give the scientists involved enough responsibility for overseeing work on the telescope: "The people with say-so weren't experienced builders who knew in the seat of their pants how things could go wrong."

In the years since the flaw appeared, NASA investigators have spent millions of dollars attempting to pinpoint its cause, and they now claim to have uncovered evidence that a contractor, owned by Perkin-Elmer Corporation for most of the 1980s, withheld information that would have exposed the flawed mirrors early on. However, Ronald Rigby, leader of a mirror-polishing team for Perkin-Elmer, reported to *The New York Times* in October 1992 that NASA is just "looking for a scapegoat." On top of the billions of dollars spent in development and launching costs, as well as the millions more in investigation expenses, NASA will spend an additional $1 billion on a shuttle mission to fit the telescope with corrective lenses.

Clearly, if anyone from NASA management to the Hubble scientists or the manufacturing contractors and the technical consultants had mustered the courage to own their circumstances and step out of the victim cycle before the Hubble telescope was ever launched, scientists might already be benefiting from the results the Hubble telescope was designed to produce. Instead, billions of dollars have been and will continue to be sucked into space.

In contrast, Bradco, the largest privately owned drywall and plaster company in California, found the heart to own its circumstances when the initial actual costs on a major project started coming in much higher than estimated. If the cost-to-budget discrepancy were allowed to continue, the company would face an enormous loss by the end of the project. Promptly, one of the estimators on the project started spending his evenings, on his own time, scouring the project plans and budgets to figure what had gone wrong. No one in the company had assigned him this responsibility and no one had blamed him for the problem, but he nevertheless chose to own the company's problem and spend countless personal hours reviewing stacks of paper and blueprints to get to the bottom of things.

To his chagrin, he not only isolated the problem but discovered he himself had caused it because, during the estimating phase of the project, he had overlooked a single wall in the detailed plan from which he had developed his estimate. In a domino effect, that same wall was omitted from all 18 floors of the building. When the estimator informed company executives of his mistake, he knew he was putting his career on the line, but instead of receiving a pink slip he won praise from higher-ups, who thanked him for his investigation and his willingness to bring the problem to light without regard to his own reputation.

Because the accountable estimator located the problem early, the estimates could be adjusted to allow the project to be completed on time and within budget. In the months following the incident, the estimator's story was told and retold throughout the company as an example of what it means to *Own It* at Bradco.

In another example, a consumer electronics manufacturer, and a client of ours, experienced such extraordinary growth in the 1980s that the entire company grew accustomed to the benefits of tremendous success. For example, they never worried about their budgets because the company always brought in greater than projected sales, affording them the best working environment and equipment in the industry. They hired and rewarded the best employees available, they held lavish retreats, took two-hour lunch breaks, golfed two or three times a week, and enjoyed many other opportunities for mixing business and pleasure.

Curiously, most of the people in the company knew that the flush times, the "glory days," would not last forever, but nevertheless they basked in their plush business and life-style routines when, by the early 1990s, the company began to lose its competitive edge to smaller, more determined competitors. Still no one wanted to give up the "glory days" life-style, even though conversations about why the company was experiencing such declines began to consume a good deal of the workday. Everyone talked about the problem during lunches, on golf courses, at retreats, and even after work, but since no one stepped forward to own the problem, no real action was taken to turn things around. Myopically preoccupied with rehashing why the situation had gone sour, many individuals grew eloquent in their descriptions of precisely who was responsible and exactly what had gone wrong, with most of their energy directed at identifying what others needed to do differently.

After talking to hundreds of people in this organization, we were astonished at how the problem always seemed to rest with the other department or the other guy. Unfortunately, the people in this company waited too long before owning their circumstances, so that when they finally did accept responsibility, it came too late to stave off a relentless competitive attack that resulted in a substantial loss of market share and a major decline in revenues growth and profits.

To avoid the consequences that befell NASA or this once-high-flying consumer electronics company and assume instead the attitude of ownership, you must learn to assess and develop your own ability to own your circumstances.

THE *OWN IT*ˢᴹ SELF-ASSESSMENT

Owning your circumstances depends on your seeing both the victim and accountable sides of a story. You should therefore begin your assessment by identifying a current situation in which you feel victimized, taken advantage of, or otherwise find yourself languishing *Below The Line*. If you can't think of a current situation then consider a past one, choosing a story from your work, home, personal, community, social, or church life. Once you have selected your story, complete part 1 of the *Own It* Self-assessment form that follows by listing facts that describe why you feel or felt "victimized" or "taken advantage of." Try to list the victim facts of your story in a way that will persuade someone else that you really weren't at fault!

PART 1—VICTIM FACTS ABOUT A CURRENT OR PAST CIRCUMSTANCE
▼

1. _____
   _____

2. _____
   _____

3. _____
   _____

4. _____
   _____

5. _____
   _____

6. _____
   _____

7. _____
    _____

8. _____
    _____

9. _____
    _____

10. _____
     _____

As we discussed earlier in this chapter, most people quite naturally "lock-in" on the victim facts that make them feel "had" or "let down" or "victimized," while they "lock-out" the accountable facts that support their own role in creating the situation. Therefore, in part 2 of the *Own It* Self-assessment, you want to move beyond the selective perception that stems from locking-in to the victim facts of your story, and instead consider the accountable facts of your story: that is, the other version of your story where you delineate your own actions or inactions which contributed to your circumstances. The following six key questions will help guide your assessment.

1. Are there things you are (were) pretending not to know?

2. What questions could you ask (have asked) but are (were) afraid to consider?

3. What extra steps could you take (have taken) to help you achieve a better outcome?

4. Are there facts you are ignoring (have ignored)?

5. Are there people you are avoiding (have avoided) speaking with?

6. Have you experienced this same thing before? What learning can (could) apply?

7. Can you see how your behavior or actions are (were) preventing you from getting desired results?

With the aid of these seven questions, complete part 2 of the *Own It* Self-assessment by listing at least four accountable facts. Once you've done that, we'll show you how to score your responses.

PART 2—ACCOUNTABLE FACTS
ABOUT A CURRENT OR PAST CIRCUMSTANCE
▼

1. _____
   _____ Score _____

2. _____
   _____ Score _____

3. _____
   _____ Score _____

4. _____
   _____ Score _____

5. _____
   _____ Score _____

6. _____
   _____ Score _____

7. _____
   _____ Score _____

8. _____
   _____ Score _____

9. _____
   _____ Score _____

10. _____
    _____ Score _____

After you have listed an accountable fact, score your willingness to *Own It* by asking yourself how "accountable" you feel for that fact on a scale of 1 to 10. A score of "1" means you do not feel at all accountable for a fact, whereas, a score of "10" signifies that you feel fully accountable for a fact. Then add up your total combined score and divide that score by the number of facts that you listed. Finally, evaluate your cumulative score by using the table that follows.

Score	*Evaluation Guidelines*
8 to 10	Indicates that you see your accountability and own your circumstances.
5 to 7	Suggests that you only partially own your circumstances or vacillate between owning and not owning them.
1 to 4	Reveals that you have probably gotten stuck *Below The Line*, and are unable or unwilling to see your accountability and own your circumstances.

While a low score indicates that you are failing to assume ownership for your situation, it may also indicate that you truly are a victim in your current circumstances. Even so, you do not want to remain in the victim cycle. A person who owns his or her circumstances never allows the actions of someone or something else to keep them stuck *Below The Line*. Instead, the accountable person accepts how his or her own behavior contributed to their situation and sets about overcoming those circumstances, no matter how difficult.

At the same time people tell compelling legitimate stories everyday about how they were truly victimized without any opportunity to have changed the outcome. Whether they be victims of violent crimes, victims of natural disasters, or victims of a slow economy with layoffs and prolonged unemployment, we feel it is largely indisputable that these people are truly victims of circumstances beyond their control. However, even those whom we would consider to be "true victims" must acknowledge that in order to have a better future for themselves, they must be accountable for where they go from here.

In one case, we heard about a husband and wife in Florida whose home was destroyed by Hurricane Andrew in 1992. Devastated by the loss of all their personal belongings, the couple retreated to their vacation home on the island of Kauai to recuperate and to wait out the rebuilding of their Florida home. Shortly after their arrival, another hurricane struck the Hawaiian Islands, demolishing their vacation home. Clearly, these two people had suffered genuine victimization by these natural disasters, suffering deep grief and frustration as a result. While these disasters had destroyed their homes and most of all of their belongings, they were determined to not allow these calamities to destroy their lives as well. Instead, they acknowledged the fact they had built their homes in areas vulnerable to such disasters, and they resolved to relocate and rebuild with optimism and faith. After all, they had survived two disasters, and they had done so with their health and human abilities still intact. Owning our circumstances gives us the power to avoid the powerlessness that comes from being a victim and allows us to move forward and achieve the results in life that we seek.

▲
_____

THE BENEFITS OF FINDING THE HEART TO *OWN IT*^{SM}

The Japanese people exemplify the *Own It* attitude in making sure their trains run on time. *The Wall Street Journal* recently reported, "In the Tokyo area, millions of rail commuters can count on reaching their destination at pretty much the same minute every day—and that says as much about the Japanese as it does about their trains. . . . 'It's the people that delay the trains,' says Shoji Yanagawa, a spokesman for Tokyo's Eidan subway company. 'But then again it's people that keep the trains running on time.' . . . Tokyo's train system is so finely tuned that it has eliminated almost all sources of extended delay, to the point where a major cause of lateness is the 'jumper,' or suicide. . . . Tokyo elementary schools teach children the basics of train riding. In the stations, riders are bombarded with messages in schoolmarmish voices: 'It's dangerous, so please don't run onto the trains.' (People who rush often get stuck in the closing doors, which delays departure.) To keep straphangers from cramming into doorways, the railways lash them with a bit of shame. 'We put extra workers on the platforms, and mostly they stand there and look at the passengers,' says Mr. Yanagawa. 'That usually works.' Rigorous, maybe, but the commuters thronging the platform at Otemachi Station one recent evening are eager adherents." That could only work in Japan, you might say, but the principle of ownership cuts across all cultures and companies: when everyone buys into the problem or situation and treats it as their "own," results always improve.

In another example, Josh Tanner traveled the fast track with his former "blue-chip" company and had been referred to as a "star" by the human resources department largely because of his analytical prowess and political savvy. In four short years, he had learned how to get things done in the large, bureaucratic organizational structure until most everyone argued that Josh was a "high-potential" employee, capable of making it to the top. Josh's reputation not only spread throughout the company but also captured the attention of headhunters who were always looking for good people, talented people.

It didn't take long for an executive recruiter, offering an intriguing opportunity to work for a small start-up company with enormous potential, to grab Josh's interest. Within a few weeks Josh left the security of his large company job for a smaller, albeit riskier one, with a start-up firm where he knew he could shine, even more than before. How much he relished working in a more entrepreneurial, fast-paced environment where he could really put his analytical and management process skills to the test! The company was not just buying him, it was buying his knowledge of how blue-chip companies operate, knowledge that would ensure the success of the smaller company as it grew.

Not long after Josh joined the new firm, however, he was hit with a landslide of feedback that threw him for a loop. Given his political savvy, Josh knew how to listen, but he just couldn't believe the feedback he was hearing. People at the new company just weren't impressed with Josh's analytical bent and bureaucratic orientation. For several weeks, Josh denied the feedback, thinking to himself, "I've already accomplished so much in my career; I was a star in a 'blue-chip' company; people here should feel lucky to get someone with my experience; I gave up a lot to come here." Eventually, Josh learned that he would not receive the promised promotion to vice president of marketing, and worse, if his performance did not improve, he would not be with the organization much longer. This turn of events dealt a shocking blow to Josh who still could not believe what was happening to him. "This is worse than a bad dream, it's my worst nightmare!" Soon he began to mourn the loss of his "fast track" career with his former company and lament the fact he had reached a "dead end" in his current situation.

At this point, the management asked us to work with Josh. Immediately after contacting Josh, we began coaching him to move *Above The Line*. It wasn't easy, but Josh was at least willing to acknowledge the reality that "he was no longer the "star" in his old company, but someone who "needed to improve" in his new company." Still, even though accepting the fact that he needed to change, he continued feeling victimized by the new job and other people. He told us, very convincingly, one side of the story, moving through the victim cycle with ease and familiarity as he identified each level and anxiously explained how "they" had stuck him *Below The Line*. Finally, he explained what we recognized as a "wait-and-see" attitude: he was hoping that time would convince his new associates that their initial assessment of him was wrong.

As we worked with Josh, it became clear that his greatest challenge lay in forging the link between his own behavior and the perceptions of his new associates. While he saw the reality of the perceptions, his disagreement with their accuracy was rendering him unable to *Own It*. At this point, we asked Josh to retell his story, this time focusing on the "accountable" facts of his circumstances instead of just the "victim" facts. Slowly, he began describing how people might have misinterpreted some of the things he had done after joining the company, but after each such admission he would say something like, "but only someone with half a brain would draw that kind of conclusion." As he continued to identify how his actions could have contributed to the perceptions of others, however, he gradually found it easier to recognize the things he did or did not do to contribute to his present predicament. As he did so, his anger began to abate. We explained to Josh that "owning" his circumstances did not mean admitting that the perceptions of his new associates were completely accurate but rather acknowledging that there was a linkage between his behavior and their perceptions.

Finally, when we asked him the question, "What extra steps could you have taken?" Josh stopped to reflect on how he could have taken more initiative by asking people what kind of job they thought he was doing. Recognizing the differences between his new and old environments and acknowledging that he had ignored the new culture's bias against excessive analysis and bureaucratic process, Josh finally admitted that he could have taken more care explaining to others the motives and principles behind his actions.

As Josh's sense of accountability increased, so did his feelings of liberation: "I should have worked more closely with the people and the culture of the new company to obtain their ideas and involvement in the programs I was trying to implement. I could have been more open to the suggestions, and I should have involved myself more with their plans, purposes, and priorities. Wow, did I make a mistake by withdrawing from others when the negative feedback started coming in!" Not until that moment did Josh fully address the other side of the story and own all the facts, particularly those that linked his behavior with his circumstances. He was not saying that he should shoulder responsibility for everything that had happened, nor was he saying that the people in the new company were 100 percent fair in their assessment, but he was finally admitting that he himself had done or not done certain things that contributed to his circumstances. "Man," he said during our final coaching session, "getting stuck *Below The Line* feels like being trapped in a room with no windows or doors. Now that the doors are open, and I see the whole story, I can start changing my circumstances. Things can only get better!"

Josh came to "own" his circumstances when he made the connection between his behavior and the perceptions of his new associates. When he saw the reality that his past behavior had something to do with his present circumstances, he then realized that his behavior from now on could create an entirely different and better future. This realization gave him the heart he needed to begin working to shift the perceptions of those with whom he worked, and, before long, he lost all the distaste he had developed for his new associates. After a little more than three months of *Above The Line* behavior, Josh had so completely shifted the perceptions of his subordinates, peers, and boss that he won that promotion to vice president of marketing.

The benefits of owning your circumstances more than compensate for the heart-wrenching effort involved. When you find the heart to own your circumstances, you automatically gain the commitment to overcome and change those circumstances for the better.

THE NEXT PHASE OF ACCOUNTABILITY

As this chapter shows, the Tin Woodsman from the land of Oz symbolizes the second dimension of accountability, finding the heart to own your circumstances, and it further fuels Dorothy's realization that results come from within ourselves. In the next chapter, the Scarecrow will show you how to acquire the wisdom to *Solve It*. And he will teach you how to put your *See It* and *Own It* abilities to work in conjunction with a new *Solve It* attitude that can help you remove the obstacles on your path to results.

CHAPTER 6

THE SCARECROW: OBTAINING THE WISDOM TO *SOLVE IT*℠

▼

"Who are you?" asked the Scarecrow when he had stretched himself and yawned, "and where are you going?"

"My name is Dorothy," said the girl, "and I am going to the Emerald City, to ask the great Oz to send me back to Kansas."

"Where is the Emerald City?" he inquired; "and who is Oz?"

"Why, don't you know?" she returned, in surprise.

"No, indeed; I don't know anything. You see, I am stuffed, so I have no brains at all," he answered, sadly.

"Oh," said Dorothy; "I'm awfully sorry for you."

"Do you think," he asked, "if I go to the Emerald City with you, that Oz would give me some brains?"

"I cannot tell," she returned; "but you may come with me, if you like. If Oz will not give you any brains, you will be no worse off than you are now."

THE WIZARD OF OZ
By L. Frank Baum

Toyota has been putting its brain to work solving a problem others don't yet "see" or "own." The world's third largest automaker has been expanding capacity and building new plants despite an environment of serious global overcapacity, sluggish sales, and plant closings around the world because the plant wants to solve its problems before its problems dissolve the plant. Using its head, while others are losing theirs, the $80 billion company is literally rethinking everything. A recent *Fortune* magazine article tells the story: "Toyota is big, famously conservative, and hugely successful. Why mess with a good thing? In fact, the company that the authoritative 1990 Massachusetts Institute of Technology report, 'The Machine That Changed the World,' called the most efficient automaker anywhere, is rethinking almost everything it does. Turning Japan's unnerving stubborn economic slump into an opportunity, Toyota is reorganizing its operations, putting still more high technology into its factories, and reworking its legendary 'lean production' system. Even if some of the measures fail, Toyota is likely to emerge an even more vigorous global competitor." Not overreacting to declining profits for a second year, the company continues hammering out solutions for the future. While some European and American automakers are closing plants, Toyota keeps opening new ones, increasing the company's total capacity to one million vehicles. Instead of shrinking capacity, Toyota would rather rely on cost cutting to improve efficiency. Characteristic of a *Solve It* company, Toyota is setting the pace for competitors: According to *Fortune,* "Just when the rest of the world started to catch on to Toyota's lean production system, Toyota is adapting it to accommodate new workers and advanced technology." A perpetual problem solver, Toyota thrives on challenges. Always searching for ways to do things better, Toyota executives quickly adapt to change. Donald N. Smith, a manufacturing expert at the University of Michigan's engineering school and a long-time Toyota watcher warns Toyota's competitors to assume that Toyota will constantly improve in the future. To think otherwise would be a costly mistake. We agree. Toyota's undying and unwavering *Solve It* attitude will undoubtedly ensure its standout performance among global corporations for years to come.

We must issue this warning, however: *Solve It* means solving real problems, not tackling illusionary ones or just changing for change's sake. In another *Fortune* magazine article, reporters recount the saga of Ann Taylor Stores: "Through the 1980s, Ann Taylor was the place for women to shop for stylish, well-made career clothes at better than department store prices. That strategy was still sound in 1989 when Joseph Brooks, former head of Lord & Taylor, and Merrill Lynch bought the company from Campeau Corp. for $430 million. Brooks took Ann Taylor public in May 1991 for $26 a share. Merrill Lynch owns 54 percent of the shares outstanding." As chief executive officer, Brooks began what appeared to be changing things for change's sake, substituting synthetics for silk, linen, and wool blends and squeezing suppliers. One supplier, Irving Benson, president of Cygne Design, bemoaned the situation to *Fortune*'s reporters: "You get nothing for nothing. When Brooks told me he wanted to pay less to make a jacket, cuts had to come from either the fabric or how the garment was made." At the same time, Brooks expanded the operation from 139 to 200 stores. When customers did not materialize, the board forced Brooks to resign in November 1991. The cost? In fiscal 1991, Ann Taylor lost $15.8 million on sales of $438 million. To redirect the company's problem-solving efforts, the board picked Frame Kasaks who had run Ann Taylor from 1983 to 1985 before she left to take over Talbots and then the Limited's Abercrombie and Fitch division. She returned to Ann Taylor in February 1992. According to the *Fortune* article, "Frame Kasaks is making progress. She has upgraded Ann Taylor's mostly private-label fashions, installed procedures to monitor sales, and hired specialty retailing veterans. To broaden the store's appeal, she has added more casual and weekend clothes." While the results of Kasaks's efforts have not yet come in, prospects look promising. It doesn't take a genius to solve the sort of problems Kasaks inherited; it just takes persistent functioning *Above The Line*, discovering real problems, and designing appropriate solutions.

Unfortunately, many people attempt to solve problems without "seeing" or "owning" reality, which makes the whole problem-solving effort nonsensical and misguided, as in the case of the U.S. Air Force's fight against ozone depletion. *The Wall Street Journal*'s sarcastic article entitled "Survivors Will Glow in Happiness, Knowing the World Is a Safer Place," provides an apt example: "Fear not: The U.S. government will protect the ozone layer in the event of a nuclear holocaust. To do its bit to save the planet, the U.S. Air Force plans to retrofit its nuclear missiles with cooling systems that don't use chlorofluorocarbons. Those CFCs are blamed for depleting the atmosphere's ozone layer, which protects people from skin cancer, glaucoma and other diseases by screening out harmful rays from the sun. Never mind that each intercontinental ballistic missile packs three to 10 bombs that can wipe out entire cities, making skin cancer and glaucoma moot concerns." Good PR, perhaps, but silly problem solving.

Simply acknowledging reality and accepting your role in creating your circumstances will achieve little if you fail to take action, solving real problems and removing real obstacles on your road to results. To do so, you must exercise wisdom.

ATTAINING THE THIRD STEP
ABOVE THE LINE^{SM}

The *Solve It* attitude and behavior stem from continually asking the question: *What else can I do to achieve the results I want?* Constant and rigorous application of this question helps you avoid slipping back down into the victim cycle whenever certain events occur that seem to block the road to results. Since solutions to pesky problems often do not readily reveal themselves, you must diligently search for them, but beware of time spent *Below The Line* because it will dull your senses and discourage your imagination from discovering solutions you may have otherwise uncovered. Remember, getting *Above The Line* is a process, not a singular event, and the road to results is strewn with hindrances and obstacles that can easily thrust even the most accountable person back *Below The Line*—particularly if he or she stops asking the central question: *What else can I do to rise above my circumstances and achieve the results I want?*

In a Harvard Business Review article entitled "Empowerment or Else," author and company owner Robert Frey describes how he got his organization *Above The Line* to *Solve It*. He recounts how bad the situation was when he and a partner purchased a small Cincinnati company in April, 1984. Cin-Made was a "troubled" company, founded in 1902. The company manufactured composite cans (sturdy paper containers with metal ends) and mailing tubes. Shortly after purchase, things began to take a turn for the worse. Poorly negotiated labor contracts that drove wages to an unsustainable level, a stagnant product line that had not changed in 20 years, and old plant equipment—combined to drive profits from a meager 2 percent on sales to absolutely no profits at all. Unless something happened quickly, the company would soon go under.

It quickly became clear to Frey, president of Cin-Made, that renewed profitability meant that he needed to help the company *get out of the victim cycle.* People were slow and lethargic when the company desperately needed action. Ocelia Williams, then a sheet-metal worker recalled, "When I first came to Cin-Made, the place was like a circus. There was a ten-minute break every hour, and people walked off the line anytime at all to go to the ladies' room or get a candy bar." People just did not "see it." They didn't understand the severity of the company's situation or the need to significantly change the way they were doing things.

Frey and his partner immediately set out to make the necessary changes to move the organization *Above The Line* and "solve" the problems the company faced. After some difficult negotiations and concessions with the union, people finally began acknowledging the dire circumstances the company was in. And for the first time, Frey began to openly share previously guarded information on the company's performance with all of the employees.

While Frey was making progress on moving the organization *Above The Line*, he still struggled to get employees to take the step to *Own It* and personally *Solve It*. He daily faced the realization that only with the help of the employees would he be able to solve the dilemma the company faced. Frey recalls some earlier thoughts, "I wanted the workers to worry. Did any one of them ever spend a moment on a weekend wondering how the company was doing, asking themself if they'd made the right decisions the week before? Maybe I was unrealistic, but I wanted that level of involvement." He continued, "After a bad start, I had begun to see that the workers knew more about the company and its operation than I or the new managers I'd hired. They were better qualified to plan production for the next day, the coming week, the month ahead. They had more immediate knowledge of materials, workload, and production problems. They were ideally placed to control costs and cut waste. But how could I give them some reason to care?"

In moving the organization *Above The Line,* Frey describes how critical it was to change the way people viewed their responsibility and accountability. He states, "change of any kind is a struggle with fear, anger, and uncertainty, a war against old habits, hide-bound thinking, and entrenched interests. No company can change any faster than it can change the hearts and minds of its people . . ." The key to change at Cin-Made was to get people thinking differently about their jobs and their accountability; to get them to see that they "could," and indeed, "must" solve the problems which they faced on a daily basis in order to "solve" the long term problems of the company.

To help create this personal level of accountability where people spontaneously acted in the *Solve It* mode, Frey implemented an innovative profit-sharing plan, "establishing a pattern of cause and effect" that would link what people *did*, with what people *got*.

After realizing that his managers were used to a command-and-control, "tell them what to do" approach to the job, he found that "the workers were not much better. My managers believed that managers should manage and that hourly workers should do what they were told. The trouble was, most of the workers were perfectly happy with that arrangement. They wanted generous wages and benefits, of course, but they did not want to take responsibility for anything more than doing their own jobs the way they had always done them . . ." He realized that such behavior kept people from doing anything more than just complaining about the problems of the company. They took no ownership for solving the problems. He knew that such a culture of "complaint" would spell the death of Cin-Made.

Frey continues, "It was bad enough forcing them to use new equipment, but I was also forcing them to change job descriptions, to change work habits, to think differently about themselves and the company. What my employees were telling me, in deeds and words, was, 'We don't want to change, and we're much too old to change. Anyway, we don't come to work to think.'" Ocelia Williams recalls how the union president actually thought it was "nonunion" for employees to take on so much responsibility. "That bothered me," said Williams. "I kept asking myself if I was truly union. But I couldn't see how we were going to protect ourselves and keep our jobs if the company went under. And I couldn't see how the company could work unless we all took our share of the responsibility. A lot of people thought those ideas were off the wall." Frey observes, "But which of us is ever eager to take on new responsibilities?" Relating how his people reacted, he says, "They never dreamed how much responsibility I wanted to lay on their shoulders, but they disliked what little they had seen so far."

Coaching people into the *Solve It* mode was easy. Frey states "I made people meet with me, then instead of telling them what to do, I asked them. They resisted. 'How can we cut the waste on this run?' I'd say, or, 'How are we going to allocate the overtime on this order?' 'That's not my job,' they'd say. 'Why not?' I'd say. 'Well, it just isn't,' they'd say. 'How in the world can we have participative management if you won't participate?' 'I don't know,' they'd say. 'Because that's not my job either. That's your job.' And I'd lose my temper. In the beginning, I really did lose my temper every time I heard the words, 'It's not my job!'"

With persistent effort to coach people to step into the *Solve It* mode and help them understand that "solving it" is not an extra activity, but part of the job, Frey recalls that "gradually hourly workers in general began to take on some of the work of problem solving and cost control. I pushed and prodded and required people to help solve problems related to their own jobs. Sometimes I felt like a fool, albeit a very pleased fool, when they came up with simple solutions to problems that had persistently stumped me and my managers."

Having moved the organization *Above The Line* and taken the *Solve It* step, Cin-Made is well on its way to prosperity. It is now a company with a highly differentiated product line that "is doing well in a demanding market and making a lot of money." On-time customer delivery is at 98 percent, absenteeism is practically non-existent, temporary workers are now monitored by full time employees in an effort to reduce waste, productivity is up 30 percent, grievances are down, "strict adherence to job descriptions is a thing of the past," and people are making more money than other workers in comparable industries.

As the Cin-Made story illustrates, "solving it" requires a personal commitment to continually asking the question, "what else can I do to achieve the result?" Moving *Above The Line* and adopting the *Solve It* attitude is the ingredient that will help fledgling companies to become robust and thriving companies retain their leadership.

Michael Eagle, then president of IVAC corporation, a mid-sized medical instruments company, helped his senior team and people throughout the company take the *Solve It* step and stay *Above The Line* when they could have easily dropped *Below The Line*. The company developed a new Model 570 set of instruments, composed of 70 different pieces of equipment, and promised Sparrow Hospital in Lansing, Michigan, one of IVAC's first customers for the new product, delivery before Christmas. On December 10, Mike learned that the delivery could not take place as promised because the new Model 570 instruments required last-minute changes in their printed circuit boards. Determined to keep IVAC's commitment and to solve this problem, he asked what else IVAC people could do to hit the target date. After intense discussion, a possible solution emerged. Could a concerted effort from an ad hoc project team close the gap? Some said, "maybe." Mike said, "Yes!" Immediately he assembled the ad hoc team with representatives from product development, instrument operations, engineering, quality assurance, and shipping, urging them to invest every brain cell in effecting the circuit board changes within a week.

On Monday, December 17, the Model 570 instruments were ready for shipping, but suddenly a new obstacle arose: due to the holiday season, all the commercial shipping services were already overbooked. Once again, the president asked, "What else can we do?" And the answer came, "There is nothing else we can do short of renting a Lear jet to get this product there on time." Mike Eagle quickly responded, "So why don't we rent a Lear jet?"

Astonished at Mike's "Get it done" attitude, the team enthusiastically went to work. The shipping department raced to rent a Lear jet and reconfigure its interior to accommodate all the packages that contained the Model 570. Then, at the last minute, it turned out that the company had miscalculated the size of the order. Even with the reconfigured jet interior, all the boxes simply would not fit. Unwilling to accept defeat so close to the goal line, freight packers opened each box and repacked all 70 different instruments. Finally, at 3:00 P.M. on December 17, the Lear jet left the San Diego airport for Lansing, Michigan.

In anticipation of any further problems and intent upon doing whatever else it took to get the result, a product manager from IVAC accompanied the flight. A few hours later, the jet arrived in Wichita, Kansas, for refueling. While taxiing down the runway to take off again, the pilot detected a broken altimeter. Able to fly but a short distance at low altitude, the pilot took the aircraft 200 miles to Lincoln, Nebraska, where the product manager got on the telephone with the company's Traffic Coordination Department to track down the faulty altimeter part, a task quite out of the ordinary for this department. After five hours of focused communications with airlines and manufacturers, the part was secured, flown to the airport, and installed in the Lear. At 3:30 A.M., on December 18, the shipment left Lincoln for Lansing, where it arrived at 5:45 A.M. Meanwhile, IVAC's in-service and training personnel who were scheduled to instruct the people at Sparrow Hospital in the use of the new Model 570 instruments had gotten stuck in a snow storm in Chicago on December 17 and had chosen to travel all night by car to arrive at the hospital on time the next morning.

At 7:30 A.M., on December 18, IVAC unveiled the Model 570 instruments at Sparrow Hospital and commenced with its service and training operations.

Unlike the people at Cin-Made and IVAC, many in other organizations do not ask the question, "What else can we do to rise above our circumstances and achieve the results we desire?" and ultimately fail to solve their problems.

WHY PEOPLE FAIL TO *SOLVE IT*^{SM}

As people begin solving problems they often encounter obstacles, expected and unexpected, that can stimulate a temptation to fall

Below The Line into the victim cycle. To avoid this, people must be committed to stay *Above The Line* during problem solving, particularly in the face of an unanticipated crisis.

One of our clients has demonstrated an uncanny ability to cope with and beat the often powerful temptation to fall *Below The Line*. Again, to protect the privacy of this client organization and the individuals involved, we have disguised the circumstances and details of the story, but we assure you it's otherwise true.

Michael Gilbert, the store operations vice president for a midsized department store chain, had experienced a trying year in which retail sales declined in general. Without any new merchandising or marketing programs over the last three years, Michael and his 84 store managers felt as if they were fighting a battle without any bullets. However, as those in the company began to recognize and own the circumstances, new life and hope spread throughout the organization, and along with it a new merchandising campaign that breathed new optimism and a "can-do" attitude into the store managers. Even the sales clerks agreed that things were getting better. Though sales started to increase and morale climbed higher, the company still needed to do a lot more just to catch up with their more successful competitors. Yes, the department store chain was making progress, and, thankfully, people were attempting to stay *Above The Line* with a strong problem-solving attitude, but it wasn't easy, particularly for the store managers, who battled in the trenches for retail sales each and every day.

Late one night, in a hotel at the Dallas-Fort Worth International Airport, Michael Gilbert met with his five regional managers, each one of whom supervised 15 to 18 stores, for a brief meeting. All six of them were on their way somewhere else and had arranged to meet for a few hours on this particular evening. As they gathered in a small conference room for their meeting, each person wanted to appear accountable, willing to own their circumstances and commit to operating *Above The Line,* but all of them were feeling the pain of their difficult circumstances (e.g., the high expectations of senior management for continued improvements in performance, the diminishing effect of the latest merchandising program, and the delay of promised incentive compensation plans).

Before the meeting officially started, one of the regional managers asked somewhat hesitantly, "Before we begin, can we drop *Below The Line* for just a few minutes? Let's talk about what's going on." Everyone laughed but then unleashed a lot of pent-up anxieties by blurting out their thoughts about what was going wrong in the company, who was at fault, and why the situation was terribly unfair. After about 15 minutes and Michael's final salvo, he said, "Okay, now that we've gotten that off our chests, let's get back *Above The Line* so we can determine what else we can do to achieve the results we want." Having aired their frustrations, the regional managers could finally move forward with a productive discussion of what they could do to solve the problems and remove the obstacles that confronted them. They all knew that remaining *Below The Line* would get them nowhere, but they had consciously dropped into the victim cycle for a brief moment to vent their frustrations and recite their discouragement with their current circumstances. Without their increased awareness of the fruitlessness of remaining *Below The Line,* Michael Gilbert and his five regional managers may have unwittingly prevented themselves from rising *Above The Line* to solve their problems. Without such awareness, it's awfully easy to succumb to the urge to stay *Below The Line.* In fact, Michael and his regional managers commented on how productive their session had been. Ordinarily, they would have remained *Below The Line* and carried their victim attitudes back to their store managers.

When people give up asking the *Solve It* question, as Michael Gilbert and his five regional managers felt tempted to do, they drop back *Below The Line* into the victim cycle and do not seek out creative and proactive ways they can achieve the results they want. In a recent *Fortune* magazine article by Brian Dumaine, "Leaving the Rat Race Early," the author cites a recent Roper survey in which a mere 18 percent of those polled (1296 people) felt that their "careers were personally and financially rewarding." According to the *Fortune* article, the dissatisfaction with full-time work is growing as more and more Americans find themselves overworked and overstressed. The article makes an intriguing and revealing point but fails to make another more important one: that 82 percent of those surveyed are stuck *Below The Line,* victimized by their circumstances, and could, in fact, make their jobs more personally and financially rewarding if they would only accept accountability for that result. The *Fortune* article makes the point that you can gain greater personal and financial satisfaction by retiring early, but it never explores the possibility of making the workplace itself more personally and financially rewarding. Instead, the article reflects the general attitude that people in organizations have no control or influence over their circumstances; they are simply pawns and victims, helpless to do anything but take what they can get. People at all levels of an organization who recognize the realities and own the circumstances of their job dissatisfaction can remove the obstacles encumbering their paths to greater satisfaction by developing the wisdom to *Solve It.*

Anyone who chooses, as the *Fortune* article urges, the early retirement path will run into plenty of obstacles there, too. It claims that "dropping out (i.e. early retirement) requires foresight and discipline but isn't as difficult as you might have feared." Perhaps so, but that doesn't mean you'll stroll down an obstacle-free path. You'll still need the wisdom to *Solve It.* Whether you stay employed full time or "drop out," you can always sink *Below The Line.* To its credit, the *Fortune* article does spell out what someone must look out for if he or she drops out of the rat race early: "Sounds great, but how on earth can you leave your job with no pension or social security and hope to survive? Financial planners recommend a three-pronged approach. First, expect to cut back on your life-style. You might have to buy a smaller house in a less expensive part of the country, tell your kids they can't count on Ivy League tuition and buy used cars rather than new ones. Second, you'll probably have to work a few months a year or hours a week, either for your old employer or for a new one (including yourself). Third, you'll have to save enough money to supplement your newly reduced income." In other words, even when you retire early, you must go on asking yourself what else you will need to do to attain your goals. Retiring early changes the landscape, but not the journey. You must still learn to rise *Above The Line* as you encounter the new challenges and obstacles you will face. If it sounds like the process of moving *Above The Line* to solve your problems requires some personal risk, that's good, because it does. But to think that residing *Below The Line* does not have its own risks is folly. The risk in getting stuck *Below The Line* is never obtaining the results you most earnestly seek.

Regardless of whether you're trying to keep, revolutionize, or retire from your current job, you'll never do it successfully unless you overcome the temptation to fall *Below The Line*. Indeed, you must focus your efforts on removing the obstacles standing between you and the outcomes you desire. As always, unhappy consequences await those who fail to do so.

THE CONSEQUENCES OF NOT *SOLVING IT*

According to a recent *Wall Street Journal* article, college textbook publishers stand to lose their entire market unless they assume a *Solve It* attitude: "A technology revolution is sweeping higher education. At Drew University, every entering freshman is given a high-powered notebook-style computer, and some professors assign software instead of books. Professor Norman Lowrey teaches musical composition using a floppy disk that enables students to compose music on their computers and then play it back. Students at Cornell's veterinary school work on computer simulations that allow them to examine animals, complete with audible heartbeats, before experimenting with treatments. 'They get really upset if they kill Fluffy the dog,' says Kathy Edmondson, an administrator, 'even though it's just on computer.' But most college textbook publishers aren't ready for this high-tech conversion. Despite such advances as CD-ROM, interactive computer software, and other so-called multimedia developments, the publishers in the $2.6 billion market for college books could miss a potential gold mine in new product sales. They have a fortune sunk in the making and marketing of standard textbooks that are increasingly behind the times and technology." While most publishers "see" this rapidly emerging reality, and some even *Own It,* few have started converting their problems into opportunities. An exception is Robert Lynch, director of McGraw-Hill's Primis service, a database operation that allows professors to customize textbooks, who says, "If we do things right and develop the full potential of high-tech educational publishing, this could be a $50 billion business instead of a $2.6 billion business." If college students will someday buy more computer disks than books and more books that their professors tailor for their needs from databases, then textbook publishers must respond by seeing it, owning it, solving it, and ultimately providing these products.

As our next case demonstrates, it's not uncommon for people to *See It, Own It,* and then fail to *Solve It.* At General-Ware, a computer software company disguised to protect the privacy of one of our clients, four directors in the programming and development area had come to their wits' end dealing with their boss, the vice president of programming and development. He would not fully accept responsibility for meeting product development deadlines and product quality standards. Brilliant in other regards, he would blithely promise to meet impossible target dates and then release a rushed and compromised product.

On the other hand, the four directors, each responsible for a different segment of the programming and development operation, saw the reality of the situation clearly and even owned their circumstances, but they could not move forward to *Solve It.* They had become stuck in their inability to move beyond the *Own It* step. Their attitude of "we're trying, but nothing's working," dampened their willingness to continue asking the *Solve It* question.

With the four directors manifesting all the familiar signs of the victim cycle, the programming and development function continued to languish under the mismanagement of the vice president. Each time they moved *Above The Line* to *Solve It*, they would fall back *Below The Line,* frustrated and discouraged. Because of the vice president's approach they felt helpless to change the circumstances and powerless to impact the things that really needed to change. Without new products, GeneralWare's credibility in the marketplace declined as dealers, distributors, and retailers began to discount the company's promises regarding product introduction dates and continued to expect faulty products even when they did materialize on time—a heavy price paid for a failure to *Solve It.*

In a similar example, General Electric's and Emerson Electric's *Below The Line* behavior brought tragedy and heartache to hundreds of families. In an ABC News, "PrimeTime Live" broadcast, Chris Wallace reported how a malfunction in General Electric's coffeemakers, manufactured with Emerson Electric fuses, caused the appliance to burst into flames, destroying homes and families. Both manufacturers knew about the problem, but ignored it. According to Wallace: "Over the past 12 years, hundreds of people have had problems with GE coffeemakers. Defective machines have burned down houses, caused serious injuries, even killed people. But GE for years denied responsibility, contesting claims against its coffeemakers with all the resources a big corporation can muster." General Electric documents from ten years prior to the "PrimeTime Live" report show that the company expected an estimated 168 claims that year and rated the prospect of "no injuries" associated with the claims at only 42 percent, evidence that the company had the data to recognize reality. One year later, GE recalled 200,000 coffeemakers, proof that the company even owned the problem.

However, the company's efforts to improve the appliance didn't stop fires from breaking out. As Wallace reported, "GE considered adding a second backup fuse, but didn't do it." A couple of years later, GE sold its coffeemaker division to Black & Decker, which, to its credit, solved the problem by adding a second fuse. During this same period of time, GE sued Emerson Electric for its faulty fuses and won. One GE official testified that the company had been "disgusted with the reliability" of the Emerson fuses for several years. Nevertheless, prior to selling the division, GE failed to solve the coffeemaker's problems because as it appeared, an otherwise accountable company was stuck *Below The Line.*

In light of the tragic results and in the face of the collective talent, wisdom, experience, and integrity of G.E. and Emerson, it goes without saying that people and organizations need to do more than just *See It* and *Own It.*

THE *SOLVE IT*^{SM} SELF-ASSESSMENT

Over the years we have helped friends and clients translate their understanding and ownership into problem-solving action with a list of key skills that are central to the *Solve It* attitude. These skills provide a solid foundation for an assessment of your ability to move from *See It* and *Own It* to *Solve It.*

SOLVE IT℠ SKILLS
▼

1. *Stay Engaged.* Often, when a pesky problem persists, the natural human tendency is to give up and stop trying—to "wait and see" if things will get better on their own. As you move through the *Solve It* step, it is important to avoid this trap by staying engaged in the process of finding solutions. Too often, we "lock-in" on what can't be done and, as a result, stop looking for and stop thinking about other alternatives. By so doing, we "lock-out" all the other possible solutions that exist, but are not yet seen.

2. *Be Persistent.* You must constantly ask the *Solve It* question: *What else can I do to achieve the desired result?* The repeated asking of this question makes it possible for an individual or a group to formulate new and creative solutions that make progress possible. One leader once said, "That which we persist in doing becomes easier for us to do; not that the nature of the thing itself is changed, but that our power to do it is increased."

3. *Use A New Paradigm.* Albert Einstein once said that "The significant problems we face cannot be solved at the same level of thinking we were at when we created them." In other words, the same thinking that got you into the problem won't get you out. Your ability to solicit and understand perspectives other than your own is key to successfully taking the *Solve It* step.

4. *Create New Linkages.* Many solutions require new approaches that tap into new ways of thinking and implementation. Often, such approaches involve forging new relationships that involve others you may not have previously considered to be a part of the solution. Such relationships may include your competitors, your suppliers and vendors, or someone in another department in the company.

Many business solutions today are formed by creating new linkages.

5. *Take The Initiative.* The *Solve It* step requires that one assume full accountability for discovering solutions that will ultimately deliver the desired results. Such solutions generally come only when one takes the initiative to explore, search and question *after* you have done everything. Understanding that others often do not share the same level of ownership or desire to achieve your goal, you must take the initiative to get the result. As has been said many times, there are three kinds of people in the world: those that make things happen, those that watch things happen, and those that wonder what happened.

6. *Stay Conscious.* Perhaps this sounds unusual, but we assure you, it is pertinent to the process of "solving it." Staying conscious means overcoming the "auto-pilot" mode and paying attention to everything that may have a bearing on potential solutions, particularly those things that we may be taking for granted which have become accepted ways of operating or thinking. You must be willing to challenge current assumptions and beliefs that you hold about the way things "are" or "have to be," in order to breakthrough to a new level of thinking that may take you out of your "comfort zone."

To assess whether, and to what extent, you practice these six skills, you can complete the following *Solve It* Self-assessment. Evaluate each of the skills by determining whether your attitudes and behavior always, never or sometimes show evidence of them.

SOLVE IT℠ SELF-ASSESSMENT
▼

Circle the description after each skill that best characterizes your attitudes and behavior:

1. Do you stay engaged in solving a problem when things get difficult?

Often	Sometimes	Never
3	2	1

2. Do you persistently ask the *Solve It* question: "What else can I do to achieve the desired results?"

Often	Sometimes	Never
3	2	1

3. Do you take the initiative to explore, search and question when solutions are not forthcoming?

Often	Sometimes	Never
3	2	1

4. Do you stay concious by challenging your current assumptions and beliefs about how things are done?

Often	Sometimes	Never
3	2	1

5. Do you create new interdependent "linkages" in order to arrive at solutions?

Often	Sometimes	Never
3	2	1

6. Do you consciously work to discover new paradigms that help you think about problems differently than you would otherwise?

Often	Sometimes	Never
3	2	1

Now, take a few minutes to weigh the implications of your assessments. An honest appraisal of each of the *Solve It* indicators will reveal areas where you can work to obtain the wisdom you need to *Solve It.*

Score	Evaluation Guidelines
Often 18 to 13	Indicates that you see your accountability, own your circumstances, and diligently pursue a problem-solving course of action. Congratulations!
Sometimes 12 to 7	Shows that you feel ambivalent about solving your problems. Such wavering courage, heart, and wisdom will only take you on a roller-coaster ride, *Above* and *Below The Line*. Work on it!
Never 6 to 1	Reveals a need for much greater effort. Reread this chapter!

By taking this third step to greater accountability you will enhance your wisdom to solve problems and remove the obstacles you will encounter as you progress in your journey *Above The Line*. The benefits are enormous.

THE BENEFITS OF DEVELOPING THE WISDOM TO *SOLVE IT*^{SM}

You'll recall that the four directors in GeneralWare's programming and development function recognized their reality and even owned it but felt so powerless to *Solve It* that they had stopped looking for any new solutions. After a lot of soul searching and debate, they finally decided to overcome their feelings of powerlessness and take the *Solve It* step by asking the question, "What else can we do to rise above our circumstances and get the results we want?" In answering this question they decided to air their concerns at a company retreat during a series of group discussions. As you might imagine, it didn't take long for the focus of the retreat to turn exclusively to the new product development projections. Just three weeks prior to the meeting, GeneralWare had presented an annual profit plan to the parent company describing how three new product introductions would account for 25 percent of their projected profit. Undaunted, however, the four directors announced to the participants at the company retreat that the projected product introductions from the profit plan were actually six months to one year off schedule. An audible moan could be heard across the room as every participant took in the information.

After two days of intense scrutiny of why the company had bought into such unrealistic projections, GeneralWare's president acknowledged the reality that the company would not be able to introduce any new products in the coming 6 to 12 months. He then encouraged all his senior managers to acknowledge that same reality. Then came the determination to own and solve the problem. Immediately, a series of intense actions were implemented throughout the organization. Companywide, people became focused on asking the question, "What else can we do to get these products to market?" At once, the entire company progressed up the steps to accountability as they took a collective step upward to *Solve It.*

While the four directors kept their jobs, none of them moved up to the vice president's position. They had each learned a valuable lesson, but they needed more seasoning in their attitudes of accountability before they would be ready for such a promotion. Over the next 18 months, GeneralWare successfully introduced three new products and reversed the rising credibility concerns among the company's dealers, distributors, and retailers.

Despite the pressure to perform in the short term, the president of GeneralWare and, ultimately, his people, patiently worked through the *See It* and *Own It* steps before attempting to solve the problem. Impatience would have resulted in just the sort of scheduling mishaps and quality defects the company was trying to eliminate.

Once everyone had fully seen and owned the problem, then people could start asking the *Solve It* question, which they did persistently until solutions began to take shape. Their persistence led to the new and creative solutions that would never have materialized otherwise.

Feelings of powerlessness had prevented the four directors from getting out of a rut from which the problem appeared insoluble. While the vice president never did come to grips with that issue, and, as a result, lost his job, the four directors did finally accept the fact that the power to get the results the company desired really did lie within themselves.

Each journey *Above The Line* begins, and is fueled by, a single question: What else can we do to achieve the result? The journey is not over until a solution has been discovered. GeneralWare may not have perfected its delivery of new products, but it had achieved measurable progress in that direction; the journey continues.

As the GeneralWare case suggests, getting *Above The Line* to *Solve It* can make all the difference in the world, no matter what you're trying to do or achieve. Languishing *Below The Line,* you can expect only lackluster performance.

THE FINAL STAGE OF ACCOUNTABILITY

The Scarecrow symbolizes the wisdom to solve problems, a capability it turned out he possessed all along. By this time in the story, Dorothy herself was coming closer and closer to realizing that the results she was seeking would also come from within, but she would need to discover one more dimension of accountability before she could click her heels and return to Kansas. Having learned a great deal from her Oz companions, she finally reached the threshold of fully understanding the power of living *Above The Line.* In the next and final chapter in Part Two, you will discover how Dorothy pulls all four *Steps To Accountability* together to *Do It.*

DOROTHY: EXERCISING THE MEANS TO *DO IT*^{SM}

▼

*"Oz, left to himself, smiled to think of his success in giving
the Scarecrow and the Tin Woodsman and the Lion exactly
what they thought they wanted "How can I help being a hum-
bug," he said, "when all these people make me do things that
everybody knows can't be done? It was easy to make the
Scarecrow and the Lion and the Woodsman happy, because
they imagined I could do anything. But it will take more than
imagination to carry Dorothy back to Kansas, and I'm sure I
don't know how it can be done."*

THE WIZARD OF OZ
By L. Frank Baum

169

Wal-Mart CEO, David Glass, emerged as the most admired CEO
of the most admired companies in *Fortune* magazine's 1993 survey. *Fortune's* article, "David Glass Won't Crack Under Fire,"
explains why this *Do It* executive deserves the praise of his
peers: "Sam Walton had to try several times before he could persuade Glass to join the company as executive vice president of
finance 16 years ago from the Consumer Markets chain in his
home state of Missouri. Walton was forever stirring the management pot. In 1984 he pulled a high-level job swap, naming
Glass, then the CFO, president and chief operating officer and
requiring vice chairman Jack Shewmaker to give up the stores
for the financial chores. The switch created a very public succession race in which Glass became the front-runner." Now, as
CEO of the $55 billion retailing powerhouse, Glass lives in the
stores more than in his headquarters office because that's where
the action is. Wal-Mart's success hinges, he recognizes, on
knowing what's going on in store aisles, in competitors' show-
rooms, and in each employee's daily work. Notebook in hand,
Glass asks a million questions for every answer he gives. Glass's
constant questioning and searching for better ways to do things
personifies the *See It*, *Own It*, *Solve It*, and *Do It* executive, who
consistently strives to work *Above The Line*. Employees never
fear a visit from Glass because they know he shares their hopes
and concerns. And Wal-Mart executives respect him as well,
knowing that Glass's down-to-earth style does not mean he'll
tolerate mediocrity. As a senior executive told *Fortune,* "There's
no question that his expectation is 110%. I mean, he never has to
tell you. You know what it is before you ever talk to him." Not
surprisingly, a lot of companies and executives want to learn
from Glass. As the *Fortune* article points out, "Although Wal-
Mart's rah-rah style is sometimes criticized by sophisticated
types, a steady stream of corporate heavyweights finds its way
to Bentonville to see what the noise is all about. GE boss Jack
Welch is a welcome visitor. . . . When former Procter & Gamble
CEO John Smale took over as chairman of General Motors, one

of his first exercises was to cart CEO Jack Smith and other GM executives to a Wal-Mart management meeting, presumably to learn how to make a decision without using a calendar. Executives from IBM, Eastman Kodak, Southwest Airlines, Sara Lee, P&G, and Anheuser Busch have all made the trek." Despite Wal-Mart's impressive growth and success, David Glass believes the best is yet to come. In other words, you don't just *Do It* and then rest on your laurels, you keep on "doing it" day in and day out.

When you combine the first three steps of accountability with the fourth and final step, *Do It*, then and only then will you experience the full power of living *Above The Line* and enable yourself to get the results you want. The words of another highly visible executive, Louis Gerstner, CEO of IBM, "We need to adopt that legendary Noah principle: No more prizes for predicting rain. Prizes only for building arks," point to what the fourth and final step to accountability is all about.

▲

REACHING THE FOURTH AND FINAL STEP OF ACCOUNTABILITY

Ultimately, personal accountability means accepting full responsibility for results. It requires the sort of attitude popularized in the Nike footwear television commercials: "Just Do It." If you don't *Do It*, you'll never reap the most valuable benefit that is derived from full accountability: overcoming your circumstances and achieving the results you want. Despite the many benefits that accrue from applying the other three steps, results only come when you put all four steps together and *Do It!*

The *Do It* step bestows accountability, not just for activities, circumstances, or feelings but for future accomplishment. When you combine the notion of accountability with the objective of accomplishing better results, you create an empowering and guiding beacon for both personal and organizational activity. This form of accountability comes after you have progressed through all four steps *Above The Line*. By stopping at any step short of *Do It*, you may keep yourself out of the victim cycle, but you will never fully achieve a permanent position *Above The Line*. Any effort that falls short of making it happen and getting it done simply indicates a lack of full acceptance of accountability.

"Doing it" requires that you work continuously to stay *Above The Line*, avoiding the occurrences inherent in daily circumstances and problems that can tempt you back *Below The Line*. As we constantly stress in this book, accountability is a process, and you can fall into the victim cycle just as easily from the fourth step to accountability as from any of the others. Staying *Above The Line* requires diligence, perseverance, and vigilance. It also requires a willingness to accept risk and to take the giant step that's often necessary to accomplish what you want to have happen in your life or your organization. Fear of the risk of failing can be so debilitating that many people build walls between *Solve It* and *Do It*. However, only by accepting the risk can you penetrate the walls and break down all the barriers to success.

In the final analysis, *Do It* means embracing your full responsibility for results and remaining answerable for your progress in attaining those results, regardless of how or why you managed to get into your current situation. Consider the example of an American Van Lines driver who established his accountability and stayed *Above The Line*, even when the going got tough. It all started at the Teradata Corporation, a company founded in a garage in Los Angeles now a part of Unisys. Teradata strove to fill a niche in the computer database market unserved by larger companies such as IBM. After the first two years of hard effort they finally sold the first Teradata computer to a *Fortune* 500 company headquartered on the East Coast. That accomplishment prompted quite a celebration among Teradata's

52 employees, who had worked together as a veritable family for two long years. Now, after all that effort, the company had turned the corner and was about to ship its first product.

On the Saturday morning scheduled for shipment of the computer, all the employees and their families gathered at the Teradata facility, a renovated warehouse that had replaced the garage in which the company had begun its operations, to give it a rousing send-off. Streamers and signs hung from the rafters and the eaves of the warehouse roof. Everyone sported T-shirts with the words "The Big One" screened on the front and back. Even the American Van Lines driver who had contracted to deliver the shipment got caught up in the festivities as he climbed into the cab of his 18-wheeler.

As the contract driver pulled out of the parking lot with "The Big One" in tow, the Teradata families formed a parade route to cheer his departure. Moved by the moment, the driver waved back, shouting that he would not let them down. Indeed, the driver felt he had joined the Teradata team, even if for only this one haul, and he felt a strong sense of ownership and pride over the role he was playing in Teradata's first major achievement.

Almost eight hours into his trip, the American Van Lines driver pulled into his first weigh station only to discover that his load was 500 pounds over the legal limit. He knew the overweight problem would require additional paper processing and approvals that could create a full day's delay and prevent Teradata from meeting the promised delivery date. At this point, you can imagine how easy it would have been for this driver to fall *Below The Line*, blaming the company for the overweight problem. After all, it wasn't his fault. You can also imagine how easy it would have been for the driver to check into a motel to await further instructions. However, the driver stayed *Above The Line* by choosing to "own" the situation. Only he could "save" the delivery date. Recognizing the reality of his situation and owning the circumstances, he quickly moved to *Solve It*. In minutes he turned the truck around and drove to the nearest truck stop where he dismantled the truck's front and rear bumpers, removed its extra water containers, and hid all the apparatus in a nearby ditch under some brush. He recalled thinking of the risk of losing the hidden items; after all, he would be held accountable by the company that owned the rig, but such thoughts were only momentary as he accepted the risk as the only way to get the shipment delivered on schedule. When he returned to the weigh station, the truck checked in 50 pounds under weight. With a great deal of pride and satisfaction in his accomplishment, he drove on to the East Coast where he delivered "The Big One" on time. He had done it!

After hearing about the driver's experience, the people at Teradata celebrated the driver's *See It, Own It, Solve It, Do It* attitude by, among other things, incorporating his story into the company's new employee orientation program as a symbol to reinforce the power of working *Above The Line*.

In another example of how seeing, owning, solving and doing combine to make extraordinary things happen, consider what Tracy Sullivan (not her real name) did for her product testing department at a mid-sized company.

The Southwestern Micro-Chip Corporation (SMC, also a disguised name) faced a problem: how to get its products to market faster. Although everyone at SMC was scrambling to accomplish this goal, no group in the company felt more responsible for it than the product testing department. Tracy, among the first in the company to "see" the need several months earlier, had been working diligently with her department to "own" the company's current circumstances and figure out a way to "solve" the problem. As she told the members of her department, who serviced all of SMC's product management groups, "Seeing, owning and solving this problem won't make any difference unless we put our solutions into action and get results."

With perseverance and determination, the product testing department, which the company's product managers had all too often perceived as a serious bottleneck, began investigating the "best practices" in the industry and related industries to find out how they could streamline the company's product testing process. Equipped with those findings, the department had developed three different alternatives for cutting the product testing period by two-thirds without compromising its fundamental purpose or its market research value.

In a special meeting with all the product management and marketing personnel at SMC, Tracy presented her department's recommendations, led a discussion of the pros and cons of each alternative, and invited all present to vote on the best alternative. When one of the alternatives outpolled the others, the product testing department quickly put it into practice and managed not only to slash product testing time in half but gained the recognition of everyone in the company.

Tracy Sullivan's efforts inspired the entire company to stay *Above The Line* in all its endeavors and to foster greater accountability throughout the organization. Once Tracy and others at SMC experienced the power of staying *Above The Line*, no matter how grim their circumstances became, they constantly reminded themselves that they could accomplish anything if they set their minds to it. Of course, that's more easily said than done.

▲
WHY PEOPLE FAIL TO *DO IT*^{SM}

Most people who fail to *Do It* can't or won't resist the gravitational pull from *Below The Line* which can so easily drag someone back into the victim cycle, wasting valuable time, energy, and resources, ignoring and denying, making excuses, developing explanations, pointing fingers, getting confused, and waiting to see if things will get better. In our experience, this happens most often because people naturally resist the perceived risks associated with becoming fully responsible for results. A fear of failure can create a terrible burden that makes taking the final step to accountability virtually impossible. It seems so much easier to hide in a false sense of security, citing excuses for avoiding the dangers associated with risk. Nothing will keep you in the victim cycle more surely than a risk-avoiding attitude.

This happens to organizations all the time. Just as the line between the *Steps To Accountability* and the victim cycle separates effective organizations from ineffective ones, the unseen line between *Solve It* and *Do It* separates good companies from great ones. Great organizations welcome the risks associated with action, regardless of the inherent danger in those risks.

To get people personally involved and accountable for results, many companies are finding new ways to empower workers to take risks. Such organizations have learned what it means to create a "sense of urgency" around "doing it," regardless of the existing structure or past traditions. A story in *USA Today* shows what happens when a group of people do get personally involved: "Chevrolet had a problem. Its Camaro muscle car—an important lure for young buyers and a big part of Chevy's performance image—had become a clunky rattletrap as the 1990s began. *Consumer Reports* magazine condemned it. Even sympathetic auto-enthusiast magazines couldn't ignore loose gearshift levers, leaky windows, chattering dashboards. Pontiac—Chevy's sibling division at General Motors—was suffering too. Its Firebird shared hardware with, and was built alongside, the better-selling Camaro. GM's generic designation for these cars is F-car. 'Sales were off. Quality ratings were way down,' says F-car engineering manager Richard DeVogelaere, 43. 'Water leaks, squeaks and rattles, poor driveability, electrical problems—probably no secret to any Camaro or Firebird owner. We just hadn't paid as much attention as we should have.'"

However, a relatively small and underfinanced team of GM engineers led by DeVogelaere did not let bureaucracy stand in the way of improvement. Given the fact that headquarters did not constantly look over its shoulder, the team was able to improve quality and cut defects so much that warranty claims fell by half in just two years. Richard DeVogelaere described how his team did it: "The budget was very, very small, but it was all blessed upfront, so we didn't have to justify anything. They gave me the money and said, 'Get it done.' That really made it work. It didn't take several signatures. If you say it, it gets done. That was refreshing. You hear about driving the responsibility down to the levels where people really know. Well, this is a case of it." On the other hand, companies that fail to engender this kind of accountability in their people pay a dear price by having to tell people what to do, all the way down the line.

Recall that the 1980s ushered in an era of debt financing that helped bankrupt many companies and eventually helped plunge the country and the world into a nagging recession. So few investors avoided the temptations of the junk bond craze that Morgan Stanley's behavior stands out in stark contrast. As reported in *Time* magazine: "During the heyday of takeover lending and junk bond financing, the patrician investment firm Morgan Stanley was often the butt of ridicule. While more aggressive firms plunged into risky new techniques, Morgan, despite a leading role in corporate takeovers, seemed stuck in its stodgy habit of underwriting stock for blue-chip companies and selling investment-grade bonds. The new breed was playing high-stakes Monopoly, the joke went, while the stuffed shirts at Morgan were playing Trivial Pursuit." To its credit Morgan Stanley was willing to risk losing investors with its conservative policy, but in the long run it turned out that the company did the right thing.

In hindsight, analysts value Morgan Stanley's position. This investment banking establishment, almost without peer, stood solidly *Above The Line* by accepting full responsibility for the consequences of its actions. It did "see" the shortsightedness of the junk bond craze, it did "own" its circumstances despite ridicule and criticism, it did "solve" its problems by diversifying into various other fields rather than jumping on the junk bond bandwagon, and it did *Do It* by sticking to the well-established values of trust and integrity. In the end, what Morgan Stanley did was become the most profitable Wall Street investment banking firm of the early 1990s.

From another part of the world comes another insight into why people fail to *Do It*. According to an article in *The Wall Street Journal*, "Desert Drift: Their Nation Saved, Kuwaitis Wait for Others to Fix It," reporter Tony Horwitz describes how Kuwait may have lost a perfect opportunity to rise *Above The Line* after the Gulf War by becoming mired in *Below The Line* attitudes and behavior:

"Before August 2, (1990) Kuwaitis lived in a gilded welfare society. They made up only 27% of the population, relying on outsiders to do virtually all the gritty work. They were entitled to retirement benefits at age 40, as well as free land and interest-free housing loans. As a result, the Interior Minister, Sheik Ahmed al-Sabah says, Kuwaitis lacked 'the will to work.'"

Such a widespread loss of will among Kuwaitis made their country easy prey to Iraq's dictator, Sadam Hussein. Even after the United Nations and the U.S. military rode to their rescue, the Kuwaitis did not wake up to the need to climb *Above The Line*. Instead, as at least one high-ranking Kuwaiti, former Planning Minister Sulaiman Mutawa, argues, "We've dribbled away a heaven-sent opportunity to kill off the Kuwait of August 1, and build a leaner, more independent society...Now it looks as though the crisis was just a Dracula film that scared us for a while." Mutawa laments, "We didn't learn a thing."

Unless the Kuwaiti people decide to work their way out of the victim cycle, they will not gain the independence and self-sufficiency they need both to respect and protect themselves. Not surprisingly, many people find it much easier to go with the status quo and allow themselves to be "acted upon" even when that behavior gets them into trouble, rather than confront the risks that so often attend moving from *Solve It* to *Do It*. With a good deal more vigilance concerning the dangers of *Below The Line* behavior, companies and nations may learn how shunning the risks associated with action can prevent them from creating a better future.

COUNTING THE CONSEQUENCES
OF NOT "DOING IT"

If you fail to *Do It*, you not only fail to improve your circumstances or obtain the results you want, but you also set yourself up for a continuing cycle of disappointment. The following story illustrates the consequences of not "doing it."

As do many small-sized service organizations, Strategic Associates (not its real name) ran into difficulty sustaining its overhead and continuing its growth. During the past three years, the firm had learned to pinpoint the "cliff" of "no sales" that usually lay two to four months beyond current engagements. Strategic Associates (SA) executives used the cliff metaphor to represent the point on the company's financial pro formas that showed no projected sales revenues in the future. As in many small professional service firms, the key people in the organization both sold and delivered the company's services. Naturally, these key people watched for the "cliff" and turned their attention from delivering service to sales whenever they saw themselves swerving too close to the edge.

While SA's organizational culture had become adept at avoiding the cliff, the situation began to change in early 1988 when the "cliff" became steeper and more threatening. In fact, unknown to the rank-and-file employees of the firm, the president himself had to mortgage his home to meet payroll demands for two months. As word of the predicament got out, however, people began to wonder about just how bad the situation had become and started speculating on who among them might be laid off if things didn't get better.

In this atmosphere of dread, the entire firm dropped *Below The Line* as everyone began blaming various people, programs, and occurrences for lack of performance and for the recurrence of the "cliff" problem. Although SA's management conducted objective personal interviews with all employees to assess their performance, most people felt they were getting blamed unfairly for the company's problems, which lay outside their control. After a lot of emotional venting at a weekly staff meeting, management and employees agreed that the time had come to move *Above The Line* and turn the situation around.

Subsequently, management invested a lot of time interviewing all the employees to better understand the real nature of the problem. Then, at an historic company-wide meeting, they laid everything they had discovered on the table, holding nothing back, and unveiling charts and graphs that summarized all the pertinent facts of the situation. Open discussion and dialogue ensued, with the express aim of solving the overriding issue of sales. Everyone worked hard to *See It* because the problem had become so pervasive. As the meeting progressed tumultuously, no one held anything back because everyone figured they had nothing to lose. Clearly, unless the current situation changed, SA would have no choice but to start laying off people within the next two months. The meeting sounded a loud wake-up call for every employee as each came to appreciate both the gravity of the situation and the fact that they personally were doing little to help solve the problem.

Senior management had certainly made its share of mistakes, but employees, too, had avoided the sales issue because they felt it lay outside their control. Even those who had tried to sell in the past had failed to get good results, while others had not even tried to sell because they received no incentive beyond delivering services sold by others. While some blamed management for poor training or the lack of attractive commissions, they also started seeing the limitations of their own comfort levels and unwillingness to challenge themselves and assume responsibility for SA's problem. Everyone had allowed the burden of sales to rest upon the shoulders of the executive group, and in particular, upon the president. After all, since those key executives had always made the necessary sales to sustain the firm's growth, why should anyone else worry about it? Now, of course, with the very life of the organization at stake, the realization dawned that everyone must worry about it.

Management, too, obtained from the meeting a growing realization that they had not acknowledged some important realities. In the past the top salespeople had received a lot of recognition for "saving the day" and bringing in the sales, and until now, they had to admit, they had shied away from sharing the glory and the wealth. With luck, they had always steered SA away from the cliff, but at this juncture luck seemed to be in short supply. As the senior staff listened to their people, they realized that all SA's sales success stories starred the president and the chairman. In fact, the chairman always bestowed upon the selling of intangible consulting services a certain mystique reserved for only the elite among consultants. Whenever SA dug up promising leads for new business, the firm invariably put its very best salespeople, the chairman and the president, to work on them, a habit that had further fostered the perception that sales remained the domain of people at the highest executive levels.

As a result of the meeting, the chairman and president also came to appreciate that while they knew how to sell, they did not feel confident that they could train others to do so. Their own experience over the years had made them good salespeople, but they did not believe they could pass that along to another person through training alone. Finally, they admitted that their behavior stemmed, in part, from their own need to feel good about their accomplishments. After all, successful selling cemented their positions as stars in the company.

As the chairman and president owned the facts surrounding SA's dilemma, they realized that all their employees needed to gain confidence that they could help solve it. If they could define themselves as part of the problem and own their own circumstances, they could help everyone else see themselves not only as part of the problem but as part of the solution. Given the gravity of the situation, each person must grasp 110 percent ownership of the situation, no matter how small their contribution to the problem, before SA could turn things around permanently.

As the president and chairman shared this insight during the meeting, more and more people began talking about how they could and would do whatever it took to accomplish the firm's objectives. Emotion ran high as people spontaneously recounted their feelings and expressed their eagerness to solve the problem. In a very real sense, the organization's power to get results increased tenfold as everyone developed a strong sense of ownership.

As the president led the group into a *Solve It* phase, he in essence asked, "What else can we do to achieve the results we want?" The ensuing discussion revealed a pent-up enthusiasm for solving the firm's ever-recurring sales problem, not only for the immediate-term but for the long-term as well. The group began crafting a sales plan that listed the immediate involvement of every person in the firm, outlining what each might do to keep SA from falling over the "cliff." For the first time in SA's history, each and every employee began thinking of what they could personally do to increase sales leads and impact the overall sales performance of the company. Some even considered friends and acquaintances they could tap for sales leads.

Even more important than this short-term effort, everyone engaged in hammering out a longer-term plan to involve the entire consulting staff in keeping the firm well away from the "cliff." This plan centered on developing the sales skills of all the consultants. Eventually, everyone bought into the long-term solution: categorizing all incoming business into three different groups based on income potential. Any lead for a company with annual sales under $250 million fell into the "C" category, which would be courted by any consultant without the aid of a member of the executive team. This aspect of the solution would immediately expand the sales team by allowing more people to call on prospective clients without risking the loss of more lucrative accounts. Over time, all consultants would gain selling experience that would eventually prepare them for selling to bigger prospects.

The "B" category included companies with over $250 million but under $1 billion in annual sales. These prospective clients would be contacted by consultants and a member of the executive team other than the chairman or president. The "A" companies exceeded $1 billion in annual sales, and they would receive the direct attention of the chairman or the president, along with one of the consultants who might lead the ultimate engagement.

To implement this program, the senior consultants outlined a training and certification process for each category, and by the end of the meeting the entire group felt both enthusiastic and empowered to meet the challenge ahead. Most people felt they now stood in a position to benefit both themselves and the company with the new sales approach, and the president himself felt that the new program would remove all limits and boundaries to the firm's successful future. Not only would the solution expand the sales force immediately, it would further develop all SA's people, creating a machine capable of producing sales and keeping SA permanently away from the "cliff."

After the meeting, SA's people moved swiftly *Above The Line*, with everyone "seeing it, owning it, and solving it." Now, finally, they were ready to *Do It*. However, as people turned their attention to the need for immediate sales during the weeks after the memorable meeting, the president managed to snare the firm's largest contract ever, causing everyone to heave a sigh of relief that SA had solved its immediate crisis.

Almost overnight the longer-term concern of permanently avoiding the "cliff" and sustaining perpetual growth became a dim memory as all the consultants went back to doing what they had always done: implementing the work sold by top executives. The picture looked rosy because this one huge sale, combined with SA's annual sales to date enabled the firm to achieve its best revenue year ever. As a result, the chairman and the president perpetuated the myth that only they could slay the big dragons when they needed slaying, and they let the training and certification program fall by the wayside. While from time to time an employee lamented the return to "business as usual," none of the new sales development plans ever materialized. With neither management nor the consultants willing to take the risks associated with the new approach, SA soon fell back *Below The Line*, waiting for the next "cliff" to appear, hoping that it wouldn't be so steep the next time.

Of course, a year later, the "cliff" reappeared, and SA found itself right back where it started. Once again, the chairman and president shouldered the responsibility. Unfortunately, by not taking the step from *Solve It* to *Do It*, the firm could not stay *Above The Line* and get the results it really needed. Imagine what might have happened had SA followed through on its original plan. Not surprisingly, SA has grown sluggishly over the past five years because it keeps bumping up against the growth limits imposed when only the top people worry about sales. While the firm has expanded from $3.5 million to $7 million in annual sales, at least one competitor has grown from $3 million to $45 million over the same period of time. That competitor knew how to *Do It*.

*DO IT*SM SELF ASSESSMENT

Your own ability to *Do It* will stem from your willingness to hold yourself fully responsible for your circumstances and totally accountable for your progress toward results. The following questionnaire will help you determine whether you are willing to take the risks associated with "doing it." If you find yourself unwilling or hesitant to *Do It*, go back to Chapters 4 through 7, to renew your understanding of the *Steps To Accountability*.

Now, take a few minutes to weigh your behavior and attitudes when it comes to "doing it."

DO IT℠ SELF ASSESSMENT
▼

	Always	Often	Sometimes	Seldom	Never
1. You recognize the forces, when they present themselves, that could pull you back down *Below The Line*.	7	5	3	1	0
2. You are effective at avoiding additional excursions *Below The Line* as you work to *Do It!*	7	5	3	1	0
3. You proactively report on your accountability no matter what the results are.	7	5	3	1	0
4. You take the initiative to clarify your own responsibilities and accountabilities.	7	5	3	1	0
5. You encourage others to proactively clarify their own responsibilities and accountabilities.	7	5	3	1	0
6. You are willing to take risks in order to *Do It*.	7	5	3	1	0

	Always	Often	Sometimes	Seldom	Never
7. You do not easily give up and are not easily overcome by obstacles, but continue to persist in seeking to make it happen.	7	5	3	1	0
8. Once personal or organizational goals have been set, you actively measure progress toward those goals.	7	5	3	1	0
9. As circumstances change, your commitment to getting the result does not vary— you remain determined to *Do It!*	7	5	3	1	0
10. You always keep yourself "seeing, owning, solving, and doing" until you achieve the desired results.	7	5	3	1	0

Once you have completed the *Do It* Self-assessment, total up your scores then consult the following table for some guidelines on evaluating your ability to stay *Above The Line* and *Do It*.

Total Score	Evaluation Guidelines
55 to 70	Verifies a strong *Do It* attitude. However, you should avoid intolerance of those

who feel less accountable, lest you lose your ability to influence their journeys *Above The Line*.

40 to 54	Indicates fair to good *Do It* attitudes and behavior, but you can improve.
25 to 39	Suggests a problem with taking the risks associated with the *Do It* step.
0 to 20	Reveals serious *Below The Line* problems. You should go back to Chapter 4 and start climbing the *Steps To Accountability* again.

The benefits of climbing the fourth and final step to accountability can be astonishing.

SEEKING FEEDBACK TO HEIGHTEN YOUR ABILITY TO WORK *ABOVE THE LINE*^{SM}

At this point, you probably have a pretty good feeling for how you view yourself on the *Steps To Accountability*. As we mentioned in Chapter 4, the honest input from others may help you to learn ways in which you can operate from a more accountable perspective. Remember, accountable people seek feedback and feedback creates accountable people. Those of you who desire to further heighten your accountability can turn to the Appendix at the back of *The Oz Principle*. In the Appendix we describe how to share the concept of accountability with four or five individuals, discuss with those individuals times when you have been *Below* and *Above The Line* and capture their insights on how you can heighten your overall ability and commitment to work *Above The Line*. In the Appendix you will find a Feedback Worksheet as well as some suggestions on how to make the feedback sessions with others most effective.

▲
_____

THE BENEFITS OF EXERCISING THE MEANS TO *DO IT*^{SM}

We know from first-hand experience that it's a lot easier to preach accountability than it is to practice it. That's why it heartens us so much when we encounter that rare individual who, no matter how great the obstacle, refuses to get stuck *Below The Line*. Such people vigilantly and diligently strive to improve their circumstances and invariably create stunning results for themselves and others. Karsten Solheim deserves special recognition in this regard.

During the great depression of the 1930s Karsten dropped out of college in order to earn enough money to survive, though he hoped he could return to school one day. He worked as a cobbler, then as an apprentice engineer at Ryan Aeronautical and Convair, gaining valuable on-the-job training but never quite saving enough money to continue his formal education.

Eventually, Karsten left Ryan for General Electric, where he helped develop the first portable television set. Shortly thereafter, on his own time, Karsten created the first "rabbit ears" antenna, but when GE executives dismissed the invention, he shared the idea and design with another company that went on to make a fortune with the device. Unfortunately, Karsten received no remuneration for his innovation except a set of gold-plated antennas after the company reached 2 million units in sales. Rather than give in to resentment, however, Karsten learned from his experience, faced the reality, owned his circumstances, and vowed, with a genuine *Solve It* attitude: "The next time I invent something, I'll make it myself." And that's exactly what he did.

While still employed by GE, Karsten spent his evenings and weekends developing innovative golf clubs in his garage. No one took him seriously in the beginning as a *Sports Illustrated* article noted: "Karsten Solheim was considered a kook when he began showing up at tour events around 1960, but he was perceptive enough to head straight for the practice putting green. That is where the tour's sick and wounded pull in for repairs, and they always are looking for a miracle 'cure.'" Refining his inventions with the responses of professional golfers, Karsten finally developed a putter that provided a larger "sweet spot," facilitated lining up the ball with the hole, and worked beautifully on all kinds of grasses. Once he succeeded in convincing a few professionals to use the putter, he was delighted when they soon began winning tournaments. Word of the new "Ping" putter spread quickly, fueling demand not only for the putter but for other Ping irons and clubs as well.

Having learned from earlier experiences, Karsten knew that he himself must guide the future development of this new product. This meant he would have to take calculated risks, such as leaving his successful career at GE. But knowing that he could not realize the results he wanted unless he took such risks, he didn't think twice, he just "did it." After leaving his job at GE, Karsten engineered a full-scale golf club manufacturing line, and, in just over two years, he grew his business from $50,000 to $800,000. By 1992 Karsten was leading the industry. Today, Karsten continues to stay *Above The Line*, even in the face of adversity. When he received some bad news not long ago from the United States Golf Association, which claimed that the distance between the grooves on Karsten's Ping "Eye 2" clubs did not conform to USGA standards, Karsten began contesting the allegations in court, all the while steadfastly developing more innovations at his plant. Karsten refuses to abandon his commitment to *Do It* and he refuses to fall *Below The Line*. Without doubt his continued application of an *Above The Line* attitude, a drive for performance, and a commitment to *Do It* will enable him to lead the field in innovation and gain an even greater share in the world golf club market.

Cardiac Pacemakers, Inc. recently encountered a problem with its implantable defibrillator, the primary product that had fueled the company's tremendous growth. The problem could not have come at a worse time, with patents on the defibrillator running out and competition poised to flood the market with rival products. If CPI didn't aggressively address the defibrillator problem, it would soon go out of business.

The defibrillator problem stemmed from a diode within the unit that was designed to protect employees during tests of the instrument during the final stage of manufacturing. Chloride contamination in the diode, it found out, might in some cases cause the defibrillator unit not to operate according to its design. Thorough tests, however, convinced CPI that the contamination problem would not in all likelihood cause a life-threatening failure. Some attributed the problem to the diode vendor, while others chalked the problem up to a certain bad lot of diodes, even though further investigation could not trace the problem to a specific diode lot. While innumerable excuses and explanations mounted, the basic problem of predicting the performance of the defibrillator remained. Was the problem rate high enough to warrant action? The product evaluation committee thought not, but others in the company disagreed. Some argued that certain people were overreacting or instigating a "witch-hunt," while others accused people of rationalizing the situation.

In the midst of this debate, the company could have easily dropped *Below The Line*, hiding from the problem and its consequences. In fact, at first, the statisticians waved away the problem, arguing that even if a problem existed, the vendor, not the company, could be at fault. Also, in light of all the confusing and inconclusive data on the diode, the company could ask the Food and Drug Administration (FDA) to monitor the product, thus temporarily taking CPI off the hook. Why shouldn't company employees just wait for the company's officers to tell them what to do? Why shouldn't CPI just wait to see if its customers experienced any problems with the product, hoping, of course, that nothing would go wrong? After all, no defibrillator unit had actually failed in any patient who had had it implanted.

Since CPI was working to create greater accountability throughout the organization at the time, they avoided getting stuck in the victim cycle and quickly made an *Above The Line* commitment to its business and its customers. The senior management team recognized that getting stuck *Below The Line* would waste critical time and could compromise physician and patient trust in CPI. Together, the senior team acknowledged that the diode issue had to be resolved, accepted the fact that it could not have come at a worse time, and agreed that it must do everything to resolve the issue. Their ability to *See It* empowered the rest of the organization to move from paralysis, finger-pointing, and confusion to a level of organizational accountability that allowed the entire organization to "own" the company's circumstances.

Now, with a high level of ownership spreading among the senior team and the whole organization, CPI stood ready to *Solve It*. As groups and teams throughout the company worked on solving the problem, they constantly asked the question, "What else can we do to achieve the result," until it became commonplace for individuals to break the news that a desired path of progress had become blocked or that the necessary resources had not come into play. As a result, the company eventually identified a few viable options that could yield the results the company desired, the best of which entailed removing the faulty diode from the faulty product. Having reached this conclusion, CPI finally stood ready to *Do It*, despite one remaining challenge: FDA approval.

Manifesting the highest degree of accountability, the senior team aligned CPI's management ranks behind the objectives and schedule for developing and introducing the diode-free defibrillator, communicating their plans and expectations throughout the company and providing vital information updates as implementation proceeded. To overcome the hurdle of FDA approval, CPI provided early supplemental information to the FDA on the

diode-free defibrillator; then the company began building the
new defibrillator even before FDA approval so that it could put
it on the market the instant the FDA granted its approval. The
early supplemental information to the FDA, combined with
CPI's honest reports about the situation and its decision to
design out the diode, engendered trust at the FDA, trust that CPI
was trying with all its might to do the right thing for patients.
That trust encouraged the FDA to work closely with CPI to
achieve premarket approval for the new defibrillator in just two
weeks. In the end, CPI replaced all the units currently implanted
in patients as physicians recommended doing so, and the company quickly created a strong inventory of the new product in
record time.

Without question, the diode problem created a difficult and
costly episode in CPI's recent history, but to the credit of Jay
Graf, his senior team, and all the people who work at CPI, they
never wavered from their commitment to stay *Above The Line*,
except for a few momentary dips along the way. CPI could easily have spent its time, energy, and resources deflecting blame and
drafting politically correct explanations rather than resolving to
stay *Above The Line* and *Do It*. CPI did what many organizations
fail to do. It overcame the gravitational pull of the victim cycle
and moved resolutely from "solving it" to "doing it," despite all
the associated risks. Its actions paid off, not only in terms of satisfied customers, a cooperative government agency, more quality
conscious suppliers, and fully accountable employees, but also in
terms of the inner power, confidence, and peace that only come
from doing what it takes to get the result. CPI may still suffer the
lingering consequences of the diode problem, but the entire company will face the future with a greatly strengthened corporate
culture, driven first and foremost by a sense of complete accountability.

The benefits of exercising the means to *Do It* were readily
seen in the story of a young business school graduate who we will

call Terry. Terry was just out of graduate school with his MBA and was interviewed by the director of development of a mid-sized company for a position in their product development organization. During the interviews, the director told Terry that his experience in graduate school was just what the company was looking for. In fact, he promised this young man that if he were to come on board, he would be given a team to work with, a budget, and the time necessary to lead the product development effort. Needless to say, Terry enthusiastically accepted the job opportunity with a great deal of confidence. He knew from interviews with people in the company that he had skills and knowledge beyond the capabilities of people currently in the organization.

Things unfolded just as the director had suggested they would. Upon beginning work, Terry was given a budget, a timeline, a project team, and all the freedom he could have ever desired to make decisions and put his knowledge to work. Although others could be heard to mumble about why someone just out of school would be given such an opportunity, the director outwardly manifested his confidence and faith in Terry's ability to pull it off.

Over the next few months, Terry's team worked very hard at developing the product. They found that co-locating (moving people from different functional areas in the company out of their respective departments and into the same working area) helped them focus and not get distracted by other daily issues facing the company. Things were developing quite nicely, and Terry was feeling fully empowered, even to the point that when people, including the President of the company, would ask him how it was going, he would simply respond that it was going great, "wait till you see what we're developing, it is everything you wanted and more." Given that this was his first real management opportunity, Terry was determined to meet the time line and deliver the promised product as agreed.

To reach the milestone which the Director had set, the team worked around the clock. They would even take turns sleeping on the couch in one of the conference rooms. Never had the individuals on the team worked so hard and with so much enthusiasm. Each of them believed that this is what the company expected. As time passed, the need for the product had become more apparent. Everyone in the company anxiously awaiting the completed project.

The morning of the deadline came and the team was ready to unveil its work. Having worked the previous 2 days straight, members of the teams were tired, but their enthusiasm and excitement about making the date and completing the project with what they felt was an even better than expected outcome filled them with energy. They met with the director of development in his office. It was readily apparent that it was a busy morning. The director was feverishly working at his desk. He looked up at the clock when the team entered his office and inquired as to what they needed. They eagerly replied that they had finished the project and had a written presentation with all the information regarding the new product. To the team's surprise, and to Terry's utter frustration, the director looked up and said, "Thank you, I will get to it as soon as I can. Do you need anything else?" Stunned, the team said "no." Confused at the director's response, the team marched out of his office. Quickly, the confusion turned to frustration and then anger. Making matters even worse, not another word was heard from the director regarding the project in the days following.

A week later, Terry asked the director what he thought of the work he and his team had done. The director replied that he had not been able to look over the material because he had misplaced it. He would need another copy.

Terry could not believe what had happened. He went back to the team, dismayed by what he had heard. When he told the team what had happened, it seemed that a mutiny of sorts was in the making. People began talking about updating their resumes and looking for other opportunities. Terry felt he had been "had." If ever someone felt like a legitimate victim, it was Terry. He hesitated telling other people about the story, after all, who would believe it? It did not take long for word to get around the company that senior management was not pleased with the efforts of Terry and his team. Terry could not remember being more unfairly treated in his entire life. What's more, others in the company seemed to accept what the director and others were saying about Terry's efforts. No one really seemed to question what was being said or even asked to see the team's work.

As with many MBA's out of school only a year or so, Terry began considering his options. He began talking to classmates about opportunities in their organizations, trying to get a feeling for what the job market was like. However, as Terry began thinking about the situation, he realized that if it happened here, it could happen somewhere else. If he walked away a "victim," who's to say it would not happen again? So Terry resolved to move *Above The Line*. He knew that it would not be easy, but he also knew he had to do it.

As Terry took the *See It* step, he began talking to others in the company about what had happened. As he asked for their opinions and perspectives, he learned some interesting things. First, he found out that the company was on the verge of collapse as a result of some failed product introductions. Having focused solely on their development efforts, the team was quite unaware of the severity of the situation. Right in the middle of all the turmoil was the director of development who remained responsible not only for the problem, but also for coming up with the solution. As far as the director was concerned, Terry's project stood near the bottom of the list, something Terry was surprised to find out because he thought the team's efforts would capture the attention of the company. After all, his team considered the project "central" to the company's future. It seemed that everyone in development was working night and day on solving the urgent product problems. But Terry, having kept himself and the team fairly insulated, was not fully aware of the circumstances.

To make matters worse, the day Terry's team made the presentation, he received feedback that his boss, the director, had six months to turn things around "or else!" The director had just bought a new large home near corporate headquarters—the prospect of being out of work or even needing to move and uproot his family was very distracting and discomforting. Further, Terry was told by more than one person that many in the department resented the team's efforts. The team would never share any of their work or even ask for input. They were secretive about everything related to the project. The culture of the department had been one of a high level of teamwork, even to the point that you could leave something out on your desk that you had been working on and others strolling by could stop and look at it and give input. Teamwork was key to the way things were done in this organization.

After having heard the feedback, Terry could not believe what he had done. Somehow, he had managed to alienate the entire department, which would explain why no one had any sympathy for him or the team and why no one even questioned the unsubstantiated opinions of the director. While it was clear to Terry that the director could have helped the team better understand what they should have done differently, it was also clear to Terry that they had put up huge barriers that prevented people from seeing that they could be part of the solution. Terry began to realize that maybe he had not been as "had" as he first thought.

As he moved to the *Own It* step he began to recount more fully in his mind the things he could have done differently that could have made a big difference: understanding the teamwork culture of the department, creating open communication with his peers, asking for feedback as he went along, and paying more attention to what else was going on in the department and in the company. As Terry came to realize that maybe he had some accountability in all this too, he came to feel more strongly that he wanted to stay and change things. He wanted to work it through and be successful. After meeting with his team and talking through his new insights, he found everyone able to easily list those things that could have been done differently and produced a better outcome. Terry, a little surprised at how easy it was for everyone to tick these things off, began to coach the group in the same way he coached himself. Everyone responded with the determination to do the things necessary to make things better.

As Terry moved to the *Solve It* mode, he knew he would have to demonstrate to the department that he was a team player and that he was interested in more than just seeing himself succeed. He also knew that this would take some time. He determined that he would need to sit down with the director and discuss what had happened and what he had learned from the experience.

As he considered his circumstances, Terry knew that he had climbed *Above The Line* by taking the *See It*, *Own It*, and *Solve It* *Steps To Accountability*. While it was difficult to hear the feedback and perceptions of other people and equally difficult to acknowledge that there were things that he had done to help create this situation, he also knew that there was a way to change how people felt about him and what he had to offer. All that awaited him now was to *Do It!*, the fourth and final step to accountability. Terry knew full well that there was a huge difference between "knowing what to do" and actually "doing it." While he knew there were some risks in acknowledging he had made some mistakes, particularly when many had predicted that this young MBA would not be able to deliver, he also knew that if he were going to stay with the company with hope of succeeding, he must implement his plan to meet with his director and to find new opportunities to demonstrate he was a team player.

And so he did. Having moved fully *Above The Line* by taking the final step to *Do It!*, Terry was able to take the steps to change the way people viewed him which enabled him to grow with the organization. By taking an accountable point of view of his organizational experience, he was able to overcome the forces that would drag him *Below The Line* and keep him feeling like a "victim" of his circumstances, never able to learn what he could do differently in the future to succeed. Over time, Terry brought his new product knowledge and innovative ideas into proper focus and application, making him a part of the larger team. Terry eventually became director of development within the organization where he spends many an hour coaching new employees to *See It*, *Own It*, *Solve It*, and, most importantly, *DO IT!*

▲
PREPARING TO APPLY ACCOUNTABILITY THROUGHOUT YOUR ORGANIZATION

In the end, Dorothy exercised the means to *Do It*. Only when she recognized and utilized the skills she possessed all along could she cement her own accountability for her circumstances and for the result she wanted. With new-found determination, she finally clicked her heels and returned to Kansas. While Dorothy had worn the magic slippers throughout her journey, she had not tapped their power until she had learned *The Oz Principle*: people hold inside themselves the power to rise above their circumstances and get the results they want.

Accountable people have grasped this principle for centuries. For instance, we read in the Bible a statement which was made over 2,000 years ago: "Arise, for this matter belongeth unto thee…be of good courage, and do it!"

W. E. Henley, the English poet, characterized the determination not to fall victim to circumstances by remaining committed to manage one's own fate. During one of the most trying periods of his life, after losing his left leg to tuberculosis of the bone and while fighting to save his right leg at the Royal Infirmary, he composed what has become one of his most famous poems, Invictus:

Out of the night that covers me,
Black as the Pit, from pole to pole,
I thank whatever gods may be
For my unconquerable soul.

In the fell clutch of circumstance
I have not winced nor cried aloud.
Under the bludgeonings of chance
My head is bloody, but unbowed.

Beyond this place of wrath and tears
Looms the horror of the shade,
And yet the menace of the years

Finds, and shall find me, unafraid.

It matters not how strait the gate,
How charged with punishments the scroll,
I am the master of my fate:
I am the captain of my soul.

Back home in Kansas, Dorothy would never be the same because she had learned, through her arduous journey, that she was the master of her own fate. Breathlessly, she told her family and friends about the marvelous things she had experienced and learned in the land of Oz, a sharing you can now commence yourself as you apply *The Oz Principle* throughout your organization, the subject of Part III.

RESULTS THROUGH COLLECTIVE ACCOUNTABILITY: HELPING YOUR ORGANIZATION PERFORM *ABOVE THE LINE*SM

PART 3

Getting your entire organization **Above The Line** *requires helping every employee accept both individual and joint accountability for results, which demands effective* **Above The Line** *leadership. In Part III, we show you how to incorporate* **The Oz Principle** *into your own leadership, implement it in your own organization, and apply it to today's toughest business and management issues. In the end, we think you'll agree with us that accountability for results rests at the core of every business success.*

THE GOOD WITCH GLINDA: MASTERING *ABOVE THE LINE*ᔆᴹ LEADERSHIP

▼

Dorothy then gave her the Golden Cap, and the Witch said to the Scarecrow, "What will you do when Dorothy has left us?"

"I will return to the Emerald City," he replied, "for Oz has made me its ruler and the people like me. The only thing that worries me is how to cross the hill of the Hammer-Heads."

"By means of the Golden Cap I shall command the Winged Monkeys to carry you to the gates of the Emerald City," said Glinda, "for it would be a shame to deprive the people of so wonderful a ruler."

"Am I really wonderful?" asked the Scarecrow.

"You are unusual," replied Glinda.

THE WIZARD OF OZ
By L. Frank Baum

203

Like a wise and powerful mentor, the good witch Glinda watched over and nurtured Dorothy, the Scarecrow, the Tin Woodsman, and the Lion as they journeyed toward the realization that they already possessed the power to get the results they sought, never intervening unless absolutely necessary. Glinda didn't tell them everything at the beginning because she knew how important it was for them to develop their own sense of powerfulness, but neither did she refuse to help when she saw that the companions had reached a point where they could advantageously apply the resources she could bring to bear. By so doing, she symbolizes the leader who operates from *Above The Line*.

▲
_____
*ABOVE THE LINE*ˢᴹ LEADERSHIP

So far in this book we've described how you can get *Above The Line*. Now, we'd like to discuss how you as a leader can help other people discover the secret of *The Oz Principle* and move *Above The Line* to rise above their circumstances and get the results they want.

Above The Line leaders display a number of personal characteristics: while they may fall *Below The Line* on occasion, they don't stay there for long; they actively seek and provide feedback; they hold themselves to the same accountability standard as everyone else; and they desire to help others rise and stay *Above The Line*. Motivated by a desire to empower the human spirit, *Above The Line* leaders work hard to free people who cage themselves in the victim cycle. Consider this metaphor of a caged animal:

> A Bengal tiger prowls its narrow cage. Yellow eyes smoulder with angry fire, the switching tail bespeaks an energy too long confined. Now and then the cat rears back to slap the steel bars, but slowly, as the weeks pass, it ceases even that token rebellion and lies down in weariness. Its once-

bright spirit dimmed, its once-mighty body robbed of vitality, it gazes beyond its small world, dreaming perhaps of a freer one.

The image of an imprisoned creature, unable to exercise its basic nature, aptly applies to many people in our society who have become caged by the victim cycle and who fail to get results because they cannot or do not accept accountability for better results in the future. They have become immobilized. It's saddening to see any creature with pent-up potential languishing in a cage, unable to pursue and accomplish its dreams. It's depressing, too, to see people in organizations with their spirits locked up and diminishing. Imagine, however, the caged spirit free at last, no longer a victim, regaining responsibility for its own life. Imagine, too, people in organizations finally unfettered, reclaiming their own accountability for results. This dream motivates *Above The Line* leaders, who work to free others from their cages so they can regain responsibility for their own lives.

In a recent survey of 726 corporate directors conducted by Korn-Ferry, the international executive recruiting and organizational consulting firm, respondents indicated they would be more likely to remove a chief executive officer for leadership flaws than for poor financial returns. This increasing emphasis on effective leadership at the top has been further augmented by the power shift taking place in most organizations in which senior executives seek to spread decision-making authority more widely to the lowest levels of the enterprise. As a result, *Above The Line* leadership is becoming a requirement, not merely an advantage, for most organizations.

In this chapter we want to share with you the experiences we have gained helping people become effective *Above The Line* leaders. First, of course, you must feel motivated to become such a leader. Assuming you have experienced the power and freedom that comes from rising *Above The Line,* you must now decide whether or not you genuinely want to help others accomplish the same. If you want to brow-beat them with your new-found knowledge, compete against them with your superior account-ability, control them for your own personal gain, or ridicule their *Below The Line* behavior, then this chapter will not interest you. If, on the other hand, you want to help others escape their *Below The Line* patterns of behavior, then you should find this chapter especially rewarding.

RECOGNIZING WHEN IT'S TIME TO INTERVENE

First and foremost, *Above The Line* leaders recognize when other people are stuck *Below The Line* and are failing to obtain the results they want. By this point you should have developed an increased ability to identify *Below The Line* attitudes and behavior in yourself and others, and you should have come to appreciate how people can develop elaborate explanations for their behavior. Such "victim stories" can make it difficult for you to discern when it's time to intervene.

At IBM it became too difficult for management and employees to recognize the illusions of their own victim stories, so John Akers and other executives failed to intervene soon enough to get the organization and its people back up *Above The Line*. Now, Louis Gerstner, IBM's new CEO, will demonstrate whether he can turn things around. Many analysts believe IBM faces three major issues: as many as 100,000 too many people, products and services that are late to market and cost too much, and an inward-focused culture that has established an "IBM Way" that isn't working anymore.

According to a watchful Steven Jobs, chairman of NeXT Computer, as reported in a *USA Today* article, "There are a lot of talented people in IBM if management would just tap the talent it has. If [Gerstner] can bring out the technical talent already in that company and find the right people to trust, he might do fine." In other words, if Gerstner can get IBMers to stop preparing their victim stories and rise *Above The Line,* he has a lot of talent to draw upon to put IBM on the path to renewal and transformation, but that won't happen without solid *Above The Line* leadership from Louis Gerstner himself. However, in our view, the key to an IBM turnaround is getting every IBMer *Above The Line* as soon as possible, which means quickly developing and deploying a cadre of *Above The Line* leaders throughout the company.

Above The Line leaders risk their own comfort and security by going beyond symptoms to the core problems that spring from a lack of accountability. When they see *Below The Line* behavior, they rip away the disguises worn by self-proclaimed victims to reveal the underlying problem. Unwilling to let themselves or others be fooled by the masks people wear to hide the reality of a situation, they drive relentlessly to determine the real reasons why people aren't achieving results. Not even the most elaborate and creative victim stories fool them into thinking that if someone else would just do the right thing everything would be fine. They understand that symptomatic cures continue to hide and even exacerbate the problem, not solve it. They do not get trapped in the excessive activity syndromes, they are not blinded by the smoke screen of programmatic solutions offered by organizational special interest groups desiring to mask their lack of results; they are not persuaded by the many voices that would have them believe "if only we did this or that" everything would be fine. They understand that changes in structures and systems often only hide the real problems—they have the ability to rise above the haze to see things as they really are.

When *Above The Line* leaders hear about a particular problem such as "we are not producing quality products," they don't bemoan that fact, but move immediately to discern to what extent people at all levels of the organization have failed to shoulder responsibility for the quality of their own individual contributions. Such leaders know that whenever results fail to materialize, they must look behind the excuses and finger-pointing to the real reason why people are operating *Below The Line*. When they detect *Below The Line* behavior, they begin coaching the person or people out of the victim cycle, a process we will explore later in this chapter. By recognizing when it's time to intervene and helping others to rise above the victim cycle, *Above The Line* leaders can help people focus on the right issues in the right way. Then, and only then, can the group and the organization begin creating a better future.

▲
_____

NOT ALLOWING YOURSELF TO TAKE ACCOUNTABILITY TO THE EXTREME

Continually seeking out *Below The Line* behavior in others can create dire consequences if you push it too far. Any virtue or strength taken to an extreme can eventually become a vice that actually gets in the way of achieving the performance and results you desire. One leader likened such an over-preoccupation to persistently pounding on a single piano key to the irritation and dismay of everyone present. In such a situation, the leader's effectiveness diminishes, and he or she loses the benefit and strength that comes from calling upon a broad range of resources, skills, and solutions. If you define everything that happens as an accountability problem, you may misinterpret the complete picture. However, if you fail to discern the accountability factor in every problem, you will also make a mistake. Skillful intervention requires a delicate, yet firm, touch.

Over the years we have watched people take accountability to an extreme as they tried to force people to accept accountability for anything and everything that occurs in their lives. This may sound outlandish, but such extremists go so far as to argue that if a pedestrian walking down the sidewalk gets hit by a runaway car, the pedestrian is to blame because he or she chose to walk down that street at that particular time, instead of taking an alternate route. This is simply not true. What *is* true is that the pedestrian or the pedestrian's survivors cannot get their lives back on track unless they accept responsibility for moving beyond the accident to a better future.

Additionally, some people go so far as to blame a person's illness on his or her lack of accountability in working out the emotional issues and stresses of life. While a certain level of physical illness may result from pent-up anxieties or unresolved issues, it is both erroneous and destructive, in our view, to believe that all illness, tragedy, misfortune, and calamity occur as a result of something a person did or did not do. *The Oz Principle* teaches that people's circumstances result not *just* from what they do or did (although a person should always identify how his or her action or inaction have contributed to current circumstances) but also from things outside their control. However, rather than continuing to suffer as a victim of circumstance, *The Oz Principle* shows people how to overcome those circumstances and achieve the results they desire. Even in the most extreme cases where people have been severely victimized, such individuals can be accountable for how they allow those past circumstances to affect the rest of their lives.

People can also take accountability to the extreme by trying to control other people. Operating like self-appointed "thought police," such people try to force people *Above The Line* into a world they themselves have created to suit their own beliefs and prejudices. As we mentioned in Chapter 1, a *Time* magazine article recently labeled these overzealous extremists as "busybodies." No one can or should try to force another person to be more effective, more righteous, more knowledgeable, more productive, friendlier, braver, more trustworthy, or in any other way more politically or socially "correct." Coach them, encourage them, teach them, give them feedback, admonish them, love them and lead them, but don't try to coerce them. In *Time*'s article, author John Elson tells the story of a Los Angeles security guard who was fired for being overweight: "Jesse Mercado was dismissed from his job as a security guard at the *Times* despite an excellent performance record." No one should be removed from or refused a job because they violate some whimsical, unprincipled standard of correctness, and, in Mercado's case the courts upheld that view: "Overweight Mercado sued, won and got a judgment of more than $500,000, plus a return to his old post."

RECOGNIZING THAT YOU CANNOT CONTROL EVERYTHING

Wise *Above The Line* leaders, on the other hand, know that a delicate touch works best when things lie completely or partially beyond one's control, both in life and at work. They recognize that many things lie outside their control, including but not limited to, weather, natural disasters, other people's choices, taxes, global economy, physical appearance, the family a person inherits, place of birth, the boss, the parent company, size or makeup of the organization, competitors' moves, government regulations, and so on. However, too many leaders today worry about things over which they have very little control or influence as shown in a *Wall Street Journal* survey of chief executive officers, which identified what keeps today's CEOs up at night worrying. The top five vote-getters in the "worry" survey received more than 50 percent of the votes. They were, in order, 1) the economy, 2) the competition, 3) the political environment, 4) the employees, and 5) government regulation.

The wise leader separates those factors that remain beyond his or her control from those he or she can do something about. For example, since you cannot control whether economic conditions will be favorable or unfavorable, spending a lot of time complaining about the economy will only squander your time and effort. However, if you spent your time trying to develop strategies you could implement under a variety of economic scenarios, you will probably increase the likelihood of success in a significant way.

Effective *Above The Line* leaders quickly recognize the "uncontrollable" issues, separating them from the controllable ones, thus enabling others both to avoid falling into the *Below The Line* trap of complaining or worrying about what they cannot affect and to resist rising too zealously high *Above The Line* in an attempt to refashion everything and everyone to their own liking.

Before we offer a model of accountable leadership, we'd like you to write down a few of the "uncontrollables" that currently receive too much of your attention at work or at home. Try to confine your list to characteristics, traits, situations, and events over which you truly can exert little or no influence. Creating such a list will help you isolate those aspects of your work and personal life over which you really can exert some influence. As you ponder your list, consider how much more productive and effective you could be if you stopped getting stuck *Below The Line* worrying about what you cannot control.

At one of our training sessions a woman told the group about her experience as a young girl listening to her father recount his workday at the dinner table. With great emotion, her father would often describe all the day's ills with particular emphasis on the "miscarriages of justice" that had been wrought against him. While the family ate, he worked hard to convince his wife and children that he had been dealt with unfairly and that his boss was an unappreciative, unfeeling, and unrighteous man. As dessert arrived, everyone tried to make father feel better by confirming his perceptions and agreeing that he had been victimized. Expressions of sympathy and support for father allowed the family to continue with its nightly activities. Looking back, she realized that her mother and the rest of the family had not done her father or themselves any favor by accepting his *Below The Line* explanations of life. Her father's unhappiness and the resultant disruption in the family were high prices to pay for failing to acknowledge that much of what happens in life lies outside a person's span of control or influence. Ironically, many studies have indicated that over 90 percent of the things people worry about are completely outside their control; however, being accountable means worrying about things you can do something about. Imagine what additional good might have come into the life of the woman in our training session had her family's dinner discussions been more focused on what could be done in each of the family member's lives instead of on what was outside her father's control.

Correctly understood and properly applied, accountability is an empowering principle that can give people a new sense of control and influence over their circumstances so they can achieve the results they desire. Ultimately, helping people get *Above The Line* involves assisting them to *See It*, *Own It*, *Solve It*, and *Do It*.

PROVIDING A MODEL FOR OTHERS

As people seek to create accountability in their organization, it is critical to remember that they must always provide a model for those with whom they work or associate. It is imperative that they remain accountable for the consequences that flow from whatever role-model they provide. If it is a negative model, then they are likely to take not only themselves, but also the entire organization *Below The Line*. For example, in a *Wall Street Journal* article entitled, "Bosses Who Deflect Blame Put Employees in A Tough Spot," Joann Lublin discusses one such negative role-model— working for a boss who blames his or her personal blunders on subordinates. Lublin states, "Of all problem bosses, a 'blamer' is among the toughest to handle. Limiting damage from misplaced blame requires delicate judgments, sharp bureaucratic instincts and varying levels of risk tolerance. It's no wonder that many people end up doing nothing more than grinding their teeth." We have interviewed thousands of individuals who state emphatically that a boss who deflects blame is a boss you don't want.

Such bosses that lead from *Below The Line* may in some cases experience short-term gain. In the long run, however, such *Below The Line* behavior will only result in the loss of the trust, cooperation and focus needed to maximize results. This model of leadership will ultimately and consistently give people permission to fall into the conscious-and-careful mode of "cover your tail." As Lublin advises, "A paper trail also can vindicate an unfairly accused subordinate, especially if the mistake comes up later during a performance appraisal. Dr. Grothe, the Boston psychologist, proposes that you give yourself an account of an incident and verify its date by sending yourself a certified letter and keeping the envelope sealed. 'It's a little form of self-protection,' he says." Imagine the time, resources, and energy people waste trying to protect themselves from such *Below The Line* behavior of bosses.

Successful *Above The Line* leaders become models of accountability for everyone within their sphere of influence. In this sense, leaders must remain accountable for how they model accountability. If, like Glinda, a leader knows when to intervene and when to hold back, he or she will avoid particularly ugly situations in which others chafe under the leader's constant follow-up on their activities in a misguided effort to make sure they are honoring their commitment to accountability. In such cases, the leader has forgotten to adhere to a well-tempered model of accountability. Such behavior will only undermine people's confidence and even infuriate them. Again, good leadership demands a delicate, yet firm, touch.

We read with great interest Noel Tichy and Stratford Sherman's book *Control Your Destiny or Someone Else Will,* about how Jack Welch has been transforming General Electric since 1981. The book struck a chord with us because its core message

promoted accountability: "The remarkable story of GE's revital-
ization teaches lessons essential for the well-being of managers
and layperson alike. Control your destiny is more than a useful
business idea. For every individual, corporation, and nation, it is
the essence of responsibility and the most basic requirement for
success. As the world endlessly changes, so must we. The greatest power we have is the ability to envision our own fate—and to
change ourselves." The secret to GE's transformation lies in the
Above The Line leadership of Jack Welch, who set as his overriding goal empowering his people with the values of "self-con-
fidence, candor, and an unflinching willingness to face reality,
even when it's painful." Even though we have cited examples of
General Electric operating *Below The Line,* Jack Welch offers a
compelling example of *Above The Line* leadership because he
models *Above The Line* accountability in his own life, even when
a problem besets him or his company. Like every leader, he
knows he's not perfect. The following excerpt from his own
words at the end of *Control Your Destiny or Someone Else Will*
reveals his own misgivings as well as his personal commitment
and conviction to staying *Above The Line*:

> I've made my share of mistakes—plenty of them—but my biggest
> mistake by far was not moving faster. Pulling off an old Band-Aid
> one hair at a time hurts a lot more than a sudden yank. Of course
> you want to avoid breaking things or stretching the organization
> too far—but generally, human nature holds you back. You want
> to be liked, to be thought of as reasonable. So you don't move as
> fast as you should. Besides hurting more, it costs you competi-
> tiveness.
>
> Everything should have been done in half the time. When you're
> running an institution like this you're always scared at first.
> You're afraid you'll break it. People don't think about leaders this
> way, but it's true. Everyone who's running something goes home
> at night and wrestles with the same fear: Am I going to be the one
> who blows this place up? In retrospect, I was too cautious and too
> timid.

Effective leaders like Jack Welch strive to keep themselves and their organizations climbing the accountability ladder, applying a delicate, firm touch whenever they or others fall *Below The Line* momentarily. The following list identifies ways in which you can demonstrate the right touch to people in your organization:

▼ You constantly ask yourself the question, "What else can I do to achieve the result I desire?"

▼ You ask people to give you feedback on whether they perceive you operating *Above The Line* on a particular issue.

▼ You provide honest, yet encouraging, feedback to others when they drop *Below The Line.*

▼ You actively observe activities and offer coaching, rather than wait for others to report on their progress on any given project or assignment. You never wait to report progress to your own superiors.

▼ You focus your discussions around things that you and others can affect and do rather than on things that no one can either affect or do.

▼ You acknowledge when you fall *Below The Line* and do not react defensively when others point that fact out to you.

Once you master these traits and personally exhibit and model *Above The Line* behavior yourself, you can begin successfully coaching others to do likewise.

COACHING PEOPLE *ABOVE THE LINE*ᔆᴹ

Creating accountability in others is a process and doesn't happen as a result of some singular event. Many leaders mistakenly think that once their people have been exposed to the concept of accountability and understand it, they will never fall *Below The Line* again. This "event" approach to accountability, the notion that accountability happens at an identifiable moment, doesn't work.

Leaders who make this mistake tend to use accountability as a hammer, nailing people when they fall *Below The Line* in an unending game of "I gotcha." Such hammering will only propel people back into the victim cycle. Therefore, you must help people feel empowered by the concept of accountability, not trapped by it. While it is not effective to allow victim stories and victim behaviors to go unchecked, you must bear in mind that the process of coaching people *Above The Line* requires patience, nurturing, and appropriate follow-up. Keep in mind that the people you want to help climb the *Steps to Accountability* have developed ingrained perspectives and personalities they cannot quickly discard or consider from a new viewpoint, especially if they feel cornered by an ever-vigilant "Big Brother." Too heavy a hand tends to make people feel excluded from the process ("I'm right, you're wrong"), while a firm, delicate touch helps people feel included in the process ("We've got a problem, let's figure out how to *Solve It*).

A friend of ours, Jim, recently told us how betrayed he felt over a particular experience he had earlier in his career. Working as an accountant in a well-known regional accounting firm in Boston, he began looking, as so often happens in successful accounting firms, for opportunities to move over to the controllership of one of his firm's client organizations. Before long, an opportunity for just such a career move arose with a company he greatly respected. Eagerly, he started the interviewing process with the chief financial officer who was leaving the company and then continued interviewing with the new CFO who would be joining the company from the outside in a few months. The interviews went well and Jim landed the job. Excited about his new responsibilities as controller of a $35 million company, he relished the initial autonomy he enjoyed. He was actually running the financial side of the house by himself while he awaited the arrival of the new CFO. Jim felt good about his future. He felt like the sky was the limit.

He dug into his new job by thoroughly reviewing the company's financial statements. As he did so, he discovered that there was a great deal of work to be done. He started in on the financial statements which were poorly organized. When he approached the outgoing CFO with a few questions concerning the statements, he found that his concerns were deflected and treated lightly. The CFO told Jim that his questions could wait until next week. After all, there was no emergency and it would take some time for Jim to get into the swing of things.

The next Monday the outgoing CFO met with Jim again and quickly reviewed the company's books. He asked Jim to sign his final check. And since the check only amounted to a few thousand dollars, and given his tenure as CFO, Jim didn't think twice about handing him the check and wishing him well. To his alarm, as he dug further into the records over the next week, he found that the former CFO had persuaded three other people to sign his "last" paycheck. With continued scrutiny of the books over the next couple of months, Jim uncovered evidence that the former CFO had embezzled over $1 million through phony purchasing requisitions.

As he gathered evidence of the former CFO's wrongdoing, he shared it with the new CFO who had begun coming into the office one day a week while still wrapping up his job with his former employer. The new CFO asked him to keep the situation to himself, and not even share it with the president of the company, until they had constructed an airtight case. Jim worked many 14-hour days and weekends trying to unravel the scheme and amass the necessary evidence against the former CFO and his collaborators.

When the president of the company stopped by one morning to speak with Jim, he casually mentioned that he suspected his former CFO of embezzlement but still couldn't believe the man could have actually done it. To Jim's utter disbelief, the president praised the new CFO for uncovering the mess, and wondered why Jim had not seen it himself. Pointing an accusing finger at his new controller, he said, "You have been here three months, Jim. Why in the world didn't you uncover any of this?" Shocked by the revelation that his new CFO had taken credit for all his hard work, he vowed he would never trust another superior.

Jim's story is familiar to many people in organizations who have found themselves victimized by someone in authority over them. As an *Above The Line* leader you cannot assume that the people over whom you have responsibility will automatically trust your coaching efforts to get them *Above The Line*. Instead, your people may suspect you of having ulterior motives, particularly if you have participated with them in preparing victim stories in the past or if you have not previously established feedback as a pattern of communication in your relationship with them. Keep this in mind the next time you attempt to coach someone *Above The Line*.

Whenever you hear a victim story or a *Below The Line* excuse, we suggest you use the following five key steps to coach that person away from reacting and toward learning:

1. **Listening.** Look for instances of victim behavior, and when you engage someone in a discussion of their victim story (for the purpose of coaching them) or hear *Below The Line* excuses, listen sympathetically to what they have to say.

2. **Acknowledging.** Acknowledge the victim facts and obstacles that someone thinks has kept him or her from getting desired results. Show the person that you understand their feelings and know yourself how hard it is to overcome those feelings. Agree that the challenges are real or that bad things do happen to good people.

3. **Asking.** If someone seems deeply attached to a victim story or a *Below The Line* excuse, gently move the discussion toward the accountable version of the story. Continually pose the question: "What else can you do to achieve the result you desire or overcome the circumstance that plagues you?"

4. **Coaching.** Use the steps to accountability to help a person identify where he or she currently stands and where the person needs to go to obtain desired results. Take a few minutes to explain *The Oz Principle* using the specific instance as an example, but also share an incident when you yourself got stuck *Below The Line.* Emphasize that falling *Below The Line* on occasion is only natural but staying there never yields results. Stress how rising *Above The Line* will produce positive outcomes. Walk through the *See It, Own It, Solve It,* and *Do It* steps. Then, adapt each of the *Steps To Accountability* to this particular situation.

5. **Committing.** Commit yourself to helping a person create an *Above The Line* action plan and encourage him or her to report on their activities and progress. Don't end a coaching session without setting a specific time for follow-up, allowing sufficient time, but not too much time, to elapse. If the person does not approach you at the appointed time, take the initiative yourself. During these follow-up sessions, continue to look, listen, acknowledge, ask, coach, and recommit. Provide honest, caring feedback about progress, and express congratulations for every improvement.

Once you begin coaching others *Above The Line* you will quickly see the value of a person's accounting for his or her progress.

ACCOUNTING FOR PROGRESS

In an ideal world it wouldn't be necessary for leaders to coach accountability because everyone would acknowledge their accountability in every situation. However, since this is not an ideal world, and since everyone is fallible, leaders must make coaching a daily habit. And while we have emphasized proactive coaching, which focuses on the present and the future, we have also come to appreciate the need for review of the past, what we call accounting for progress. When handled properly, an after-the-fact accounting can provide a person with an opportunity to measure progress toward results, learn from previous experience, establish a sense of accomplishment, and determine what else can be done to get the desired results.

While most leaders intuitively know the value of urging people to account for their actions, many often fail to do it well. Too many leaders

▼ Wait for their people to do the right thing. Rather than asking for regular reports, they let them go, hoping that people will automatically measure their own progress.

▼ Avoid unpleasant confrontation that might possibly result from an unacceptable report. They fear that such a confrontation will damage their relationships with people.

▼ Allow skeletons to remain in the closet, rather than squarely facing troublesome issues that have gotten in the way of results. They assume that people simply cannot surmount some issues and therefore choose to ignore them.

▼ Tolerate excuses as true representations of reality when they know in their hearts that the excuses prevent people from accepting the true reality of a situation. They allow this to happen in the hope that the problem will simply fix itself over time.

- ▼ Let their other responsibilities consume all their time. They don't make regular accounting a top priority. They simply wait for the results to speak for themselves.

- ▼ Fail to convince people of the importance of reporting on progress. Their own low priority becomes their people's low priority.

- ▼ Insufficiently clarify their expectations or inadequately explain the purpose of accounting. They accept vague reports because they have set vague goals.

- ▼ Do not set a specific reporting timetable or schedule. They let people decide when and how they will account for progress.

- ▼ Fail to use accounting sessions to coach individuals toward desired outcomes. They simply applaud or criticize progress.

- ▼ Do not understand that holding people accountable need not be a negative, hand-wringing, knuckle-crunching, head-bashing, life-threatening experience for those involved. They make sessions so painful that people come to dread them.

If you can overcome these common mistakes, you will obtain the tremendous benefits of effective accounting, which include pinpointing what else people can do to achieve desired results, disseminating vital information people can use to break down barriers to results, identifying legitimate needs for the organization, and helping people look forward to their accounting sessions as a positive personal and organizational experience.

Above The Line leaders both give and require *Above The Line* accounting. Note the differences between effective accounting and accounting that falls *Below The Line*:

From Above The Line[SM]	*From Below The Line*[SM]
▼ People report regularly and thoroughly.	▼ People report only when asked to do so.
▼ People analyze their activities in an effort to determine what more they can do to get results.	▼ People justify or explain their activities.
▼ People stand and deliver when it's time to report.	▼ People run and hide when it's time to report.
▼ People own their circumstances.	▼ People blame others for lack of results.
▼ People welcome feedback.	▼ People react defensively to suggestions for improvement.

If a leader accounts for progress from *Below The Line,* everyone else in the organization will do likewise, but if a leader always accounts for his or her own progress from *Above The Line,* everyone else will follow suit.

LEADING FROM *ABOVE THE LINE*[SM]

To help our clients master the art of accountable leadership we have constructed a checklist that covers the most important "do's" and "don't's" of *Above The Line* leadership behavior. Reviewing this list periodically should help you maintain a good example for your people.

ABOVE THE LINE[SM] LEADERSHIP CHECKLIST
▼

1. *I Do* model accountability and set an example.

   I Don't hold others accountable without holding myself equally responsible.

2. *I Do* allow people to drop *Below The Line* from time to time to vent their frustrations.

   I Don't let victim stories and *Below The Line* excuses go unchecked or unresolved.

3. *I Do* recognize victim stories and *Below The Line* excuses when I hear them.

   I Don't avoid my responsibility to hold people accountable and to expect *Above The Line* behavior.

4. *I Do* use accountability as a way to empower people toward results.

   I Don't use accountability as a hammer to nail people when I catch them functioning *Below The Line.*

5. *I Do* expect people to coach me to get *Above The Line* when necessary.

   I Don't expect people to coach me if I am not seeking their feedback.

6. *I Do* practice what I preach.

   I Don't get caught thinking that accountability is something everyone else should work on.

7. *I Do* avoid focusing solely on accountability to the exclusion of everything else.

   I Don't hold everyone accountable for everything all the time—I do understand the uncontrollables.

8. *I Do* coach people *Above The Line* by listening, acknowledging, asking, coaching, and committing.

   I Don't view accountability as a principle that people ought to immediately comprehend.

With effective *Above The Line* leadership skills you can begin moving your entire organization to higher levels of accountability. Before you move on, however, take a moment to consider how it took Dorothy and her companions a good deal of time to come to the realization that they possessed the power within themselves to get what they wanted. Glinda could have told them that at the beginning, but she wisely understood the value of the journey, that the best learning comes from struggle and hard work. As an *Above The Line* leader, you should apply your leadership in ways that will help people and groups in your organization learn best, which may mean allowing for more mistakes and setbacks and smaller triumphs than you would like. If you're patient, however, you will see fewer mistakes, shorter setbacks, and amazing triumphs.

THE EMERALD CITY AND BEYOND: GETTING YOUR ENTIRE ORGANIZATION ABOVE THE LINE^{SM}

Turning to the Tin Woodsman, she [Glinda] asked:

"What will become of you when Dorothy leaves this country?"

He leaned on his axe and thought a moment. Then he said,

"The Winkies were very kind to me, and wanted me to rule over them after the Wicked Witch died. I am fond of the Winkies, and if I could get back again to the country of the West I should like nothing better than to rule over them forever."

"My second command to the Winged Monkeys," said Glinda, "will be that they carry you safely to the land of the Winkies . . . and I am sure you will rule the Winkies wisely and well."

THE WIZARD OF OZ
By L. Frank Baum

The Tin Woodsman chose to share his new-found power with others. Such a choice represents the ultimate application of accountability, helping others in your organization move *Above The Line*. Regardless of your current position in your organization, you can begin to promote *The Oz Principle* by encouraging people to climb out of the victim cycle to begin ascending the *Steps To Accountability*. The entire organization can benefit from what you've learned: your superiors, your subordinates, your peers, and all the stakeholders both inside and outside your organization.

In this chapter, we will summarize the five key elements that should inform any effort to create and sustain an organization's ability to *See It, Own It, Solve It*, and *Do It*. With these six elements, you can build accountability into the structure, processes, culture, and very fabric of your organization:

1. Training for understanding.
2. Coaching accountability.
3. Asking *Above The Line* questions.
4. Pulling the corporate culture levers.
5. Utilizing the Commitment Process.
6. Spotting opportunities to get *Above The Line*.

These six elements apply to any kind of group setting, both professional and nonprofessional. Wherever you are involved with other people, you can use them to create a foundation of accountability upon which everyone involved can build toward the results the group wishes to accomplish.

TRAINING FOR UNDERSTANDING

Training people to understand the pivotal importance of accountability in getting results represents the first crucial challenge. Most likely, not everyone in your organization consciously appreciates the central role accountability plays in both personal and organizational performance. However, once people understand the danger of thinking and acting *Below The Line* and the benefits of moving *Above The Line,* they can begin applying accountability more broadly to what they do. Much like learning to see a glass of water as half full rather than half empty, once you've seen it that way, you tend to always see it that way. To accomplish such a shift in people's perspective, you can employ three steps: help people unlock their *Below The Line* paradigm, assist them in transitioning to the new view of accountability, and work to lock in the new *Above The Line* paradigm.

1. Unlocking the *Below The Line* Paradigm

Before you can implement an accountability program in your organization, you must determine how people in your organization currently understand and define accountability. You should acknowledge that people view accountability in different ways, and often with a negative slant. When we asked a number of people in an informal survey to define accountability, here's what they said:

> "Accountability means responsibility and obligation. It's when someone outlines what you are supposed to do in a job description and then rates you A, B or C."

> "Accountability means being willing to stand up and explain what you did."

> "Accountability is the same thing as supervision."

> "Accountability is reporting."

> "Accountability equals productivity."

> "Accountability is an explanation as to why you did what you did."

> "Accountability means finding out who is at fault when something goes wrong."

"Accountability means clear and measurable goals."

"Accountability is management driven: it's external, not internal."

"Accountability means reporting on actions, not results."

"Accountability is a negative concept to me."

"Accountability means carrying a burden."

"Accountability is a tool that management uses to pressure people to perform."

"Accountability is used to punish people for poor performance."

"Accountability is something that is put on you by your boss. It causes unnecessary pressure, fear, regret, guilt, and resentment."

"Accountability is paying the piper."

"Accountability is something that nobody does around here."

Obviously, accountability means many things to many people. Some view it positively, while others see it as a negative factor in their lives. For some, talking about creating greater accountability congers up all sorts of charged feelings that lead to resistance and avoidance. Because of this, creating greater accountability within the organization requires helping people become aware of the divergent, and often negative, views of what accountability is and is not, while at the same time determining how much time and energy the organization wastes *Below The Line*. You can use the following Organizational Accountability Assessment instrument to determine to what extent accountability is an issue within your organization. We suggest you assess yourself and then encourage others to do the same as a first step toward identifying how critical an increase in accountability might be in your organization.

ORGANIZATIONAL ACCOUNTABILITY
ASSESSMENT
▼

Circle the response that best describes your situation.

1. Do you ever see people blaming others for what goes wrong in your organization?

   All the time   Often   Sometimes   Seldom   Never

2. Do you feel that people do not accept responsibility for what they do or how they do it?

   All the time   Often   Sometimes   Seldom   Never

3. Do you see people failing to proactively report on their activities and their progress toward results?

   All the time   Often   Sometimes   Seldom   Never

4. Do people fail to "dive for the ball" when it gets dropped?

   All the time   Often   Sometimes   Seldom   Never

5. Do people "wait and see" if things will get better when serious problems engulf your organization?

   All the time   Often   Sometimes   Seldom   Never

6. Do you hear people saying they feel a situation is out of control, and that they can do nothing to resolve it?

   All the time   Often   Sometimes   Seldom   Never

7. Do people spend their time "covering their tails" just in case things go wrong?

   All the time   Often   Sometimes   Seldom   Never

8. Do people seem to feel more responsible for their activity and effort than they do for their results?

   All the time   Often   Sometimes   Seldom   Never

9. Do you hear people say, "It's not my job or my department," and act as if they expect someone else to solve the problem?

All the time   Often   Sometimes   Seldom   Never

10. Do you feel that people display a low level of personal ownership and involvement when problems arise?

All the time   Often   Sometimes   Seldom   Never

Award the following points for each response—All the time = 5, Often = 4, Sometimes = 3, Seldom = 2, Never = 1—then total up your score and evaluate your organization using the scoring table that follows.

Total Score	*Evaluation Guidelines*
40 to 50	Your organizational culture operates *Below The Line.* It has adopted a self-reinforcing pattern that has become the way the organization does business. Unlocking this paradigm will take a deliberate and conscious effort.
30 to 39	Your organization spends enough time *Below The Line* that it continues to compromise organizational results and personal fulfillment. Although a glimmer of understanding exists, it will take a focused effort to shift to a more positive paradigm.
11 to 29	Your organizational culture typically operates *Above The Line.* Additional gains in productivity will come as you work to inculcate a positive definition of accountability throughout the organization.

0 to 10   Having mastered the art of living *Above The Line,* your organizational culture should continue to achieve outstanding results, as long as people remain alert for occasional dips *Below The Line.*

Unlocking the *Below The Line* paradigm requires an awareness of what accountability really means and a recognition of the extent to which your organization operates *Below The Line.* Achieving this awareness and recognition is vital to unlocking the old view of how people perceive accountability and how they have put up with *Below The Line* behavior and attitudes in their organization. Even the most accountable organizational culture can fall *Below The Line* from time to time and find itself needing to focus on the transition from the old to the new paradigm.

2. Transition to the New View of Accountability

It takes time for people to change their perspectives and adopt new attitudes and behavior. Breaking out of the old paradigm and embracing a new view of accountability within the organization sets the stage for moving the entire organization *Above The Line.* Only when everyone embraces the same positive perspective of accountability can the entire organization maximize its effectiveness at getting results. Having achieved awareness and recognition in step 1, you can begin building *Above The Line* attitudes that will improve performance throughout the organization. Without this consensus of perspective, however, *Below The Line* attitudes and behaviors will continue to form a resistive force to greater accountability and results.

Elements of the new view of accountability which your people must understand include the following:

▼ Understanding the "victim cycle" and its damaging effects

▼ Recognizing when they have fallen *Below The Line*

▼ Acknowledging when they have become trapped in the "victim cycle"

▼ Accepting *The Oz Principle's* definition of accountability and the need to ascend the *Steps To Accountability*

▼ Knowing what it means to *See It*

▼ Knowing what it means to *Own It*

▼ Knowing what it means to *Solve It*

▼ Knowing what it means to *Do It*

▼ Understanding what it means to live *Above The Line*

▼ Recognizing that "being accountable" is an organizational expectation

Making the commitment to operate in an *Above The Line* fashion and putting these precepts to work requires more than lip service and an intellectual acceptance; it also demands deep emotional and psychological commitment. If you doubt it, recall the last victim story you heard and consider the emotional and mental stress exhibited by the person telling the story. Before anyone can personally transition to a new view of accountability, they must experience, as well as intellectually understand, the difference between *Above The Line* and *Below The Line* behavior and attitudes. Since it takes time to gain experience, you must allow sufficient time for people to gain the experience they need to embrace this new paradigm. While training sessions designed to help people "experience" the concept of accountability, and not just learn "about" it, can prove extremely helpful, daily "experiences" incorporating the principle of accountability into actual practice created by leaders in the organization provide the best training of all.

You can best launch a training effort designed to unlock the old paradigm and transition to the new view of accountability by providing an experiential training session where co-workers are brought together to discuss their organizational experiences. This can occur at any level and for any team or group as you walk people through these four steps: (1) develop a common, shared frame of reference, (2) discuss and thoroughly understand how an attitude of accountability can affect the way people function as a team, (3) give and receive feedback to help everyone recognize when they are working *Below The Line* and when they are operating *Above The Line,* and (4) set the stage for effective coaching after the training session.

3. Locking In the New *Above The Line* Paradigm

To accomplish this step, you must constantly encourage people to make an all-out commitment to operate differently, by abandoning *Below The Line* attitudes and adopting consistent *Above The Line* behavior. Such a commitment comes only after deep personal reflection and a lot of real-time feedback that considers both *Above The Line* and *Below The Line* behavior. The reflection and feedback should help a person clarify and plan the specific ways in which he or she can think and act differently.

Since feedback, more than anything else, will enable people in your organization to make the 100 percent commitment to stay *Above The Line,* you must learn to give and receive feedback in a timely and effective manner, a skill we will discuss in the next section on coaching. Before we explore ways in which you can coach accountability, however, we want to emphasize the importance of using the imagery and language of the victim cycle and the steps to accountability to enable people to reflect on the distinction between *Above The Line* and *Below The Line* behavior.

Most people find it harder to think about philosophical abstractions than about concrete images. Using the terminology and language of *The Oz Principle*, people begin to develop a common frame of reference that takes on special and significant meaning. The mere mention of the phrase *Below The Line* immediately communicates that an *Above The Line* view may allow you to see things differently and thereby enhance your ability to get the results you want. Terms such as *See It, Own It, Solve It*, and *Do It*, quickly point to the kind of attitudes and behaviors that produce results. Moving *Above The Line* can become a rallying catch-phrase that signals to everyone involved that it's time to commit to making it happen, no matter what.

With the concrete images of *The Oz Principle*, you can help every person in your organization search daily for ways to weave accountable attitudes into the very fabric of your organization's operations: performance appraisals, decision-making patterns, policy formulation, mentoring, verbal and written communications, standard operating procedures, and every other aspect of day-to-day organizational life.

Personal reflection and commitment, giving and receiving feedback, applying the language of accountability, and constantly looking for ways to inject accountability into every nook and cranny of your organization will ensure that people lock in new attitudes, beliefs, and behaviors. When that occurs, your organization will achieve its goals more fully because it will be conducting its business within a common frame of reference.

COACHING ACCOUNTABILITY

In our experience, no organization can consistently behave and work *Above The Line* without constant feedback. Continuous feedback must become a living, breathing part of the accountable organization's culture. Throughout this book we have emphasized the importance of feedback, but we want to turn your attention to how it can and must be used in an ongoing coaching program.

Bill Hansen, a fictional, but representative manager with a major company, had experienced the accountability process and felt inspired to make accountability a core value in his organization. He found himself in a management meeting where one of his peers, a fellow named Stan, was presenting a status report on one of his team's priority projects. As Bill listened, he pulled out a card that contained both the victim cycle and the *Steps To Accountability* and began staring at it. Based on what he was hearing, he concluded that Stan was stuck *Below The Line* because many of his statements blamed others for his team's lack of progress on the project.

Bill's attention shifted from Stan's explanations to the others in the room because he wanted to see how everyone else was reacting to the report. As he watched the focus of the audience, he got the impression that everyone else was buying Stan's explanations for the team's poor progress. In the past, he realized, he, too, would probably have accepted Stan's *Below The Line* excuses, but now he found them quite disconcerting. Should he reveal his feelings? If he didn't, it was unlikely that anyone else would question Stan's report, but if he did, all the other managers might take offense. Pondering the personal risk associated with speaking up and attempting to pull the group *Above The Line,* he felt conflicting emotions: his own sense of accountability urged him to speak, while his sensitivity to the group counseled him to hold his peace.

Suddenly, he caught himself. "I'm just as far *Below The Line* in my thinking as everyone else in this room," he realized. "The company desperately needs me to speak up and accept accountability for moving this organization *Above The Line.*" At that moment, Bill began considering exactly how to raise the issue. Should he simply tell Stan that he thought Stan was telling a victim story? Perhaps that made sense, but then he remembered how he had been cautioned not to use accountability as a hammer. As he continued reflecting on his predicament, he wondered, again, whether anyone would see Stan's report the way he did. If so, a lively and productive discussion could ensue; if not, Bill might more wisely coach Stan away from the eyes and ears of the others.

Just then, another colleague, Julie, raised her hand. "I hear what you're saying, Stan," she said, "and I know this project has been a bearcat, but I can't help wondering what else you and the rest of us can do to make it work." Julie's observations coincided precisely with what Bill had been thinking. He couldn't have put it better himself, and he immediately felt miserable for not speaking up earlier. Almost instantly the whole room began buzzing with suggestions. Far from attacking Stan, everyone began lending him support and offering creative suggestions. To Bill's relief and chagrin, it turned out that most everyone else had seen the same problem he had, but only Julie had mustered the courage to help the group get *Above The Line.*

Before the meeting adjourned, the president of the company singled Julie out for praise: "She's shown the kind of leadership we desperately need in this company."

Bill had learned a valuable lesson and would never hesitate to speak up again. Most people respond to honest coaching, provided the coach counsels but never accuses, offers the counseling within the context of results, and invites the same sort of candid feedback he or she has given to others.

As you work on coaching others, be sure that you apply the steps to accountability to your own behavior. Good coaches always hold themselves to the same standards they wish others to follow.

ASKING *ABOVE THE LINE*ᔆᴹ QUESTIONS

Throughout this book we have stressed the importance of constantly asking the question, "What else can I do to achieve the results I want?" Now we'd like to add several more vital questions that any employee, supervisor, manager, president, group, or team can ask themselves during the ongoing task of moving an organization to greater levels of accountability:

TEN MORE *ABOVE THE LINE*^SM QUESTIONS

1. What aspects of this situation will most likely pull us *Below The Line* in the future?

2. What can we control, and what can't we control in this situation?

3. Have we fallen *Below The Line* in this situation?

4. What are we pretending not to know about our accountability in this situation?

5. Where are the areas of joint accountability that may lead to the ball getting dropped?

6. If we really "owned it," what would we do differently?

7. Given recent decisions about this situation, what do we need to do to make sure the organization stays *Above The Line*?

8. Does anyone involved with this situation still not "own" the decisions we have made?

9. Who is accountable for what and by when?

10. What have we learned from our recent experience?

Above The Line questions like these help flesh out the reality of a situation. You may want to refine these questions and add your own within the framework of the victim cycle and the *Steps To Accountability*, but we feel confident these ten, and variations of them, should remain central to your efforts to think, behave, and work *Above The Line*.

▲

PULLING THE CULTURAL LEVERS

Winston Churchill once said, "First we shape our structures, and then our structures shape us." We think that holds especially true in this era of rapidly evolving organizations. If you want accountability to become a lasting and important part of your own organization's evolution, you must consciously foster accountability throughout every aspect of your organization's culture.

Even in this age of downsized, dynamic organizations, it's not uncommon to hear people say, "You can't go against the system," "Don't rock the boat," or "You can't fight city hall," by which they mean that the organization governs people's actions, rather than vice versa. However, *The Oz Principle* insists that people can and should "own" their circumstances. That's more easily said than done, of course, because the cultural side of the organization can exert a strong influence on people's behavior. If the culture in any way accepts *Below The Line* behavior, that behavior will continue under both formal policies and informal norms which reinforce victim attitudes and responses.

The secret lies in shaping the formal and informal systems with *Above The Line* values that redefine "going against the system" as "owning your circumstances and striving for better results." By building accountability and *Above The Line* behavior into the organizational system, you can assure that your structures shape people in positive ways, stimulating continuous learning and development, rather than decline and inefficiency.

Within any organizational system there exists what we call "cultural levers" that greatly influence an organization's character. The principle of leverage implies "the increased means of accomplishing some purpose." In other words, a small effort can produce a large result, depending on how you position that small effort. Cultural levers are those small efforts that can yield major advancements (i.e., the 20 percent of effort that produces 80 percent of the results). When it comes to building accountability into your organization, some activities will produce more of the desired effect than others. When you pull the right lever, you can greatly accelerate the process. The following levers deserve your special emphasis:

1. Feedback and coaching
2. Performance appraisals
3. Promotion practices
4. Formal and informal rewards
5. Meeting agendas and discussions
6. Hiring criteria
7. Job descriptions and expectations
8. Budgeting Process
9. Communications Practices
10. Planning Process (strategic and tactical)

Although these levers exist in every organization, no matter how large or small, leaders and managers too seldom use them to promote accountability. Used improperly, as instruments to control and punish people, they can actually cause more harm than good. A performance appraisal, for example, should provide an opportunity for guiding someone toward higher achievement and giving them an opportunity to account for what they have done.

To pull the cultural lever of feedback and coaching, one CEO began providing time, usually a half hour, at every senior staff meeting for "coaching stories" from his vice presidents. He wanted to hear about his vice presidents' experiences coaching others to get *Above The Line*. The fact that he consistently devoted time during senior staff meetings to elicit coaching stories sent a message both to the staff and to everyone else who heard about it that the company placed great value on coaching. As a result the senior staff not only increased its own accountability for people development, but people themselves assumed more accountability for their own development. This CEO had successfully spotted and seized an opportunity to move his team and organization more securely *Above The Line.*

In another company with which we have spent a good deal of time, the senior team identified the senior staff meetings as a key cultural lever. Each Friday morning the senior staff would invite selected people from throughout the organization to attend the meeting and report on their activities. Those invited would spend a lot of time preparing their presentations in the weeks before the meeting, and after the meeting they would engage their colleagues in a lot of discussion about how it went (who said what, who on the senior staff attacked the presenter, etc.). Given the impact of these meetings, they certainly represented a key cultural lever, which the senior team could pull either wisely or poorly.

As the senior team began consciously trying to pull this lever more wisely and use it to build greater accountability into the organization, they saw that their own preparation for the meeting could make a world of difference. That required little effort, really, but it nevertheless represented a major shift in their thinking about their meetings. No longer would they just show up to hear and critique presentations, they would come fully prepared to use the steps to accountability as a tool to emphasize joint responsibility, detect *Below The Line* attitudes, and coach the presenter as well as each other *Above The Line* in a fair but firm manner.

At the first of these new meetings, the presenter brought several members of her project team along to help with the presentation because her last presentation had sparked a lot of heated debate. Joan knew that some members of the senior staff thought her project was in trouble, so she set up a meeting to discuss their views on how her project could be improved. After Joan summarized her project's status with a number of charts, graphs, and statistical analyses, the senior staff began asking questions. Joan was surprised when one member, Anthony, immediately dropped *Below The Line* and began blaming three people on Joan's team for the lack of progress. She was relieved when other members of the senior team pointed out Anthony's slip *Below The Line,* and he quickly brought himself back *Above The Line,* and began focusing more on what else people could do to get results than why they hadn't already done so. Throughout the discussion that ensued, the senior staff emphasized the importance of joint accountability and then used the steps to accountability to assess the status of the project and to coach Joan and her team on working through some of the problems that surrounded their project. Anthony himself shared an example of how he, too, had once been stymied by a similar problem, and he offered to share his experience in more detail after the meeting.

After the meeting the usual companywide "grapevine" discussion took place, but this time it took on a decidedly different tone. People throughout the company no longer regaled each other with "atrocity stories" but with the story of how the meeting sped Joan and her team towards results. Stories also circulated about how senior staff members had coached one another *Above The Line* in a noncontentious, productive manner. The meeting activated a powerful cultural lever that had always existed but which had never been properly pulled.

In addition to pulling similar cultural levers, you can employ six additional culture enhancing devices to instill greater levels of accountability in your organization:

SIX CULTURE-ENHANCING DEVICES

1. *Trigger words.* Trigger words drawn from the victim cycle and the *Steps To Accountability*, such as *Above The Line, Below The Line,* and *See It, Own It, Solve It, Do It,* can

serve as behavioral cues for those who become familiar with the concepts of *The Oz Principle*. The language associated with the *Steps To Accountability* and the victim cycle can trigger the right response in another person.

2. *Story telling.* Stories about falling *Below The Line* and then getting back *Above The Line* can stir people's imaginations. Such concrete examples and anecdotes can make the point much more memorably than will a lot of philosophical or theoretical description. You can use story telling to further clarify what it means to get and stay *Above The Line* and to praise those who have done it.

3. *MBWA.* Anyone with supervisory responsibilities can use "management by walking around" to seize opportunities for coaching people *Above The Line.*

4. *Attention management.* In meetings, conversations, written correspondence, contacts with customers, and so forth, you can emphasize the need for people to stress accountability in all their thoughts and actions.

5. *Role modeling.* As we have discussed earlier in the book, modeling accountable behavior and attitudes works wonders. Always set an example for others in your organization and praise others who do likewise.

6. *Creating experiences.* Look for opportunities to give people new *Above The Line* experiences. Such experiences are particularly powerful when people are anticipating or contemplating *Below The Line* responses from you or others in the organization. Consistently creating such experiences will certainly move the culture toward higher overall levels of accountability.

Used together, all these cultural levers and devices can make a big difference in your organization's progress toward higher levels of accountability.

UTILIZING THE COMMITMENT PROCESS

As you recall, *The Oz Principle* defines accountability in the following way:

> An attitude of continually asking "what else can I do to rise above my circumstances and achieve the results I desire?" It is the process of "seeing it, owning it, solving it, and doing it." It requires a level of ownership that includes making, keeping, and proactively answering for personal commitments. It is a perspective that embraces both current and future efforts rather than on reactive and historical explanations.

Central to creating accountability within the organizational context is the process of "making, keeping, and proactively answering for personal commitments." In the end, when all is said and done, personal accountability means that people individually *See It,* decide to *Own It*, personally work to *Solve It*, and then individually commit to *Do It.*

This process of making and keeping personal commitments is one that we have heard much about in our work with organizations. One of the most frequent complaints we hear from people we interview is the complaint that people are not held accountable to do what they say they are going to do. It may be interesting to note that even those who are viewed as highly accountable and productive often discover that they do not always follow through on their own commitments.

Many organizations have developed cultures that promote the practice of creating lists of active projects that just grow and continue to grow with no projects falling off the list until they're completed. In one company, we told the management group about an organization that had a list of about 60 active new product projects that were stripping the organization of the focus necessary to get things completed. The environment created by this practice of keeping an unmanageable list of projects was unmistakably *Below The Line*. Because of the enormity of the task, there were plenty of ways to run and hide. It was considered understandable when you did not follow through with your commitments because everyone knew that there was just too much to do at once. As we recounted this circumstance to the management team, they began laughing. When we asked them why, they said they had the same list, but they had 140 projects on theirs. When we asked them why they let this happen, they observed that they do not follow-up on commitments people make, they just keep adding things to the list and expect that people will figure out what is most important and then do their best to get it done. Everyone seemed to agree that there was an unspoken rule in that culture: "I will support you in adding your projects to the list as long as you support me by not confronting me when I do not follow through on my project commitments."

At some point, weaving accountability into the very fabric of the organization will require a concerted effort to improve the process of making and keeping personal commitments. To help with this, we suggest you use the four step "Commitment Process." This process will help you clarify how you can overcome those areas where accountability begins to break down and commitments begin to slide.

The first step is to understand that with every commitment there is a "coach" and an "owner." When people make commitments in an organizational context they are not just making commitments to themselves but to others, a boss, a team, a peer, etc. When a commitment is made, the "coach," who is the person to whom they are responsible, must be certain that the commitment is well defined so that everyone understands what the person is accountable for and by when. How many times have you been in a meeting when you thought certain commitments were made only to learn later that others saw it a different way? It is hard for people to be accountable for certain actions if we are uncertain about exactly what those actions are.

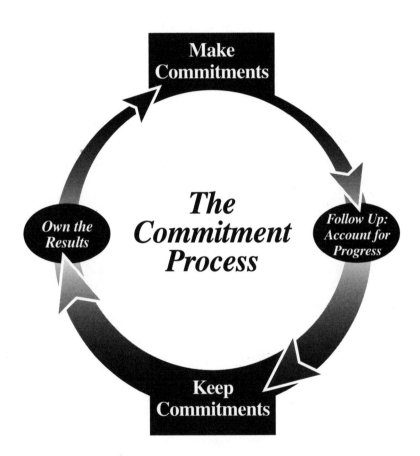

Make
Commitments

The Commitment Process

Own the
Results

Follow Up:
Account for
Progress

Keep
Commitments

Step Two involves the follow-up. All of us have probably experienced in one way or another the reality that people only keep commitments when there is some sort of follow-up. This is particularly true when people are functioning in an environment of limited resources with numerous priorities that often appear to be conflicting (or, in other words, today's business environment). One leader observed:

> When progress is measured, progress improves. When progress is measured and reported, improvement accelerates.

In the typical cycle of making and keeping commitments, reporting tends to occur at the time the commitment should have been fulfilled. At that point it is too late to impact the activity. The only thing that gets accomplished is a reporting session so that the person can either be rewarded or punished for their action or inaction. Have you ever observed people get put into a job or receive an assignment with the comment, "let's see what they can do"? A question we would ask about this all-too-frequent management practice is "why are you so anxious to test a person to see if he or she will succeed?" Might it not be better to set them up to win from the start? *The Oz Principle* suggests that follow-up occur well before the targeted completion date in order to increase everyone's chances of succeeding. There is no question that it is always in our best interest to make sure that those who make commitments to us are successful.

When we "follow up" on people, the person "following up" typically remains accountable for the activity. However, when the "owner" of the commitment doesn't just wait for follow-up to occur, but actually "returns and reports," then he has manifested that he has assumed the accountability to take the initiative to fully follow through by providing on-going updates on his progress. This follow-up step should have been previously agreed to in Step One. By pre-specifying a time to return and report, the "owner" is the one who remains primarily accountable to "return and report" on progress. So often, the people acting as coaches remain primarily responsible to make sure all the reporting happens at their request and as a result of their activity. The accountable individual will "return" and "report" on their own initiative because they *Own It* and are committed to "doing it." This follow-up stage is a perfect opportunity for the coach to use the *Steps To Accountability* chart to coach the person in order to ensure success in completing the commitment. It will be during the process of achieving the commitment, and not after-the-fact, that others will benefit most from being coached to move *Above The Line.*

Step Three primarily involves keeping the commitment; that is, "doing it." Here, people apply all four *Steps To Accountability* to make it happen; while at the same time avoiding excursions *Below The Line* that serve only to get them off track and divert their energies from getting results.

Step Four comprises the more traditional view of accountability: the opportunity to "own" the results that come from actions as people follow through on their commitments. The accountable person will "own" not only the action of fulfilling the commitment, but also the results that come from its completion. We have all seen where people go when they don't own the results: they drop *Below The Line* by crafting their explanation to "cover their tail;" they "run and hide" hoping they will not be found out, thinking no one will notice if they just lay low; they actively participate in the blame game, pointing fingers at everyone but themselves; they "wait and see" if anyone will say anything or if the results might not improve on their own. By standing up to be counted, the accountable person understands that reporting on progress and owning results is essential to an empowered and high performing organization. The "coach" understands that he or she is not on a witch hunt. The purpose of the accounting is to recognize success and coach the individual to improved performance next time. In the learning organization, this is a critical step to understanding "what people did right" so they can replicate it, learn from and understand "what they could do differently" next time in order to be more effective.

Accountable people make clear commitments, they take the initiative to "return and report" their progress, they act *Above The Line* to *Do It* and make it happen, and they stand up and take responsibility for their results. In creating clear accountability for making and keeping commitments, the two steps most often neglected by organizations are steps two (follow-up) and four (taking responsibility). By focusing on these two steps as you work to build a *Culture Of Accountability* into your organization you can begin to enjoy higher levels of accountability and greater results. By building all four steps into every aspect of your organizational process you will begin to see the transforming power of *The Oz Principle* at work in your organization.

In every organization, opportunities abound for training, coaching, asking questions, and pulling cultural levers. Rather than trying to apply them to all the issues facing your organization, we suggest you pick one issue that currently beleaguers your organization. By selecting such an issue, you can more dramatically demonstrate the impact of greater accountability.

First, create a list of the issues facing your organization that have caused at least some people to slip or remain *Below The Line*. Some possible candidates include total quality management, product defects, new product development, production schedules, people development, customer satisfaction, customer complaints, budgets, sales quotas, and company reputation. Be sure to identify major issues that relate to you and the people with whom you work most closely.

Second, choose one of the issues from your list and then identify where on the *Steps To Accountability* or in the victim cycle you think your team, group, department, function, division, or company currently stands. Begin discussing with your superiors, peers, and subordinates what realities everyone must acknowledge (*See It*), what ownership they must achieve (*Own*

It), what possible solutions they can implement (*Solve It*), and what exactly everyone should do (*Do It*).

Third, once you have started to create some awareness of your organization's position relative to this specific issue, decide on the right sequencing and mix of the five elements of creating accountability (training for understanding, coaching to create accountability, asking *Above The Line* questions, pulling the cultural levers, and looking for opportunities to get *Above The Line*) for addressing this particular issue.

Fourth, evaluate the success of your efforts both in terms of results and in terms of people's behavior and attitudes. After this experience, do you find more people in your organization thinking, behaving, and working *Above The Line* more often and more effectively?

Once you have completed your evaluation, pick another issue or move to a more broad-based approach to getting your organization to live *Above The Line*. Regardless of your next steps, you should remain constantly on the lookout for opportunities to get your organization *Above The Line*.

STAYING *ABOVE THE LINE*^{SM}

Once the Scarecrow, the Tin Woodsman, and the Lion had mastered accountability for themselves, they found others eager to benefit from their personal gains. Likewise, as you work to keep yourself and others *Above The Line,* you will undoubtedly find more chances to apply *The Oz Principle* to corporate America's toughest issues, the subject of our final chapter.

SOMEWHERE OVER THE RAINBOW: APPLYING THE OZ PRINCIPLES TO CORPORATE AMERICA'S TOUGHEST ISSUES

Then the Witch looked at the big, shaggy Lion and asked,

"When Dorothy has returned to her own home, what will become of you?"

"Over the hill of the Hammer-Heads," he answered, "lies a grand old forest, and all the beasts that live there have made me their King. If I could only get back to this forest I would pass my life very happily there."

"My third command to the Winged Monkeys," said Glinda, "shall be to carry you to your forest. Then, having used up the powers of the Golden Cap, I shall give it to the King of the Monkeys, that he and his band may thereafter be free for evermore."

THE WIZARD OF OZ
By L. Frank Baum

The Lion symbolizes courage, and nothing tests your courage more than danger. To meet and conquer danger, of course, you must be willing take a risk, a calculated risk to be sure, but one that sets aside your natural desire for safety and comfort. In his book *Technological Risk,* University of California professor and risk consultant Harold W. Lewis argues that Americans have come to fear risk and that fear, more than anything else, impedes the country's progress. "Are we over the peak in our willingness to take risks, which is the only reason we've evolved to the place we are now?" he asks. While Lewis offers his observation within the context of technology, we think his message applies equally well to the "softer" issues that beset American organizations.

In our work with hundreds of organizations—from gutsy little start-ups to huge *Fortune* 500 companies—we have observed that most of them continue to shun the risk associated with resolving several perennial and costly issues. The following is our list of the top ten most threatening unresolved organizational issues:

1. Poor communication
2. Developing People
3. Empowerment
4. Lack of alignment
5. Entitlement
6. Balancing work and personal life
7. Confronting poor performance
8. Coaching senior management
9. Cross-functional strife
10. Fascination with programs

These unresolved issues plague the full spectrum of organizations, be they nuclear power plants, financial institutions, "high-yield" bond departments, insurance companies, health care companies, high-fashion designers, construction contractors, computer manufacturers, fine jewelers, schools, and the offices of doctors, lawyers, and accountants. In some cases, individuals perceive these issues as part of the inescapable reality of complex modern organizational life. Others dismiss the cost of remaining *Below The Line* on these issues as inconsequential. In our opinion, however, these are the very problems that are hampering our organizations in their quest to become more competitive, more profitable, more successful at fulfilling the dreams of their people, and more capable of achieving results.

In this chapter we will urge you to define these issues as real and present dangers, set aside your fear of risk, and rise *Above The Line* with respect to each of them. In the sections that follow we will explore each of these universal issues, but it will remain your task to apply *The Oz Principle*—seeing it, owning it, solving it, and doing it—to resolve these issues in your own organization.

ISSUE ONE: POOR COMMUNICATION

Poor communication always stands in the way of results. Every day we hear people describe the lack of communication between employee and manager, between one function and another, between one division and another, between team members, between senior management and middle management, all as an ongoing problem that impedes progress. According to management consultant Patricia McLagan, author of *On-the-Level: Performance Communication That Works,* an emphasis on accountability places even more importance on the role of communication in the organization. As McLagan says, "When you are accountable for the work you and your team are producing, you need to keep all the channels of communication open. You need information constantly on what is working and what isn't." Conversely, without good communication, accountability cannot flourish.

From a skyscraper in New York, where people talk about the communication problem between the 2nd floor and the 11th floor, to the geographically separated sites of headquarters and manufacturing, where people just don't seem to "connect," communication issues abound. We have heard people attribute their communication problems to such physical conditions as different floors, opposite sides of the same building, and even a single wall, but behind these physical conditions we hear the hum of the victim cycle. The more people talk about their communication problems, the clearer it becomes that most of them feel victimized by poor communication. Some people may feel unheard, unlistened to, unacknowledged and uninvolved, choosing to play the "blame game," feeling misunderstood, claiming "I am not responsible because I did not know," or because "they did not listen."

Ironically, in this so-called communications age, with all its networked computers, fancy phone systems, and screeching fax machines, many people accept poor communication as an organizational reality they feel powerless to correct. Yet, as we hear those same people reflect on the price they pay for poor communication, it becomes painfully clear that they must risk something to change the situation. Otherwise, their organizations will continue to suffer the consequences of missed schedules, delayed products, wrong shipments, incorrect designs, and missed sales. While consulting with one particularly well-known high-fashion apparel organization, we couldn't quite get this point across. Rather than face the danger directly, people preferred to "wait and see" if things would improve over time. Finally, however, when we asked a group of key people to quantify what poor communications with the management group had actually cost them, they concluded that better communication could have saved the company at least $3 million over the past six months. This number drove the message home. Now that the group could *See It,* they could begin working on the problem.

To its credit, this group took action, but in most groups it's surprising how much talk and how little action surrounds a communication problem. One client CEO grew so exasperated hearing his management team talk about a vague "communication problem" that he issued an edict that no one ever again utter the phrase. Of course, that didn't work, because silence would not make the problem go away, either. He would have been much wiser to stimulate people to go beyond talking about it to doing something about it. Communication problems may be inherent in contemporary organizations, but that does not mean you can't tackle and solve them. In fact, if you leave communication problems unsolved, they will create habitual *Below The Line* behavior, employees who feel victimized, and a granite roadblock to accountability.

Moving *Above The Line* with respect to communication problems means that you become accountable for how you communicate with other people by: first, acknowledging what is causing communication to break down; second, own what you are either doing or not doing to cause ineffective communications; third, determine what else you need to do to make sure you or others are heard; and fourth, make the commitment to go out and make it happen. While this approach may appear simplistic, we have seen it work. What is not needed is another new program to improve communication. What is needed is the willingness on the part of every individual in a work group, team, or organization to own the effectiveness of the communications that take place. While exercising a higher degree of personal accountability may not magically solve all your organization's communication problems, it will set off a spark that can ignite a chain reaction, as others join you *Above The Line.*

▲

ISSUE TWO: DEVELOPING PEOPLE

Most executives claim that their people are their organization's most important asset. However, those same executives would be amazed to hear that their people don't buy that claim. If communications problems rank number one on the list of impediments to organizational progress, then people and career development problems come in a close second. And if poor communications rankles people, poor personnel development enrages them.

Rather than looking inside themselves for personal accountability in this area, employees often blame their lack of advancement on the organization for not creating the requisite systems and programs. Quite often, they blame management for a lack of timely and comprehensive performance appraisals, often stating that they haven't received an appraisal for years and sometimes disparaging the fact that a boss actually asked them to write their own appraisals. Just as often, they blame management for its inaccessibility that prevents them from getting and receiving the feedback they need to grow and improve. In the end, both end up excusing themselves from better preparing for opportunities because management let them down.

In some companies, employees continue such *Below The Line* patterns by heaping the blame on an "out-of-touch" or ineffective human resources department. Many cite job posting practices as inconsistent and unfair, claiming that the company usually hires outsiders or even insiders preselected for the jobs. Even those who work hard at their current jobs often feel powerless to affect their career paths and futures. Paralyzed by such feelings of powerlessness, they simply wait for future opportunities and hope that management will ultimately award them the promotions that will foster personal growth and professional development.

On the other hand, we have also seen many individuals in a variety of companies climb *Above The Line* with respect to their careers. One such individual, an extremely qualified and effective industrial engineer we'll call Stuart, found himself highly praised by management as an individual contributor, but he never could obtain the opportunity to play a bigger role in the management of the manufacturing site he knew so well. After years of waiting for an invitation to play that role and feeling somewhat victimized by not having been asked, Stuart decided to get *Above The Line* and actively pursue the opportunity. He let upper management know that he was interested in managing production and that he had developed ideas for what supervisors could do differently to heighten quality, increase efficiency, and improve the management strengths of supervisors. After sharing that vision with his current production manager, he set about implementing it. Later that same year, when the current production manager was transferred, management gave Stuart the job he had so long desired but only recently pursued. Management later claimed that they had never known that Stuart longed to play such a role.

While every organization shoulders responsibility for the development of its people and benefits from seeking to understand their career aspirations, individual employees who allow themselves to feel victimized by a process that doesn't work pay a huge price for doing so. For such individuals, getting stuck *Below The Line* when it comes to their personal development always results in missed opportunities for growth, progress, and career advancement. Even in organizations that manage people development poorly, talented and accountable people still grow, develop, and win promotions because they assume personal accountability for their own progress.

Without question, we agree that joint accountability for the development of people should exist between employees and their organizations, but we also believe that individuals at all levels of an organization should become personally accountable for their own development. By functioning *Above The Line*, they will actively look for what more they can do to create their own growth opportunities. They will pursue classes and training that will prepare them for advancement or increased effectiveness in their current jobs, find an appropriate mentor to help advise them on a longer-term career path, seek feedback on their performance continually to measure their overall progress, and ask themselves constantly what else they can do to get the results they want for their careers. Looking at the bigger picture, they may also work to make sure the right systems are installed so the company can improve its ability to develop people. If that sort of attitude grows from the grass roots, it becomes so pervasive that it helps the entire organization rise *Above The Line* and "own" the responsibility to overcome the short-term orientation that impedes it from making the right investment in developing its most important asset.

ISSUE THREE: EMPOWERMENT

The notion of employee empowerment has become a hot topic in recent years. Much has been written and spoken on the subject, yet with all that attention, we constantly hear people at all levels of the organization blame a lack of results on a lack of empowerment. For example, two of the questions that we hear most frequently asked by senior management are "why are the directors not directing?" and "why don't they make decisions, 'own' their areas and get results?" On the other hand, we often hear directors, managers, and employees ask why senior management does not listen to their input, trust them to make decisions and empower them to get results; they talk about having the responsibility to accomplish certain things but not having the necessary authority to get them done. At the center of the debate over empowerment lies a great deal of continuing confusion. "Just exactly what does it mean to be empowered?" asks one CEO. "I am so tired of hearing people saying that they are not empowered. What more do they want? Everybody wants it, no one seems to know what it means, and nobody feels like they have it. If they don't feel they have what they need to get the job done, then why don't they go out and make it happen? If you have to wait for someone to empower you, then how in the world can you ever be empowered?" Many contemporary managers and leaders echo this frustration.

On the other hand, employees resent what they perceive as management's dismissive attitude and feel that management should realize that it often withholds authority to direct resources, which, at the root, prevents people from becoming empowered. The confusion mounts as organizations debate whether empowerment comes in the wake of an invitation or accrues through initiative. While the debate rages, organizations remain stuck *Below The Line,* employees allow themselves to feel like victims of managers, management behaves accordingly, and results get held "hostage" by indecision and inaction.

The director of a midsized high-tech company, whom we'll call Mark, found himself in charge of the development of a key new product. Mark got the job because management prized his ability to make things happen, just what the development of this new product demanded. Most people in the company saw this move as an incredible career opportunity for Mark, and everyone assumed that Mark would soon become vice president.

However, as Mark launched into the task, which required a great deal of functional cooperation, he became frustrated with his inability to move ahead as quickly as he had hoped. Over a short period of time his reputation among teammates suffered as others began to perceive him as a person who demanded that things be done his way. Empowerment to Mark meant doing whatever he felt needed to be done regardless of the needs of other players. While the organization had, in truth, given Mark more authority, resources, and autonomy than it had to any other project team leader in its history, Mark routinely insisted, "If you don't do this by Friday, I will not be responsible for the result." In essence, Mark turned his back on accountability whenever he felt he lacked empowerment, or, as he saw it, the willingness of people to do what he wanted, when he wanted. With this attitude, he held the company hostage to his own limited definition of empowerment. Ultimately, Mark left the organization in frustration, and the product he left behind was introduced to the market two years behind schedule.

To our way of thinking, being "empowered" to get results and being "accountable" for results are inextricably entwined, but confusion over the meaning of "empowerment" has been getting in the way of getting *Above The Line* and creating greater accountability. Why not simply drop the word from your vocabulary and replace it with "what else can I do to get the result?" Yes, management should "own" the responsibility for empowering people throughout the organization, but at some point everyone must realize that, ultimately, you must empower yourself. Rather than focusing on what someone else "should" do for you, focus more on what you must do yourself. Rather than shouting, "Empower me!" just ask yourself the question "What else can I do to achieve the result?" and then take the steps to *See It, Own It, Solve It,* and *Do It.*

These steps, if replicated throughout the organization, will yield tremendous benefits in terms of improved results; and, in the end, will deliver to the company an empowered organization and workplace. It is an invaluable insight to understand that empowerment is much more an outcome, like happiness, than it is an activity. It is an outcome which stems from accountable people. You can either get lost in the debate over the meaning of empowerment or you can follow a map to greater results through accountable actions.

▲
ISSUE FOUR: LACK OF ALIGNMENT

Every organization needs a clear focus, a strategy that drives its actions in the marketplace. However, in virtually every company with which we've worked over the past ten years, we have found that members of the organization, and particularly the senior staff, hold quite different views of the organization's overall direction, a misalignment of visions that invariably permeates every level of the company. Many organizations spend countless hours discussing such strategic questions as "What business are we in and where are we going?" without forging a clear answer. Without answering such questions, key people and their teams march to the tunes of their own favorite drummers, unaligned on a playing field where marching in the same direction is imperative to organizational success. As a result, teams work tentatively and never forge the full-fledged ownership necessary to bring projects to successful conclusions. Eventually, as an alarming number of projects fail, misalignment flourishes and thrusts too many people *Below The Line.*

The challenges of creating alignment does not fall solely on the shoulders of the top brass but extends to all levels of an operation, and it includes such key elements as resource allocation, desired cultural attributes, affirmative action, organizational initiatives, and, indeed, every facet of tactical implementation that requires the effort of every single individual. While the senior management team may try to ignore the alignment issue, it doesn't need to look far from the executive suite to find a group of people who suffers from poor alignment every day of their working lives. When we encounter this phenomenon, as we do most every day, a few interviews with the directors reporting to the senior management team clearly reveal the problem and its associated costs in terms of productivity and morale.

The directors and managers beneath the senior management team can usually see the effects of misalignment quite clearly. They often complain that they seem to be working at odds with their peers throughout the organization, and they cite numerous examples of mixed messages flowing from their superiors about the direction they should pursue in a given situation. The confusion caused by misalignment then trickles down to all the people management strives to lead and manage. Such confusion always signals a *Below The Line* attitude. As role models, misaligned managers give license to everyone beneath them to do the same. By allowing confusion to dictate company direction, they breed lack of respect for senior company leadership, and a need for people to be told what to do every step of the way. Eventually, they create victims. Postevaluations of bankruptcies almost always point to an alignment problem at the top that eventually permeates every part of the organization. A close friend of ours worked for International Harvester in the late 1970s before it went bankrupt. He still remembers how the misalignment among the company's senior team grew in the years before the bankruptcy from seeds of half-hearted support and whispered criticism of corporate policies into widespread, open dissension that eventually gridlocked the entire organization, forcing it to seek the umbrella protection of Chapter 11.

Even when management creates alignment, many team leaders fail to communicate the message to their people, somehow assuming that team members will intuitively figure out and buy into important decisions they have made. Thus, even when alignment does exist, management "waits" and "hopes" for effective and consistent implementation of the desired direction.

Management must accept accountability for creating and maintaining alignment within their organizations by first acknowledging that failing to do so will keep their organizations *Below The Line,* creating inefficiencies, low morale, great stress, finger-pointing, and confusion. To get *Above The Line* you should consider who will be most affected by a decision and then involve those people in discussion before making the decision. By paying close attention to a diversity of opinions, suggestions, and perspectives, by utilizing an open decision-making process to determine your course of action, by communicating the aligned message clearly to the rest of the organization, by actively promoting the decision as a collective effort, and by coaching away any misalignments, you can ensure more coherent and cohesive action throughout your organization.

ISSUE FIVE: ENTITLEMENT

Over time, and quite naturally, some people become accustomed to an organization's systems of rewards, benefits, and traditions. From the yearly bonus to celebrations of success, people tend to expect certain events to continue, an expectation that transforms such characteristics of a corporate culture into a "right" or "entitlement."

As companies seek to become more competitive by changing the way they do business, and as they strive to get closer to their customers, more efficient, more productive, and more profitable, they find that certain cultural "entitlements" do more harm than good. The right to an annual bonus, routine yearly raises, an 8-to-5 workday, regular recognition events, lifetime job security regardless of performance, and other long-established traditions and practices may have served their purposes in the past, but such "rights" or "entitlements" may undermine the future if people expect them to continue regardless of their level of performance or ability to get results. In time, every organization reaches a point where it must reconsider its "entitlements." Unfortunately, when they do so, employees tend to drop *Below The Line,* feeling victimized by the company to such an extent that morale evaporates and people begin questioning their very association with the company.

Not long ago, we observed a relatively new, fast-growing company as it encountered predictable competitive pressures that slowed its growth rate and weakened its profit picture. In its early years, the company, let's call it Nu Tech, Inc., had soared. Its product had grabbed the number one position in the market, and its profit margins outshone everyone else's in the industry. For employees, Nu Tech seemed like paradise. It operated the best equipment, ran the best computers (one on each desk in the company), offered the best benefits, threw the best parties, and generally promoted a first-class image. When executives traveled, they stayed in the best hotels and dined at the most exclusive restaurants. Throughout the industry stories of the good life at Nu Tech prompted the best and the brightest in the industry to seek jobs there.

However, when the reality of the new competitive environment hit Nu Tech, and the company began to implement far-reaching changes that reversed much of what people had come to expect as "entitlements," the organization quickly fell *Below The Line*. Each time management questioned or abandoned an entitlement, new victims emerged, each disgruntled that management had "taken away" something they deserved. No one had ever tied the benefit to performance when performance came so easily, so the new emphasis on performance shocked the culture to its foundation. Eventually, the people at Nu Tech faced up to the reality that they did not deserve anything they could not produce, but not until after a massive layoff and a precipitous decline in market share forced them to do so.

Every day in the business press you can find an example of a company once known for its full-employment policies, an Eastman Kodak, IBM, or AT&T, that has resorted to laying off people because the company's performance has fallen. To employees conditioned to think of their jobs as a lifetime guaranteed "right," they cannot easily accept the idea that their jobs depend on their company's ability to fund them. To help people make that shift, more and more companies are attempting to build employee ownership into their cultures. If employees "own" their circumstances, the "heart" of *The Oz Principle*, they will more readily work to solve problems and guarantee their own continued employment. In today's environment, companies must learn how to manage organizational processes in a way that does not disconnect individual accountability from organizational results. They must understand that almost everything they give to employees at any level (with the exception of fundamental values such as fairness, honesty, and sincerity) flows from individual and organizational performance.

Individual employees can avoid the feelings of victimization that attend the loss of "entitlements" by viewing all the practices, rewards, and benefits the organization offers as privileges and rewards that come by virtue of excellent performance, rather than rights that begin accruing the day you're hired. By striving to ensure that your performance places you in good standing to earn the rewards you want, and by working to make your organization as productive as possible to create such rewards, you will move yourself *Above The Line*. To paraphrase the Smith Barney commercial, "I get my rewards the old-fashioned way. I earn them."

ISSUE SIX: BALANCING WORK AND PERSONAL LIFE

Our work in hundreds of organizations has shown us that working with conflicting priorities is a major issue that every company continues to struggle with in the 1990s. Conflicting priorities include such things as: focusing on quantity while at the same time delivering a high degree of quality, making the numbers and simultaneously thinking strategically, and paying the price to succeed in business while spending the time to nurture family relationships. Success in the future will come to those who learn to master the management of conflicting priorities. To succeed, people must come to see these conflicting priorities not as mixed messages, but as challenges of balance, accomplishment and growth. Perhaps, the most difficult and the most unacknowledged of all conflicting priorities challenging organizations today is that of creating a balance between work and personal life.

As more and more companies embark on programs of downsizing, delayering, and parallel pathing in an effort to enhance productivity and profitability, employees who survive the organizational reengineering find themselves under ever more pressure to do "more with less." In most cases, "more with less" equals "stress." Since we consult to many such organizations, we hear a lot of talk about the tremendous stress major changes can cause, and most of the concern centers on the dilemma of balancing a successful career and a fulfilling personal life. John Sculley, former CEO of Apple Computer, was recently quoted by *USA Today* as saying, "A good night's sleep is a remnant of agrarian and industrial ages. The information age, with easy communication around the globe and constant access to changing data, is making a night's sleep a thing of the past. It's a 24-hour day, not an 8-to-5 day." *USA Today* reporter Kevin Maney went on to say, "A few executives share Sculley's wide-eyed approach. President Clinton often gets by on a couple hours of sleep. David Johnson, CEO of Campbell Soup, works throughout a 24-hour day so he can keep track of worldwide operations." In this same article, Maney asks, "Is Sculley's routine the model for The New Millennium executive, or is it just weird? While John Sculley may be an extreme example, there is a trend toward longer hours and less free time. If your company has downsized or flattened itself to save resources, you may expect to work longer hours, extend your average workweek, and find all too little time for family, friends and recreation."

In another *USA Today* cover story, "For Many, Morale is in the Sewer," reporter Leslie Cauley describes IBM's morale in the midst of current downsizing efforts that will take the company from 406,000 to about 200,000 employees. She indicates that, "plant workers and mangers alike say work loads are increasing, in some cases dramatically. Working on weekends is common place. IBM denies it, but at least one mainframe plant reportedly is considering 12 hour shifts." In one case, "Rudy Antalek, who handled equipment orders at IBM's Endicott, N.Y., plant, says he decided to take the buy out only after managers tried to get him to take two jobs—his own, plus another vacated by a colleague—that would have lengthened his work day several hours. He says that managers offered to pay overtime, but he declined. Antalek, who has 20 years' experience at IBM, is now unemployed and looking for a job." Even in this stressful environment of long hours and double duty, Milton Moskowitz, co-author of *The 100 Best Companies to Work for in America*, still considers IBM one of the nation's best employers. Does this not suggest a change in American culture? Without question, it does! For many in such situations, it may feel like it would if someone had changed the rules in the middle of playing a basketball game. Just imagine dribbling down the court; you begin the approach to the basket for your lay-up when, suddenly, someone raises the basket another two feet! How unfair that would probably feel! We might also say "they had no right to do that!"

Such an abrupt change in the "rules" in organizational life can disrupt your family and personal life so much that you can easily start feeling taken advantage of and betrayed by the company to which you have pledged your heart and soul. However, the reality of life in corporate America is that people are being asked to give more of their time to work, leaving less of their time for home. Learning to effectively balance the two will be a required skill for every aspiring individual who wants to succeed at both.

A few years ago, a nuclear power plant began running shifts called 7-12's, where people work 7 days a week, 12 hours a day. Many employees liked the arrangement because they could more than double their take-home pay with all the overtime. However, as we talked with people around the plant, it became obvious that many were finding it difficult to stay fully alert on the job. Some even joked with others in the plant about their ineffectiveness. They often wondered how management could justify these shifts in light of the increased errors and the decreased productivity. Naturally, we wondered about the plant's safety, not to mention the security of family relationships. We often heard people recount the toll such a schedule had on their marriages. Divorces and injured relationships were prevalent.

One of our clients dealt with this kind of problem head on. The senior management team of the company understood the added pressures their employees faced as they worked to bring several new products to market. They decided to do something about it. Aware that their people were sacrificing the quality of their personal lives for the company, the management team invited candid feedback so they could understand exactly how people felt about the situation. Then the management team came together and talked at length about the increased pressures on employees. After some tough deliberation, they agreed to make balancing personal and professional life one of the six corporate beliefs that would guide their organizational culture. As a result, any employee could say "no" to a late-night meeting without fear of retribution. If someone seemed to be feeling that saying no would evidence disloyalty, a manager would quickly send that person home with a pat on the back. In effect, the company promised to support its people if they assumed their own accountability for what they chose to do and not to do. We admired their handling of the issue. Full of young, aspiring, professional people who want to make a difference and succeed, the company has turned in incredible growth and profits, all the while nurturing a culture imbued with accountability for both corporate and personal goals.

Resource constraints will continue to rule business life. Few organizations can escape the reality of a world where you must do more with less. To avoid falling *Below The Line* on this issue, management must acknowledge the personal price it asks its employees to pay and then work to find ways to help them strike a balance between a fulfilling personal life and a successful work life.

By the same token, employees must get *Above The Line* and "own" their own circumstances. The storm of change will not abate. The average workweek will grow longer. More will be required of everyone. Understanding this reality will help you adjust to it, making the personal and professional trade-offs that work best for you.

▲
ISSUE SEVEN: CONFRONTING POOR PERFORMANCE

Throughout this book we have talked about the pivotal role feedback plays in creating high levels of accountability within an organization. Yet it continually amazes us that few organizations establish an environment where feedback freely flows. In such cases, obviously, you cannot expect to confront poor performance skillfully or coach performance effectively. By failing to confront poor performance, organizations unwittingly foster feelings of victimization among people who perform poorly but don't know it and thus can't effect improvements, as well as among people who must pick up the slack because of poor performance. Poor performance leads to poor results, and poor results keep entire organizations *Below The Line.*

When we confront executives, managers, and supervisors with this problem, they tend to cite several reasons for failing to deal with performance issues: the specter of lawsuits by poor performers who claim wrongful dismissal, a reluctance to hurt people's feelings, the difficulty of establishing a fair but effective review process, a tendency to shy away from time-consuming documentation, and a general fear of the risk involved in confronting poor performance. Others cite loyalty to co-workers as a transcendent cultural code—a twisted application of the golden rule (be nice to them, and others will be nice to you), while still others cite a lack of training on how to handle such situations, especially when they are personality types who hate confrontation. A few organizations claim that they enjoy sufficient resources to "carry" nonperformers whose efforts neither hurt nor help, but even those companies end up paying a price eventually.

Everyone has heard about a person who suffered great trauma when fired from one job but after grueling months of searching, found another job for which that person was much better suited. One such case occurred with a young MBA, whom we'll call Ted. Ted was very aggressive and had set his eyes on a marketing management position that he hoped to attain in relatively short order. He accepted any and every project with great enthusiasm and worked nights and weekends to do it better and faster than it had ever been done before. To get things done quickly, Ted applied a great deal of pressure to co-workers and soon developed an abrasive style that seemed to get results. In particular, he insulated his own project teams from the demands and needs of other parts of the organization to fulfill his own fast-track objectives. Ted's projects received a great deal of praise within the company as they came in on time and under budget, and Ted's apparent ability to get results won him distinction as the best marketing project leader in the company's history.

However, in the midst all this glory, Ted's boss, along with several other senior managers, grew deeply concerned about Ted's actual performance. The way he ran roughshod over people and destroyed relationships would, management felt, eventually undermine his effectiveness, but rather than confront Ted over these issues, they decided to let Ted learn his lesson the hard way. Shunning the uncomfortable prospect of confronting Ted over his style and coaching him beyond it, they let him run loose, hoping he'd end up learning the error of his ways all on his own.

Over time, however, Ted's behavior got worse, not better, as he continued to burn bridges and force outcomes. Eventually, the head of the department began privately approaching Ted's boss demanding that she do something about Ted's abrasiveness. Finally, when Ted's boss sat Ted down and gave him specific feedback on the problem, Ted blew up: "I thought results were the only thing that mattered around here!" Now he felt betrayed and confused. "Why didn't you say something earlier?" he demanded. As it turned out, the feedback came too late, as Ted concluded that he could never be happy in this organization. He left, but to his credit, he took a greater awareness of himself to his next job, where, after a few short years, he forged a reputation not only as a guy who gets results but as one who get results as a respectful team player. Ted eventually won. But his original organization paid a price by losing their investment in all the learning and experience they had given Ted; a price that was paid because they had not learned how to confront performance issues in a proper and timely way.

We strongly believe American management must learn how to confront poor performance in a precise, constructive, and supportive way. By dealing head-on with this universal issue, you can move more surely *Above The Line*, improving results while at the same time making people happier. Very simply you must learn to confront poor performance when you see it and accept constructive feedback when you receive it. If you pretend the issue doesn't exist, or wait to see if it will solve itself, stop right now. Make confronting performance a daily habit. Don't let the problems build and get handed down from one generation of managers to the next.

▲
ISSUE EIGHT: COACHING SENIOR MANAGEMENT

Who will tell the emperor that he has no clothes? Many of the CEOs and senior managers we know lament the loneliness of leadership, and most would agree that they receive all too little feedback on their effectiveness, style, or impact on their organizations. However, if a senior manager thinks he or she cannot affect the flow of feedback, that individual is operating *Below The Line*. We have heard CEO after CEO say, "No matter how much I ask my people for feedback, I just cannot get them to muster up the courage to give it to me straight." Given the fact that employees also tend to function here *Below The Line,* believing that coaching senior management can spell career suicide, senior managers would do well to take the first step by opening themselves up to coaching. If they don't learn to do so in these perilous times, they stand to lose everything they have worked so hard to achieve. It's happening to Steven Jobs, for the second time. As reported in *The Wall Street Journal,* "His computer company, NeXT Inc., stopped making computers. In March (of 1993), his president and his chief financial officer quit. Then, several big computer makers—some of which he had hoped would use his software—formed a software alliance that excluded NeXT." Just like at Apple Computer, the company he founded and eventually lost to John Sculley, Steven Jobs's unwillingness to receive feedback may have destroyed any opportunity for him to attain stardom once again. "His insistence on complete control over a project with IBM, for example, doomed a 1989 agreement that would have lent Big Blue's backing to NeXT's software. And he lost valuable time last year when he ignored advisers' repeated warnings that NeXT couldn't compete in hardware and should become a software company." The result of Steven Jobs's inability to welcome coaching, "amounts to a steep fall from a very lofty perch." According to the same article, "His NeXT workstation seems destined to become a high-tech museum relic. He himself is fighting to show he still matters in the computer industry." According to Richard Shaffer, editor of *Computer Letter,* "People have stopped paying attention to him; it's sad."

Both employees and senior management must accept the fact that feedback creates accountability. Every action by a member of senior management affects the organization, and, being human, every senior manager has both strengths and weaknesses. No company can grow unless the senior managers grow. Even the CEO is not immune; he or she must also grow. If they do not, either the organization will falter or it will outgrow them. The best senior managers not only search for ways they can improve their performance, they encourage those around them to tell them the truth, no matter how painful.

Most leaders want feedback from their people. Consider a case in point, Ginger Howard, president and CEO of Advanced Cardiovascular Systems, began her tenure as president of the company by soliciting candid feedback from all levels of the organization on how both she and the company could grow in the future. People who would have otherwise ducked the danger inherent in offering a new CEO honest feedback eagerly accepted the risk. Howard went out of her way to follow up on all feedback, letting people know how much she valued it and describing exactly how she was going to use it to improve herself and ACS. Now Ginger receives feedback every day from operators on the assembly line to managers of every department.

We urge CEOs to assume personal accountability for obtaining feedback by making it widely known that they want it and value it. Openly thanking those who give them "tough" feedback will cause others to do likewise. For their part, employees must overcome the fear of risk and tell inquiring senior managers what they really need to hear.

ISSUE NINE: CROSS-FUNCTIONAL STRIFE

Marketing against manufacturing, manufacturing against research and development, R&D against sales, and sales against the world. Sound familiar? We hear it everywhere we go: cross-functional strife. In fact, these battles have become something of a tradition in corporate America, even though they represent one of the most shortsighted *Below The Line* issues in business today. Why can't corporate functions rise *Above The Line* and finally recognize, to misquote Pogo, that "we have met the enemy, and the enemy is not us?"

One organization we worked with came to a virtual standstill as the research and development department and the marketing department waged a feud that would have made the Hatfields and the McCoys look like pikers. Each of the combatants consistently worked as if the other were its nemesis. The vice presidents literally hated each other and openly discussed their disdain for one another's style and competence. As a result, this company, which once led its industry in product innovation, failed to turn out any breakthrough products for over an entire year. Furthermore, the products that did make it to market did so way over budget and far behind schedule. We could clearly see that the future of the entire organization depended on the two departments getting *Above The Line* and bringing the blame game to a screeching halt. It took a year, but vigorous application to move *Above The Line* resulted, after not a little stress and strain, in a renewed sense of cooperation and camaraderie. "We were nuts," one vice president told us later. "We were both in the same boat, but were doing our level best to sink each other. We still get into tussles over priorities, but now we're at least rowing in the same direction."

This scenario repeats itself every minute of every working day in thousands of organizations. However, you can eliminate cross-function strife more easily than you think. All it takes is a constant reminder that your organization's real enemy is not Joe or Sally down the hall but your mistaken assumption that Joe or Sally is not on your team. *Above The Line* leadership requires people and functions across the organization to acknowledge the reality that the market will not forgive the damage caused by cross-functional strife. People and functions must give each other the benefit of the doubt and the feedback essential to making appropriate and necessary performance improvements. They must step out of their functional "silos" and create a correlated effort between departments that is based on a productive give and take attitude that can drive a concerted focus on producing the greatest good for the overall company. As Pogo might have put it, "We have met the enemy, and the enemy is our own divisiveness."

▲

ISSUE TEN: FASCINATION WITH PROGRAMS

A list of all the management fads that have come along in the last 20 years would look like the Manhattan telephone directory. An abbreviated list might include the following entries: strategic planning, total quality management, just-in-time manufacturing, management by objectives, customer satisfaction, learning organizations, core competencies, business reengineering, zero-based budgeting, and horizontal organizations. In a recent *Sloan Management Review* article entitled "Consulting: Has the Solution Become Part of the Problem?" authors Shapiro, Eccles, and Soske make this observation: "Fad surfing—riding the crest of the newest panacea and then paddling out just in time to ride the crest of the next one—has been big business over the past twenty years.....Each of these concepts comes with a prepackaged set of tools, many of which existed previously and which have been repackaged and marketed as The Answer to competitiveness." Over the years we've watched many fads come and go, leaving little more than a ripple in their wake. AT&T, for example, recently laid off 1,000 out of 6,600 employees at a factory that won the Malcolm Baldrige National Quality Award in 1992. The factory, which makes transmission systems equipment, including hardware used by phone and cable TV companies, blamed the layoffs on slow sales and technological advances. The Wallace Company, a 1990 winner of the same award filed for chapter 11 in 1992. No matter how you look at this situation, it's obvious that total quality management alone does not prevent 1,000 people from losing their jobs, check a factory's sales decline, or deal with the human side of technological advancement.

The Wall Street Journal recently reported that "Some American manufacturers are discarding billions of dollars of investment they made in the 1980s to adopt Japanese manufacturing ideas. They haven't decided that the Japanese systems don't work. Rather, they realize that some of those systems, however useful in lifting productivity in Japan, haven't achieved much in their own plants." So, if the Japanese fad did not produce lasting value for most American manufacturers, where do we turn next? The *Journal* article continues, "Federal-Mogul Corp., deciding that its automation had gone too far, has removed much of the fancy equipment at an auto-parts plant, and General Motors Corp. is now relying more heavily on 'people power.' Whirlpool Corp. has soured on Japanese-style 'quality circles' as a means of tapping employees' ideas, and General Electric Co. and Corning Inc. have turned to other ways of tapping employee ideas. Losing favor at some companies is the Japanese 'just-in-time' system of minimizing inventory by having suppliers deliver parts only as needed."

In the field of computer technology, where changes come at lightning speed, downsizing has become the latest fad. According to William Zachman, the columnist and industry watcher credited with coining the term "downsizing," in another *Wall Street Journal* article, "People have gone overboard on the concept. It's like people, upon first hearing about electricity, stuck their finger in the light socket to check it out. It's become a mindless fad." Even companies with a lot of experience in managing technology have made silly mistakes by pursuing downsizing and rightsizing programs that produce more confusion than results. The problem, as we see it, is that any number of management philosophies and techniques can and do produce results, but too many organizations think the latest one will do the trick, when, in fact, results will only come through a sense of accountability for results in every member of the organization. We feel strongly that organizations must stop jumping on each new bandwagon that turns the corner and start paying attention to the basic fact that most anything will work if you get *Above The Line* and use your head. They need to act with courage, maintain a stout heart, and keep their eye on the main objective, whether that is "getting back to Kansas," getting products to market faster, or meeting the true needs of customers. These 10 issues are real and present dangers to thrusting your organization *Below The Line.* To move forward as an organization and achieve results now and in the coming years, you must forthrightly deal with these issues by seeing them for what they really are, acknowledging the price you pay for not resolving them, determining that you can do something about them, and acting on what you now know about accountability to get results.

THE UNENDING JOURNEY

So, here we are at the end of the book. The Lion has his courage, the Tin Woodsman his heart, the Scarecrow his brain, Dorothy's safely home with Auntie Em. And, if we've accomplished our own mission in these pages, you're well on the road to accountability, applying *The Oz Principle* to every aspect of your life and work.

Remember, only when you assume full accountability for your thoughts, feelings, actions, and results can you direct your own destiny; otherwise someone or something else will.

As a final note, just inside the cover of one of the many sequels to *The Wizard of Oz,* the publisher, Del Rey Books, printed the following message to readers: "When we mention Oz to people who haven't grown up with the books, they nod, mention Judy Garland and think they know all there is to know about Oz. How wrong they are!" We echo that sentiment as we write *The End* of our own book. There's a lot to learn in Oz. Enjoy the lifelong journey.

THE BEGINNING . . .

APPENDIX

▼

As we mentioned in Chapter 7, we highly recommend that you take time to get some feedback on how others perceive your ability and commitment to work *Above The Line*. We have provided some suggestions on how to make the feedback sessions most effective. After these suggestions we have included a feedback worksheet.

SUGGESTIONS FOR MAKING THE FEEDBACK SESSIONS MOST EFFECTIVE

1. Meet separately with four or five individuals.

2. Spend at least a half hour of uninterupted time with each person.

3. Take a few minutes at the beginning of each of your meetings to explain why you are meeting with them. Share with them the *Steps To Accountability* and the "Victim Cycle" charts. Explain *The Oz Principle*: "Only you can rise above

your circumstances and get results." And help them understand the concept of accountability.

4. Offer an example of accountable and victim behavior to help create a better understanding.

5. Describe how you assessed yourself in terms of your ability to work above the line to *See It, Own It, Solve It* and *Do It.*

6. Explain why you want their feedback.

7. Ask them for candid, honest perceptions.

8. Listen and record the feedback on the feedback worksheet provided below. Ask only clarifying questions. Do not go *Below The Line* and seek to justify yourself as you receive the feedback. Stay *Above The Line* as you continue to seek to understand the perspectives being shared.

FEEDBACK WORKSHEET
▼

1. Where do you think I tend to operate most, *Below The Line* or *Above The Line*?* Have you seen me operating on both sides of the line? Can you give any examples of either of these behaviors (victim or accountable)?

   * Open *The Oz Principle* to the *Steps To Accountability* Chart

   Feedback: _____
   _____
   _____
   _____

2. Can you help me list any issues or situations in which you feel I'm currently stuck *Below The Line*?

Feedback: _____

_____

_____

_____

3. Do you feel that I tend to own my circumstances by linking my behavior with my circumstances, or do I tend to see myself a victim of my circumstances? Give examples if possible.

Feedback: _____

_____

_____

_____

4. How consistently do you feel I strive to consider *what else I can personally do in order to achieve results?*

Feedback: _____

_____

_____

_____

5. Do you feel I demonstrate initiative and do all that is possible to solve problems? Are there ways in which you think I get needlessly stymied by problems?

Feedback: _____

_____

_____

_____

6. Over the past month, do you think that I acted accountable for results? What do you feel I could have done to have been even more accountable for results?

Feedback: _____

_____

_____

_____

7. Can you think of actions I can take to better demonstrate my accountability and an *Above The Line* attitude?

Feedback: _____

_____

_____

_____

8. On a scale from 1 to 10 (1=not accountable, 10=very accountable), how accountable do I behave in general?___ Rate my ability to *See It*___(using the same scale); Rate my ability to *Own It* ___; Rate my ability to *Solve It* ___; Rate my ability to *Do It* ___.

Feedback: _____

_____

_____

_____

9. What advice would you give me to help me to stay *Above The Line*?

Feedback: _____

_____

_____

_____

For assistance in moving your organization *Above The Line* and implementing *The Oz Principle*, in your work group, department, or team, please contact:

Partners In Leadership, LLC
27555 Ynez Road
Suite 201
Temecula, California 92591
1-800-504-6070
E-mail: pil@ozprinciple.com
Web site: www.ozprinciple.com

Partners In Leadership, LLC offers a broad array of consulting and training services ranging from a high-impact, results-oriented, one-day Accountability Training to presentations for national sales meetings and speeches. Their consulting services also include a well-recognized expertise in facilitating greater alighment within senior executive teams for creating a heightened sense of accountability for results throughout the entire organization.

> *"One of the most powerful aspects of using 'The Oz Principle' Accountability Training in a large manufacturing organization like ours has been the ability to utilize it at all levels of the organization, from shop floor through senior management. The tools and ideas are applicable both within and across functions, and we've found that the common language of accountability takes hold very quickly. In the Operations arena, where getting results is important every minute of every day, use of this model has really helped our people to work together and get results."*

--Jackie Schiavo
  Corporate Vice President, Worldwide Operations
  Allergan, Inc.

JOURNEY TO THE EMERALD CITY

ROGER CONNORS & TOM SMITH

Turn the page for a preview of
Journey to the Emerald City

CHAPTER ONE

THE YELLOW BRICK ROAD

ACCELERATING THE JOURNEY

In the story *The Wizard of Oz*, the Yellow Brick Road was a path to change for the story's characters. As in any "road" story, to reach their destination and to get what they were traveling for, Dorothy, the Scarecrow, the Tin Woodsman, and the Cowardly Lion had to approach their problems and challenges in a different way. To reach their destination, achieve their goal, and accomplish the desired result, each of them had to think and act in ways that were different from those that had been familiar and comfortable.

However, it wasn't until the end of the story that the characters realized that they had undergone a change in the way they viewed both themselves and the world they lived in or came from. Each of them learned a new way of thinking and acting that brought them the results they were seeking. And it wasn't until they started acting differently that they reached their destination and achieved their goals—wisdom, courage, heart, and gratitude.

The journey to the Emerald City created a new understanding of what was needed in order to achieve the goals of each person on the team. Yet the journey not only led to personal insight about what needed to change, but also a collective insight about how the team needed to think and act as a whole in order to get to where they were going.

As management consultants, we believe that every organization is on this journey of understanding. Every organization must constantly discover what needs to change about the way they think and act in order to conquer the ever-changing obstacles and challenges that arise. Every year, results become more difficult to achieve. Sustaining success, capturing market share, growing profits, and increasing returns is a never-ending requirement of even the best performing organizations. All of this occurs in an environment of smarter and better competition, fewer resources, and shorter time lines.

When an organization fails to achieve its results, managers typically look outside, casting about for some resource or pat answer that will change things. Often, they resort to making repairs by utilizing the "re-" fixes of the times. They redeploy their people or ask some to resign. They reorganize their structure, reengineer their processes, review their plans, revisit their goals, and review their efforts. Yet most discover that the company returns to its old ways. Some ultimately decide that change is impossible and that they must resign themselves to live with the situation until "something happens."

Effective organizations come to understand that achieving results—consistently, repeatedly, and effectively—requires an organizational journey that channels individual and group efforts, energy, actions, and thought in a targeted and precise manner. Those who undertake the journey of cultural transition (changing the way we think about how we do business and adopting corresponding changes in actions) invariably see that it is indeed possible to more directly focus the collective cultural energy of the organization on achieving the result.

In this book, we tell you about this process of cultural transition. More to the point, we tell you how to speed up the process of cultural change. In *The Oz Principle* we presented the *Steps To Accountability*[SM] and discussed their impact on organizational results. In *Journey to the Emerald City*, we describe how to create a *Culture Of Accountability*[SM] and show how managers can *accelerate* the transition to this culture.

FOR A CHANGE, TRY LEADERSHIP

Over the past decade, a fair amount has been written and said about organizational culture. Numerous questions have been put forward on the subject: What is culture? Is there a connection between culture and results? Can you manage or create or even change culture? And so on. We will spare you another round of this intellectualizing, as interesting as it can be, and instead take you right to the heart of our message and experience:

- An organization's leaders must create its culture
- The organization's culture will create its results
- A *Culture Of Accountability* is the most effective culture and is defined as people being accountable to think and act in the manner necessary for your organization to achieve results.
- Accelerating the transition to a *Culture Of Accountability* creates competitive and organizational advantage.

Stay with us! We think you will find the stories and examples to come in this book convincing—culture does impact results. Leaders can manage culture. A *Culture Of Accountability* is the most effective culture, and companies that have created this kind of culture get results—you'll see!

A company's culture makes all the difference. So let's look more closely at the four principles at the heart of our message and experience.

LEADERS MUST CREATE THE CULTURE

We have a saying: *Either you manage your culture, or it will manage you.* In our work we meet many managers who get batted around by their company's culture. Their culture undermines the results they want to achieve. They want strong customer focus and can't get it. They want diversity and can't get it. They want regulatory compliance and can't get it. They want growth, quality, or productivity and can't get it. They want their fast-growing, entrepreneurial firm to adopt systems and controls, and it won't. Or they want their lumbering, recently deregulated company to become entrepreneurial and nimble, and it won't.

These managers must lead their companies through a journey of organizational self-discovery like that described at the beginning of this chapter and throughout this book. They must lead this effort. When they do they will create a new culture. This is not the responsibility of the organization's human resources department, although HR can certainly help create a new culture. However, we've found that thinking of a transition to a new culture as an "HR program" promotes the wrong view of this endeavor. Creating a new culture is not an event. It is not a program. It is a leadership process. And it never stops.

Here is a comment that reveals many managers' misunderstanding of culture and how it is either created or fundamentally shifted. The November 1997 issue of *Training Magazine* reports the story of a CEO who "wanted to improve his company's performance by 'putting in a good culture.' The CEO went on to explain that his company did not currently have a culture because he and his team had not yet gotten around to developing one."

We can be certain of one thing: This fellow's company did have a culture. Every group of people, from a street gang to a church choir, from a family to a nation, has a culture. If the group's leaders have not created it, perhaps some informal leaders or "influencers" have. Or perhaps the culture has developed willy-nilly, for better or worse. Every organization has a culture. The only question is whether or not that specific culture is effective in creating the results that those people want.

The concept of business leadership demands that leaders take control of the company's culture and make it as effective as it can possibly be. This is, by the way, for the best of business reasons—which brings us to our next principle.

CULTURE CREATES RESULTS

An organization's culture determines the results that it achieves. Therefore, leaders must be careful when defining the results around which they will build the culture. They must be careful because while the culture effects results, the results affect the culture.

Here's what we mean by this. Leaders can build a company culture around any set of results they choose. Typical very broad ones might be market dominance, sales and profit growth, technological excellence, customer service, or stability of earnings. A company will need a certain culture to achieve any of these results. That's because the culture—how people think and act—is going to determine the results. Yet the results an organization achieves also reinforce the culture.

For example, Ford Motor Company decided that in 1995 the Ford Taurus was going to be the sales leader, "The Best Selling Car in America." It took a lot to do that. Ford had to cut deals on fleet sales, offer low-rate financing through Ford Credit Corporation, and run substantial rebate programs. They had, however, *decided* that the Ford Taurus—and not the Honda Accord, its chief rival—was going to be number one that year. (Did you know that the Latin root of "decide" is *decidere*, which means "to cut off"? A true decision cuts off other options.)

Achieving that result was important to Ford and it reinforced the position of the car and of Ford's place in American car culture. This goal was not just about "bragging rights"—although they're nice to have. It was about management recommitting the company to the Taurus at a time when the car was being criticized as somewhat dated and when it was about to undergo substantial redesign. Ford reinforced not only the product's position, but also the company's position in the public mind and in their own minds by beating Honda in that key year. They created the culture that would get the result, and getting the result reinforced Ford's "number one" culture.

This kind of "feedback loop" can work in negative ways, too. A company that fails also generates a result. That result reinforces a different kind of culture. We worked with a firm that had previously elevated failing to make budget into an art. Missing its sales or expense budget had been institutionalized into the culture. Management issued budgets and everyone, including management, knew that they were not to be taken seriously. We've also seen companies do this with deadlines. Other companies, commonly called "money losers" and firms in "dying industries," face similar cultural challenges. The more they generate negative results, the more their culture degenerates.

Because negative results have this feedback effect, leaders must develop the ability to maintain a winning culture during failures and setbacks. As you know, occasional failures are part of any effort to achieve something. How one handles them ultimately separates winners from losers.

Movie producer Samuel Goldwyn, who was a founder of Metro-Goldwyn-Mayer and saw his ups and downs, used to say, "We've been broke, but we've never been poor." He never allowed his family to develop a culture of poverty, even when they were out of money. (Coincidentally, his studio, MGM, produced the most famous version of *The Wizard of Oz* in 1939. Perhaps Goldwyn, who started life in America as an immigrant glove salesman, had found *The Oz Principle*.)

Culture produces results. Results produce culture. The link between a company's culture and the results that it produces represents a bedrock principle of our consulting practice and of this book. That link is the reason that creating and maintaining the right culture is one of management's most serious responsibilities. Culture is intrinsic to results.

A CULTURE OF ACCOUNTABILITY[SM] IS THE MOST EFFECTIVE CULTURE

The most effective organizational culture can be characterized as a *Culture Of Accountability*. To us, culture is the way people think *about* how we do business on a daily basis and the way we act. The word *accountability*, like culture, can have some irrelevant or inaccurate connotations in the context of leadership and business effectiveness, so let's define that term.

Webster defines *accountability* as "the state of having to report, explain or justify." This is in keeping with the command-and-control and surveillance-style management approaches that often prove ineffective in achieving results today. Unfortunately, this notion of accountability also draws forth certain behaviors from people in organizations. We call this behavior "Blamestorming." In general, people engage in Blamestorming to avoid true accountability by generating reasons and explanations for why they are not accountable for something.

From our perspective, accountability, as we explained in *The Oz Principle*, means to proactively see the reality of a situation, personally own the circumstances, relentlessly look for ways to *Solve It!*[SM], and consistently follow through and *Do It!*[SM] before it's too late. Accountability, most effectively applied, is a forward-looking concept that focuses attention on what I "can do" versus what I "did." As we see it, accountability is something people should want to take, not something they should fear.

In a *Culture Of Accountability* everyone in the organization is personally committed to achieving the results the team has targeted. To maintain the focus and effort required to get this result, everyone continually asks, *"What else can I do to achieve the result?"* This question is the mantra of those dwelling in a *Culture Of Accountability*. This question is also the sure cure for Blamestorming.

There are several other characteristics of a *Culture Of Accountability*, all of which we'll examine in the next chapter. However, the most fundamental characteristic is that people *assume accountability* in this kind of culture. They take it upon themselves. They do not have to have it foisted or forced upon them. They are not commanded to be accountable, nor are they kept under surveillance and then "called to account" for their actions. Instead, the company's leaders create this culture in a systematic manner that we have seen work effectively time after time.

ACCELERATING THE TRANSITION

Speeding up the process of change in a world where being first means everything has become essential to getting business results. While culture change takes time (and don't let anyone try to fool you—it does take time), the process of change can be accelerated—and the needed culture more quickly created. The ability of an organization to *accelerate* a transition to a *Culture Of Accountability* will create both competitive and organizational advantage.

Take, for example, the story of Cardiac Pacemakers, Inc., formerly a subsidiary of Eli Lilly and Company, and currently the fuel behind Guidant Corporation's extraordinary performance. In 1995, Guidant was split off from Eli Lilly and in just two years was considered Wall Street's most successful split-off ever. In the early 1990s, CPI was not the engine of success that it would become for Guidant. CPI President, Jay Graf, who joined the company a number of years after it was acquired by his employer, Eli Lilly, found a company that he characterized as "going 90 miles per hour on an icy road toward a cliff." This company was experiencing historic sales growth with monthly performance records. People were excited about the success of the organization. They were constantly celebrating their victories in the market. Indeed, the company was going 90 miles an hour—but it was also headed toward a cliff and nobody seemed to see it!

CPI's acquired technology was fueling its growth. But what people at CPI were failing to acknowledge was that Medtronic and Ventritex, formidable competitors, were on line to introduce technology that would leapfrog CPI's within just two years. Without the next new product, sales growth at CPI would indeed drop off a cliff.

What was the answer? Upcoming acquisition opportunities were not proving fruitful and likely would not be the solution. Internal new-product development was void of promise as well. CPI had not produced a new product in years and the common belief within the organization at the time was that they couldn't "develop their way out of a paper bag." A cultural transition was essential if they were to have any chance of creating a new-product development environment. Accelerating this transition was imperative as time was running out.

The story of CPI's transition is told throughout this book, as are those of numerous other organizations. CPI's story is worth knowing because within a few short years this company created a new-product development culture that from 1995 to 1996 produced 14 new products in 14 months. People at CPI came to view themselves as "a new-product development machine." Annual sales increased from approximately $300 million in 1993 to over $650 million in 1996. They achieved this growth with only a 20 percent increase in staff. The speed of their cultural transition gave them competitive advantage and they have become world market leaders in a number of their product lines—all of this has helped fuel Guidant's stock price to increase by nine-fold since January 1995. Speeding up cultural change means, in the end, speeding up results—providing both competitive and organizational advantage.

A CLOSER LOOK AT CULTURE

In order to most effectively shift an organization to a new culture, it's important to understand the components of culture. Figure 1-1 *The Results Pyramid*SM illustrates the essential components of organizational culture and how they relate to one another.

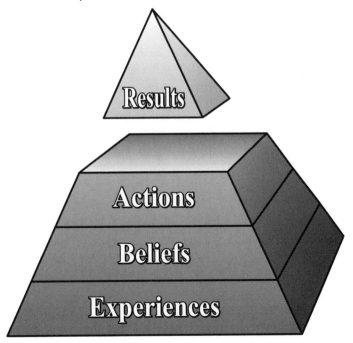

© 1997 Partners In Leadership, LLC

FIGURE 1-1   *The Results Pyramid*SM

As *The Results Pyramid* shows, three components—experiences, beliefs, and actions—working together amount to culture. The culture generates results, which as we've already noted also reinforce the culture and are part of the culture. We say these components "work together" because *experiences foster beliefs, beliefs drive actions, and actions produce results.*

This model applies to virtually any culture. Experiences foster organizational beliefs. Beliefs drive actions. Actions produce results. Results become new experiences.

In this book we will examine scores of situations and examples, but here is a small one that will show you this dynamic in action. Think about what your company says about what it values most in managerial employees. Is it technical proficiency? Operational problem-solving? Contributions to financial performance? Ability to support employees?

Now think about the people who have been promoted. Ask yourself this: How fully do the people we have promoted embody the qualities we value most?

When a management team promotes someone, that team creates a powerful experience. This experience is absorbed by the person promoted and by everyone else in the company. That experience of being promoted or seeing someone promoted fosters certain beliefs. Those beliefs will drive actions in the person promoted and in observers of the promotion. Their actions will produce results.

Promoting someone is an example of management creating an experience. So management creates experiences that foster beliefs that drive actions that produce results. This is a key point because it is how management creates the culture. The process is continual. It goes on all the time, not just when promotions or other big decisions are made. The president of a major pharmaceutical firm shared the following insightful guidance with his team in one of our senior management sessions: "Every one of us is creating the culture of this company every day. As a manager everything you do, everything you say, everywhere you go in the organization, leaves a footprint on the culture of this place." Clearly, your passage through your company will affect people in it for better or worse, every single day.

CHANGES DOWN THE ROAD

This book shows you how to *accelerate* the shift of your organization to a new culture. Specifically, it shows how to create a *Culture Of Accountability* and to do so as quickly as possible. Depending upon your company's current culture, this process may entail anything from a few slight shifts in the culture to a complete cultural transformation.

For now, let's assume that your current culture is not completely effective, that it is not motivating the right actions, the necessary thinking, the needed approaches, or the essential improvement. People may not be personally committed to achieving the targeted results. Or the results themselves may be unclear. Perhaps the organization is not achieving all of its targeted results. Some people may be more focused on failure and on avoiding blame than on achieving the result. You do not have a *Culture Of Accountability.*

Or, let's assume that you do have a solid, aligned and accountable culture, but that the business environment is going to change and you doubt that your current culture will continue to produce the desired results in the coming environment. This occurs fairly often, for example, when a company faces a new regulatory environment, or is purchased by a larger group, or is facing new competitive threats.

Figure 1-2 depicts a cultural transition, a shift from the current culture C^1 to a new culture C^2. The current culture is producing results, R^1, from experiences, beliefs, and actions, E^1, B^1, and A^1, respectively. After studying the future and considering the challenges it may present, the company has defined a new culture, C^2, as essential to success in the

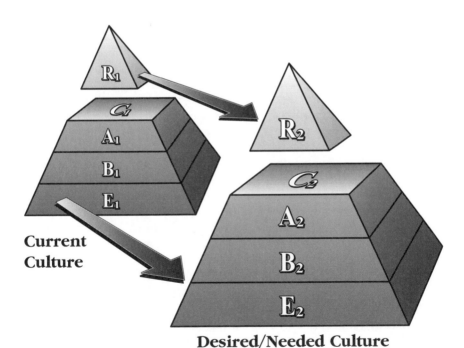

Current Culture

Desired/Needed Culture

© 1997 Partners In Leadership, LLC

FIGURE 1-2   Cultural Transition

future business environment. They have defined the C^2 culture as comprising certain experiences, beliefs, and actions, E^2, B^2, and A^2, respectively. The company expects this new culture to produce new results, R^2.

Here's an extremely important point: *You cannot take the R^2 results and superimpose them on the C^1 culture.* It just doesn't work. We are not saying that there is nothing of value in your current culture. In fact, there probably is. Nor are we saying that you must always totally transform your culture to get new results. Our experience suggests that most organizations need to focus more on a transition, not on a transformation. Usually, organizations have certain attributes in their existing cultures that will serve their businesses in their pursuit of new results. But you cannot expect to get new results from the exact same culture. Remember: Insanity has been defined as continuing to do the same thing but expecting different results.

Superimposing R^2 results onto the C^1 culture doesn't work because culture is powerful and persistent. It is powerful in that it determines results. It is persistent because it transcends individuals. Again, our president of the pharmaceutical firm said it best to his senior management group in one of our sessions: "Here's when I saw that culture was real. Early in my career I spent some time in the Italian affiliate. Then I left for a new assignment and lost touch with them. I came back five years later, and I didn't see one familiar face. They'd had 100 percent turnover. Yet the culture was exactly the same in that company. Nothing in the culture had changed, even though all the people were different!" *You can change all of the people and still have the same culture.*

That is why the traditional management fix of injecting "new blood" by moving a new person into a culture won't work, at least not by itself. This tactic works only when other aspects of the culture are shifted as well.

A division of a major business information firm learned this when its Boston sales office stopped getting results. The staff in that office had gone sour over a change in the commission structure. A fit of Blamestorming cited the change in the compensation plan as the cause of diminished performance. But senior management was committed to the new plan, which was weighted to encourage sales of new products. The division CEO terminated the head of the sales office for poor performance. Then he sent in Danny Borges, one of his star sales managers, to head the office. However, two months later, the CEO was heard complaining that Danny was "going native" up there in Boston. (The expression comes from the practice of some early European missionaries joining native cultures instead of converting the natives to European ways.)

In the Boston office Danny had enough experiences—including conversations with salespeople about "those unfair bozos at headquarters" and difficulties in selling new products in that conservative market—to change his beliefs. Eventually and inevitably his actions and results also changed, for the worse. Danny could not overcome the culture. In truth, he had been sent on something of a fool's errand, because management had to do more than change the sales manager to improve results in Boston. They had to effect a cultural transition in that office, which they eventually did.

WORKING WITH THE WHOLE PYRAMID

The power and persistence of culture explains why the usual fixes that managers use to improve results often don't work. Most of the usual fixes—new people, new marching orders, new technology, new strategies, or new structures—work only at the level of actions, when they work at all. Too often, leaders attempt to change the way people act without changing the way they think, that is, their beliefs. Figure 1-3 shows the imaginary line commonly drawn by managers who focus their attention only on actions and results when working to improve performance. By working with just the top of the pyramid, leaders leave unchanged the things that can be the hardest to change but make the greatest impact on performance.

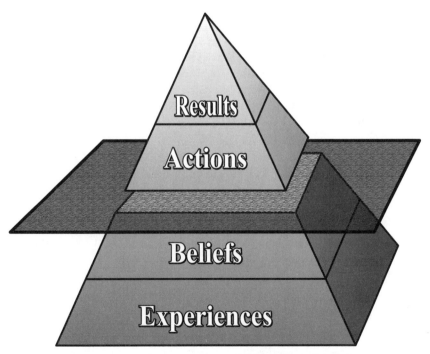

© 1997 Partners In Leadership, LLC

FIGURE 1-3   A Common Mistake: Working with Only Part of the Pyramid

We believe, on the basis of our experience, that managers will more significantly and permanently improve results by working at the level of employees' beliefs. And to impact beliefs, managers must focus on creating new experiences for people. You will see how to do this in Part Two. Without that change in beliefs, you certainly cannot shift the culture. Without a cultural shift, any improvement in actions or results will be at best both temporary and partial. To *accelerate* culture change, leaders must work with both the top and the bottom of the pyramid.

A Three-Part Process for Culture Change

Many managers find it useful to think of change in three phases: deconstructing, reconstructing, and sustaining the culture.

- In *deconstructing* the culture, the management team becomes fully aware of the current culture. Senior management and other key people examine the experiences, beliefs, and actions that constitute the culture and honestly consider their effectiveness in achieving results. They decide what is working and what isn't.

- In *reconstructing* the culture, management considers the coming business environment and defines the results the company must achieve in that environment. Then they go on to define and create the experiences, beliefs, and actions that will constitute the culture that will enable people to achieve those results. In this phase, management creates the new culture according to its designs.

- In *sustaining* the culture, management continues to provide experiences that foster and reinforce the desired beliefs. In this phase, leaders monitor the culture to maintain a focus on results and the necessary actions and beliefs required to attain these results.

Depending upon the size and structure of the company, most middle managers and other key people should be involved at some point in this process. This incorporates shop-floor reality into the analysis and facilitates broad-based buy-in, without which there can be no new culture.

Please keep this process in mind as we move through the material to come, particularly Part Two. Culture can become overwhelmingly complex, and shifting culture can be a long-term, time-consuming process without a step-by-step method of separately considering the components of the culture and their effects on one another, and then putting them back together.

BUT WE'RE JUST A SMALL COMPANY

Some managers of small companies, say those under $10 million in sales or with fewer than 50 people, believe that culture isn't an issue for their companies. However, even munchkin-sized companies have a culture. Remember, any group of people develops a culture. The only question is whether or not that culture will achieve the targeted results. So, yes, managers in small companies must definitely manage their culture. In fact, small companies face special issues that can make creating a *Culture Of Accountability* extremely important.

First, even more so than in large companies, the leader—and it is often just one leader—dictates the culture, either consciously or unconsciously. Given that culture determines results, that culture had better be positive and had better be consciously created as opposed to unconsciously dictated.

Second, small companies generally don't spawn subcultures. In large companies people can work in a subculture, find professional satisfaction, and make a solid contribution to the entire company. In large companies a strong marketing culture, as exists in Procter & Gamble, or financial culture, as in AT&T, or product development culture, as in 3M, can come to distinguish the entire company. A small company usually lacks the critical mass to offer subcultures, so the company culture is "it." So "it" had better be effective.

Third, by the same token small companies have little margin for error. If the culture doesn't work, the organization may well be doomed, particularly when a crisis arises. Typical crises that can capsize a small company with a weak, negative, or ineffective culture include the departure or death of one or more key people, loss of several major customers, acquiring venture capital financing, going public, or acquisition by or alliance with a larger company. Weathering any of these crises would demand the ability to shift to a new effective culture.

Finally, there is our view of true accountability, which as you will see calls for everyone throughout the entire organization to take accountability for the results of the company. That is another characteristic of a *Culture of Accountability*. Leaders need to seek and be open to the perspectives of others. Many an autocratic founder has sabotaged his or her company by failing to listen to reason or "let go" at the right time. An effective culture demands an openness on the part of management. This openness can be particularly beneficial—and eye-opening—in a small company.

MILESTONES ON THE YELLOW BRICK ROAD

In this chapter we've seen that creating and maintaining the right culture represents the key challenge before an organization's leaders. That is because the company's culture generates its results. Culture is the way people think and the way they act and those two things generate results. This renders the issue of culture a day-to-day, practical concern rather than one which is long-term and theoretical.

In our world, accountability means making a personal commitment to achieving the organization's results. A *Culture Of Accountability* has proven itself the most effective organizational culture. In this kind of culture people feel accountable to think and act in the manner necessary to achieve results. In this kind of culture, everyone continually asks, *What else can I do to achieve the result?* This question keeps people's efforts focused and directed toward achieving results rather than escaping responsibility. Managers must foster this kind of commitment, and this question helps people maintain top-of-mind awareness of that commitment.

Culture is made up of experiences, beliefs, actions, and results. Experiences foster beliefs. Beliefs drive actions. Actions produce results. Results become new experiences. Every organization, every group of people, has a culture. The only question is whether or not that culture is effective today and can produce the results that you need now and in the future.

Creating the culture you want and need is no longer an option. It is a business necessity. Creating that culture at all levels in the organization and doing it quickly and effectively creates organizational and competitive advantage. Unlike the characters in *The Wizard of Oz*, you don't have to walk to the Emerald City. There are things you can do, and a process you can use, to speed you on your journey to a new culture. That is what this book is about. As we take the next step to the next chapter, we look more closely at the behaviors that add up to a *Culture Of Accountability* and why this culture is so effective.

INDEX

▼

A

Above The Line behavior, 14, 29, 76, 81
and communication problems, 255
first step toward, 92-94
second step toward, 119-27
third step toward, attaining, 148-54
Above The Line leaders, 204-6
and control, 210-12
and intervention, recognizing time for, 206-8
leadership checklist, 222-24
model, providing for others, 212-15
risk taken by, 207-8
Above The Line paradigm, locking in, 233-34
Above The Line questions, asking, 236-37

Accountability, 18-20, 58-85
benefits of, 75-81
climbing steps to, 84-85
preparation for, 81-84
coaching, 234-36
creating in others, 215-19
defined, 59-65
Do It step to, 18, 169-99
and dysfunction game, 95-98
holding others accountable, 72-75
joint accountability, 66-72
line between victimization and, 28-29
and organizational success, 9-10
and ownership, 67
Own It step to, 18, 115-44
See It step to, 18, 90-114
Solve It step to, 18, 145-67
transforming power of, 18-23
transition to new view of, 231-33